JUST GO DOWN TO THE ROAD

A Memoir of Trouble and Travel

Syncopations: New Yorkers, Beats and Writers in the Dark
This Is the Beat Generation
Exiled in Paris: Richard Wright, James Baldwin,
    Samuel Beckett, and Others on the Left Bank
Talking at the Gates: A Life of James Baldwin
Gate Fever: Voices from a Prison
Invisible Country: A Journey Through Scotland
Thom Gunn in Conversation
The Picador Book of Blues and Jazz (editor)
The New Edinburgh Review Anthology (editor)

JUST GO DOWN TO THE ROAD

JAMES CAMPBELL

PAUL DRY BOOKS

Philadelphia 2022

First Paul Dry Books Edition, 2022

Paul Dry Books, Inc.
Philadelphia, Pennsylvania
www.pauldrybooks.com

Printed in the United States of America

ISBN 978-1-58988-164-8

Library of Congress Control Number: 2021951802

To Vera

CONTENTS

PART ONE

THIS LAND IS MY LAND

1. THEFT 3

2. A CONFESSION 9

3. REPORT CARD 14

4. THE LAND GIRL AND THE PETTY OFFICER:
AN INTERLUDE 40

5. THE APPRENTICE: WASHIE'S 54

6. THE SCOTIA BAR 77

7. LIFE IN THE UNDERGROUND 97

PART TWO

THE LAND OF AWAY

8. ISTANBUL AND SPETSAI 121

9. KIBBUTZ PHILOSOPHY 148

10. TROCCHI'S PAD 169

11. HITCH-HIKER'S PERSONALITY TEST 187

12. THE MAGUS 211

13. "HOW LONG . . . HAS THAT TRAIN BEEN GONE" 233

14. LEWES PRISON 269

ACKNOWLEDGMENTS 283

PART ONE

THIS LAND IS MY LAND

1

THEFT

I was fourteen when I was caught stealing books the first time. The year was 1965. The scene of the crime was a bookshop in West George Street, in the center of Glasgow, long since disappeared, and the loot consisted of three *MAD* books. My friend Bruce Dryden and I were experts on the subject. We used to create our own versions of *MAD* comics in class, with stories and drawings, while poor Mr. Donald—Ducky Donald—tried to interest us in the risqué parts of *The Merchant of Venice*. The school, King's Park Secondary, was among the first so-called comprehensives in Glasgow—but really it was only socially comprehensive. Pupils were streamed academically from A to G, with rough types included from insalubrious Southside areas such as Toryglen and Castlemilk, beyond the catchment area of the old King's Park Senior Secondary at which my elder sisters had thrived. The social experiment did not appeal to my parents. I had started out, aged twelve, in the A stream but was relegated to B in the second year, making my way down towards Bruce, one of those feared Toryglen natives.

It goes without saying that I wasn't at school, as I should have been, when I furtively slipped the three slim volumes inside my duffel coat. Not furtively enough, and as I approached the door I felt a hand on my shoulder.

The manager of the bookshop was a kindly soul, but he had to do his duty. He had already taken my name—"James Gunning"—and address (totally fictional). Now he offered me a choice: he could inform the police, the school, or my father.

The first I wasn't terribly keen on; as for the third—was there a gentle alternative, such as having my fingernails extracted? We settled on the middle course. The man who had become my courteous keeper lifted the receiver from the phone on his desk and dialed the number of King's Park Secondary, getting through to the headmaster with what now seems remarkable ease. He explained the situation and they arrived at a gentlemanly solution to the regrettable affair. I was to leave the shop as a boy on parole and return to Fetlar Drive, Simshill, where the school was, reporting to the headmaster directly. The manager might even have hinted to the headmaster that there was no need to mention it to the parents. He replaced the receiver and in my persona as James Gunning I thanked him and left the three *MAD* books behind, to be reshelved. I can't remember exactly what I thought as I stepped into the open air of West George Street, but it was probably along the lines of, "So that's how you get out of it."

The next time it happened, Bruce and I were in the large Boots at the corner of Union Street and Argyle Street, a famous Glasgow landmark, popular with young folk hopeful of romance ("See you at seven, under the clock at Boots"). We were doggin' off school again, not a rare occurrence (by now I had reached the C stream). Boots, which had once run a lending library, also stocked books for sale, and Bruce was a proper reader. It was from Bruce that I first learned of the natural evolution of a book from hardback to paperback. He informed me where to look in 007 novels for details involving Pussy Galore or some similar heroine, to which we had recently become susceptible: in the final paragraph, he said (I discovered that this wasn't always so).

He had other advanced tastes, Mickey Spillane novels being

one of them. On the first floor among the bookshelves at Boots, he constructed a little pile of novels featuring the detective Mike Hammer. Five, to be exact. My memory is precise, because the number of books taken was to feature in a Scottish legal case. I was flicking through a copy of *Peyton Place*, the televised version of which, with Mia Farrow and Ryan O'Neal, I was currently following.

"If you want it, put it on the pile," Bruce said in a low voice. Not low enough. Again, the words are precise: they were offered as evidence in court.

I did as suggested, and Bruce sheltered the lot inside the off-white shortie raincoat he wore—so much more *in* than my duffel. We went downstairs and got as far as the front door—the door beyond which lay great, garrulous, Dear Green Glasgow, Bruce's home in tough Toryglen, mine in toffier King's Park.

That hand on the shoulder again. It made a deep impression. It steered us away from freedom—a book-filled freedom—and down to a windowless room in a basement we had never imagined existed. Two plain-clothes policemen arrived and discussed matters with the Boots store detectives as if we weren't there. We gave our names and addresses. Bruce Dryden of Edinbeg Avenue, Toryglen. And James Gunning of . . . somewhere or other.

The policemen looked into my school haversack which, in addition to being plastered with inky tributes to the Rolling Stones and the Pretty Things, contained my inadequate C-stream jotters. One of the detectives pointed out the name on the cover, which was not the name I had just given him. That was easy to deal with. "This is *his* bag," I explained, referring to someone who was putatively me, Jim Campbell. "I'm taking it home for him."

The policeman fixed me with a look which remains perfectly formed in memory.

"Oh. I see."

We were taken in an unmarked car to the City of Glasgow Police Headquarters in St Andrew's Square, where our identities—ha-ha, though I wasn't feeling that way at all—were registered at the front desk. Then we were escorted down a corridor and locked in a cell. It was by then approaching 4 o'clock, the hour at which school would be getting out. Soon my mother would be expecting to hear her hungry and surly son at the front door of our nice house in Kingshill Drive, the first "bought" house either of my parents had ever lived in, a satisfying stage in a difficult journey, the fulfilment of which would be the further education and success of their four children. My elder twin sisters were already well on the way.

The cell was bare and dim, though light enough to read the graffiti, which brought a brief amusement. Bruce added to it, probably something witty. We kept each other's spirits up with MAD-type jokes, and were served bacon sandwiches on "doorstep" white bread, dripping with butter, unforgettably good, and large mugs of milky tea. The detective returned.

Name? James Gunning.

Address? Something or other.

He left, closing the cell door heavily behind him.

What can I plead in mitigation? We were fourteen. It was just a few books—value one guinea, as Scottish legal history must somewhere record (six paperbacks at 3s 6d each, amounting to 21s). And we were readers, or at least Bruce was. My interests tended towards music. I know it was a Thursday and that we languished in the cell deep into the evening, because we were missing *Top of the Pops*, the era of the Animals, the

Byrds, the Righteous Brothers, of "Little Red Rooster" and "This Old Heart of Mine."

The detective came again. Name. Address. It was getting on towards nine. This time I asked *him* a question: When do we get out? That same look he had given me in the basement at Boots. "When someone calls for you."

Even a person with my interrupted education could tell there was a problem. Excuse me . . . well . . . you see . . .

He wasn't pleased at having had his time wasted. (Come to think of it, two plain-clothes detectives had just spent six hours with a pair of zealous readers in a Glasgow famous for violent crime.) My father was likewise noticeably not pleased, when he turned up at St Andrew's Square—the first time in recognized family history—to certify the reality of what had become by then my alternative identity—i.e., me.

Bruce Dryden stepped forward straight away and made a declaration which stays with me as the epitome of honor and decency. "Mr. Campbell, I just want to say . . ." It was he, not I, who had taken the six books. "Jim didn't steal anything." He hadn't mentioned his intention to do this during our hours in the cell.

By the time the court papers were served, in person at the door of the house by a uniformed policeman—another moment of profound mortification for my poor mother—I had left school and embarked on a six-year apprenticeship in a jobbing printing firm in Ingram Street, in Glasgow's Townhead district, second in notoriety only to the Gorbals. My journey-man, or master printer, was not impressed to learn that the new boy was due in court at the same St Andrew's Square one Tues-day—only a ten-minute walk from Ingram Street—and was required to take the afternoon off (wages docked accordingly).

Sign on the wall at Central Police Headquarters, St Andrew's Square, where the two juvenile book thieves went for trial.

The charge was theft, of books to the value of one pound and one shilling. Bruce was to plead guilty. I intended to plead not guilty, although a policewoman advised my mother that this might mean going to trial by jury and hiring a lawyer, with all the costs that that would entail. Bruce had been heard to say, "If you want it, put it on the pile," and the defendant had been observed doing just that. It might be better to plead guilty now and accept the punishment—a plea bargain, in effect. "Although that could leave you with a criminal record," my mother said, unable to decide which was the less dreadful course. Future difficulties with employers were sketched. "And if you ever want to go to America . . ."

I stuck to my plea.

After much hanging around among hard-edged types of our own age, and their seasoned guardians, the case came before the judge in the Juvenile Court. Bruce was fined one pound—a shilling less than the value of the books. The second defendant was admonished. James Gunning's misdeed in the basement at Boots and later at the police station was not mentioned. He vanished from the record. Until now.

2

A CONFESSION

While I remained at school, Bruce was still my best friend and, as our brush with the law had proved, a loyal one. Toryglen was an area at least two notes below King's Park on the social octave. My mother would have disapproved of him, had I brought him home, but I wasn't encouraged to invite friends from households lower down than ours. There was only one official prediction of the future family outcome and it was upward-looking. Bruce would not have been greeted warmly, even without the regrettable business at Boots and the aftermath in the court at St Andrew's Square.

He had an older brother, from whom he had absorbed certain advanced notions in relation to sex, clothes, alcohol and up-to-date tastes in pop music. In short, he was more switched on than I was, and naturally I was attracted to this, even when the lights dimmed and the setting grew dark enough to make me feel uncomfortable. There was some joshing in the school playground among his Toryglen associates, about stripping the lead off the roofs of houses and selling it to scrap-metal merchants in Govanhill and the Gorbals. Bruce himself didn't take part in this, but he and his brother, and his brother's cavalier friends, were part of the background against which the activity took place. They could swerve to try to avoid it, but somewhere on the journey would bump up against it. Some of these future thieves and burglars in the making were, like us, fourteen years old. St Andrew's Square awaited them.

It was out of this context, so feared by my mother—the fortune teller—that our next escapade was born. Had it been executed as intended, it would have been far worse in its consequences than anything that happened at Boots or in the cell with its graffiti archive, or later on in the court and its chilling anterooms. It is the hardest confession for me to make. We planned a mugging or, to be more precise, a bag-snatching. We would target a woman in the streets near Victoria Road, grab her handbag, then make a run for the main road, hopping on to the first bus that came along.

If I say it was originally Bruce's idea, it is not to excuse myself. And why were we doing this? Not for the money, or not principally, because I doubt if we expected to get away with much. It was the pure thrill of an act that was outsiderish, both adventurous and rebellious, something that would jolt us out of the stillness of a dark Southside Glasgow evening. It was the will to step beyond ordinary life, to be in another zone, just for a few moments, to drink an otherworldly potion, be the absorbing agent of an alien force. That it was a wicked force we must have vaguely known, but that did not prevent us from going ahead with the plan.

Bruce and I met on a Friday evening outside a café in Queen's Park, a decent, more traditional district than the newer development of King's Park, about twenty minutes' walk away. There was life on Victoria Road, pubs filled with the noise and smoke and beery smell of pay day—not a single one in the officially "dry" area of King's Park—and on the wide pavements you could mix with men and women of various sorts, boulevarding up and down, from this pub to that, from the Albert Bar to the Victoria, then on to the oddly named Queen's Park Café further north, before reaching the Star Bar at Eglinton

Toll. On Friday and Saturday nights there were dances at the Plaza close to the Toll, said to be a rough-house. We were too young to be a part of it, but we enjoyed being watchers, outsiders, palms against the beating heart.

The streets behind Victoria Road were residential and mostly quiet, lined with late-nineteenth-century sandstone tenements. There we stand, at a corner, two school-blazered lads for whom shaving is in the future—whatever future we might choose. Though ignorant of it at the instant of coming together that evening, we are in the act of choosing the future right here, right now. Did we whisper between ourselves, like real thieves in fear of being overheard—the "real" being borrowed from films or the collective myth of *Oliver Twist*? The lead thieves at school apart, I had never encountered a committed robber. We must have hesitated in advance of our act—a meaningless act, practically motiveless, committed only in order to draw a breath that would light up the inner cave: on this night *I am.*

I see the two of us, from above, as if caught in a screen shot, on a street corner to the west of Victoria Road. Night can't hide us. While I know that muscles were tense, I know equally that I was unaware that this was a night on which the course of my life might be determined. On the surface, I had little or no conception of "future." There was only the stretch of limbs, the utterances of lips and tongue. The present moment. Here on a Friday after school, in Queen's Park.

A woman walks towards us on one of the streets parallel to Victoria Road, perhaps Westmoreland Street or Annette Street. We would have not wanted to go too far from Victoria Road and the getaway bus of safety—a hypothetical, perhaps non-existent bus, on which our lives depended. A middle-aged, well-dressed woman, of a sort familiar to me. She wears a hat, suggesting that she is on her way to visit a friend or a sister, a Friday-night routine, always setting out at about this time. There might have been an appointment at the hairdresser's in the afternoon. Her husband could be enjoying his Friday night in the pub, as my father often did (not far from here, in the Albert Bar). Or perhaps she is a widow. Tailored coat, gloves to match, proper choice of bag.

She draws closer to the loitering boys. She doesn't fear these streets, overseen as they are by lighted windows. The knights of that great communal Glasgow are her invisible protectors. I see spectacles beneath the hat brim, and a smile in the eyes, though her heart registers the merest hesitation. This is a nice district. The Gorbals is a mile to the north, and the tribes of Glasgow by and large remain on their reservations. When they do go hunting, it is not for her. As it happens, she could rely on them for protection from hostile strays.

The boys seem to await her approach. They're probably looking for a street—she knows all the streets—or a café or youth club. Or they want to know which bus will take them from Victoria Road to—wherever they have to get to. She can help.

To their "Excuse me . . ." she replies, "Yes," a response not posed as a question but as assurance. Goodwill, assistance, friendliness—the famous Glasgow semaphore.

What happened next I remember only vaguely, though I do recall the crucial moment. I was not the one who did the talking, but I was there. Was a distant figure seen walking towards our trio from the further reach of Allison Street? Was there a sudden, shared shaming, on the part of the two villains, of the devil that had possessed them?

Bruce asked for directions—or for the number of a bus—and with a few maternal words she set us on the right course. The Glasgow coat-of-arms ought to be composed of a great big affirmative, rather than the negatives of tree that never grew, bird that never flew, fish that never swam. "Just go down to the road . . . you'll see the stop." There is pleasure in assisting two well-spoken boys.

We thanked her and turned in the direction to which she had pointed, walking slowly, smothering our shame in giggles—a shame not shown to one another, but mine admitted to myself, in relief. The embodiment of good nature continued on her way, tossing a farewell over her shoulder as she went.

That pedestrian who approached from the direction of Allison Street—if indeed he existed—whose suspected presence interrupted us: if he had taken a different route, or left by his front door a minute later . . . we would have run towards Victoria Road . . . jumped on a bus. That is, if we had managed to reach the bus stop. Our excited state would have aroused attention of a sort we had not foreseen. The victim would have shouted or screamed. The streets of Glasgow are full of heroes.

Much later, I read Per Petterson's novel *Out Stealing Horses*. Near the end, there is this passage. It comes after the narrator (the author in light disguise) has drawn back from hitting a stranger on the mouth in a street in a Swedish town. "If I had punched the man in Karlstad, my life would have been a different life, and I a different man. And it would be foolish to maintain, as so many men do, that it would have come to the same thing. It would not. I have been lucky. I have said that before. But it's true."

3

REPORT CARD

I

By the time of my third year at King's Park Secondary—school motto: "Video meliora petoque"; I see and aim for better things—I had proved myself to be better than any of my classmates in one subject: doggin' it; playing truant; a previous generation called it hooky. There were various strategies one could employ. You could just not turn up, offering an excuse retrospectively, or bringing a forged note purporting to be from a parent, which would outline some minor malady. You might declare yourself suddenly "not well" and ask to be allowed to go home—sore tummies were neither verifiable nor deniable—taking immediately to the great, green liberty of King's Park, across the main road, or else skipping on to a bus into town (fare-dodging, naturally), to browse in the big Argyle Street shops: Fraser's or Lewis's (the Polytechnic), or in the Boots at the corner of Union Street, where it all went wrong in the books department. If Bruce's parents were known to be out, we might spend half the day at his house in Toryglen, a lush-carpeted, soft sofa-ed domain that gave me a bright and comfortable feeling of living in one of the TV sitcoms I liked. Once, we broke into the drinks cabinet, using water from the tap to make up the depleted measures in the Gordon's and Johnnie Walker bottles.

When too many sore-tummy declarations ran the risk of technical interference from a doctor, it seemed safer to resort to the dentist. From a surgery near the school someone stole a stack of dental appointment cards and put them up for sale at threepence each. With date and time filled in, one of these could be presented to a skeptical teacher, providing a pass from the horrors of Algebra or Physics.

Most of the teachers regarded me with sentiments that fluctuated on the spectrum of exasperation, from baffled to benign. I had one acknowledged minor talent beyond my doggin' skill: English composition. If we had to do it in class, I could whip up something imaginative and amusing on a suggested topic in the duration of an ordinary period, forty minutes. There was a pleasure not to be found elsewhere in the confined spaces of school in feeling the story unfold under my hand, one invention rolling neatly into another, the creative spark heartened by a reassurance that it saved us from the insupportable labor of actually learning anything. Mr. Donald—Ducky Donald—more than once had me stand to read aloud my composition in class, encouraging a merry reaction from fellow pupils. I see now that he was doing it to try to draw me into the fold of diligent scholars.

Other aspects of the English curriculum could be negotiated with a minimum of effort: the mechanics of grammar, spelling, parsing, parts of speech, the ability to précis; all these had been drummed into me at Croftfoot Primary, and from there flowed into my present written work in a natural way. It came as easily to me as kicking a ball. My twin sisters, Jean and Phyllis, were the unchallenged stars of the Art class— their individual technical competence enhanced by their twinness—and their status cast a genial light on me there, too. I wasn't particularly good at drawing and painting, but I wasn't bad. The same could be said for Physical Education and Religious Instruction: *not bad*. As for everything else: *bad*.

At the conclusion of my first year among the elect, in the A class, reserved for brainy types, poor overall results led to relegation to the B stream. This meant dropping Latin, at which I had gained a respectable 67 percent in the inaugural exam. "Amo, amas, amat," Mr. Forgie had us repeat over and over. "Ama*bo*, ama*bas*, ama—" . . . "No, you're not," old Forgie would insist, patrolling the aisles between the rows of desks, sergeant-major fashion. "You are many disgusting things, but you are not a *bo* or a *bas*."

"Am*a*bo, am*a*bas, am*a*bat."

"That's better. Campbell, greet your fellow citizen, Miss Wells, in the forum, and ask if the shepherds have guided their flocks to safety for the night."

"Safety from what, sir?"

"From boys like you, Campbell."

Much laughter. "From wolves, of course."

I did so. Aileen Wells was an old Croftfoot Primary comrade. She and I were two out of only three from a class of over forty to be selected for the A stream at the new, bigger, more competitive King's Park. She replied: "Salve, civis. Gratias ago tibi, quia doluistis."

Even down among the Bs, I hadn't yet teamed up with Bruce, who was with the Cs. Few boys or girls from Castlemilk or Toryglen made it into A or even B. Their brightness glowed with a different amplitude. One of the attractive characters seen swaggering about the playground was Big George, the son of Greek immigrants, with rocky Mediterranean features and dark curly hair, the kind of charismatic figure around whom others cluster at every school. He lived in Toryglen, naturally. When Mr. Forgie, chief belter at King's Park Secondary, summoned George for some infringement or other and told

The playground at King's Park Secondary School, mid-1960s. The school was proposed as one of Glasgow's first comprehensives, though pupils were streamed from A to G. *Courtesy of Glasgow School of Art Archives.*

him to hold out his hands in preparation for two or four or perhaps six strokes of the belt—never one, three or five—he said: "This hurts me more than it hurts you, Kavouras." To which Big George replied (or said he did): "I wouldnae want that. Let's swap places, well."

But the C stream was not far away. At the end of second year, it was suggested that I might repeat the entire course, which would mean dropping down to be among a younger lot and losing close contact with all my pals. If there was a hierarchy in the school, it was based not on social class or talent but on seniority. There was something humiliating about the idea, whereas there was nothing shameful about having failed in just about every subject in the exams and bullying weaker boys at lunchtime to yield up their homework so that we could copy it in time for the afternoon bell. It would also have meant going through the hell of second-year Chemistry and Physics all over again, as well as other subjects my brain couldn't cope with.

It couldn't cope with much. Exam marks came at the end of term: 30-something for French, 20-something for History, even lower for Geography, Maths and Physics. Only in English did I dimly glow. In Art, it was borderline.

Of course the results were far too low to be shown to my parents. There was nothing to be gained by it. My father would have punished me—not with violence, to which he resorted only in fits of impatience, but with something much worse, something that really hurt: being kept in at night. The idea was that if I could be confined to my room each evening after school for a week, instead of running off to the park to pursue in earnest the things that mattered—in the past, a ball; in the present, increasingly, a girl—I would buckle down to my subjunctives and dates and tectonic shifts and memorize the Periodic Table, ultimately performing at the level of what was alleged to be my potential. How had I got into the A stream in the first place, anyway, along with nice Aileen Wells and that swot Alan Buckley? Nobody knew. By an oversight, perhaps.

So I took the only route available to someone in my predicament: I altered the report card results to resemble something more acceptable. I used a black Biro pen. Twenty-something became 40-something—hardly a show-off improvement, but enough to evade the threat of incarceration. Thirty-six for French might have become, by two deft strokes, 86, but that would be to invent an achievement I could never live up to; 66 would do, and even that was stretching credulity.

When my father had signed the card, making much of his reluctance to do so, insisting in his look-sharpish Navy-discipline voice that I must "do better give yourself a shake boy-o pull up your socks young fellamalad," I restored the marks to their original state with the help of that modern miracle-worker, the ink rubber. The task was thus completed. No one was harmed by it. No one was exactly happy, but at least life could carry on without unpleasant interruption. The long, light, after-school evenings patrolling the streets or playing football in King's Park were my intake of oxygen. I lived for them and by them.

"He's no daft," Dad would say in lighter moments. "He only acts like it." He would also say (over and again), "If you had 20 percent more brains, you'd be an idiot," which itself took some brains to work out. And if I said something meant to be funny: "You're a bit of a wit. A half."

These remarks were supposed to be good-humored—ill humor was expressed in other terms—but they represented his genuine feelings. They exhibited just a fraction of an over-all frustration. Harry Campbell was himself a wit, a party man, gifted with an abundance of that Glasgow humor that Billy Connolly would soon make famous all over the world, handsome and intelligent and staunchly dutiful, much liked by neighbors and family friends. He had left school at the age of fourteen to work as a barrow boy in Glasgow's Fruit Market in Townhead. He and my mother, Ina—a neighbor in Shaw-lands but a pupil at a different school—met a year or two later in "the crowd," as she liked to put it, "that we went around with" in the years leading up to their envelopment in the Second World War. Her family—pedigree Protestant Scottish Lowland working class—was none the less a rung higher on the social ladder than his, which had the taint of emerald Irish in the background.

Her father, Jimmy Beveridge, was the janitor at the school

she attended, Shawlands Academy, though the word "janitor" barely describes the position of responsibility he held and the work he did, everything from odd-job carpentry and interior decoration to organizing rugby matches and the annual school sports day. It's a guess, but I imagine that the headmaster regarded Jimmy as the man who was running the school. The families visited each other during holidays in Scottish resorts, such as Dunoon, Helensburgh, and Rothesay. Grandpa had a cine camera for making short, silent films, to which he gave titles: "Doon the Water," for example, a film about pleasure steamers on the River Clyde. In one of them, the headmaster, dressed in three-piece suit and tie, can be seen on holiday, smiling broadly, with his wife and our grandmother beside him.

The job came with a house next to the school, in which my mother and her younger sister Rona were raised. They were intensely respectable, and I see her father as an essential Scottish type: a man of energy and all-round geniality from a modest background, with no feelings of inferiority, no trade or training but a multifarious artisanal talent and—a strange word to use of a church-going, self-educated Scot born almost within the lifetime of Robert Louis Stevenson—modernity.

After joining up as a teenager and serving in the Highland Light Infantry during the First World War, surviving close-up engagement by the breadth of a collarbone, Grandpa worked as an adaptable builder in different parts of Scotland, going wherever the next job took him. He cut and shaped and piled the stones one on top of the other in the construction of the Gleneagles Hotel in Perthshire in the early 1920s, and my mother retained memories of the family living in the nearby village of Blackford just after the hotel opened in 1924. In later life, she chose to return to live in a place that was within walking distance of Blackford. He measured and sawed and hammered our bunk beds, our toys—a fort, a farmyard, and a garage ("Jim's") for me—and was on call whenever Mum required practical advice. "Och, I'll ask Dad about it," she would say, when the other dad—ours—looked as if he wasn't up to the job. In the 1930s, Grandpa owned various cameras, a gypsy caravan near Helensburgh for weekends away, and a car in which to drive to get there. During the 1950s and 60s, he worked in a garage opposite the school in his free hours, and in my mental snapshots never looks happier than when something needed fixing on his Austin A40 or Wolseley Eight, with its opening windscreen. He could probably have built you a car—or a house—if you had said you needed one.

Our dad lacked these skills. He also lacked Grandpa's liking for camping, walking in the country, his shared language with domestic animals and small children, his curiosity about the names of birds and plants. Dad's father, John Campbell, had been one of ten children, and Dad himself was the youngest of eight—in themselves eyebrow-raising statistics in the poorer areas of the city, suggestive of the Roman Catholic Church. And indeed we discovered later from census returns that the first Campbell relation of record, Charles, a "blacksmith's labourer," had arrived from County Armagh sometime during the period between 1835 and 1855, the year in which he was married near Glasgow to Helen Connahan, a "scourer" from Donegal. They were united in Paisley, "according to the rites and ceremonies of the Roman Catholic Church." Both gave their ages as twenty. Helen signed the 1855 form with an X, "her mark."

Their son, the first in a succession of John Campbells, found work in the shipyards. Dad reminisced about the sound of riveters thudding through the streets around the great ship-yards on the Clyde—Fairfields of Govan, where his father had worked, Dennys of Dumbarton which could claim the phrase "steam-driven," John Brown's, Blythswood, Connell, and Yarrow. At places near the river you could hardly hear yourself speak when passing by. In George Blake's novel *The Shipbuilders* (1935), the main character Leslie Pagan recalls how "up and down the river the bows of vessels unlaunched towered over the tenement buildings of the workers" and how "the clangour of metal upon metal filled the valley from Old Kilpatrick up to Govan." Dad talked of it sometimes as ancestral lore.

My paternal grandfather, the third John of record, married Emily, née McColl, in the Roman Catholic Church in Kinning Park. She was, however, a Protestant and the last of the Irish Campbells crossed over to the Church of Scotland before Dad was born. It was not a particularly religious household and I suspect that the conversion was undertaken out of social convenience, or perhaps for reasons of education. During our childhoods, he never mentioned the crossover, even once—Mum wouldn't have liked it—only crying out, in the course of a joke, "Campbells of Donegal!" When at the age of about six or seven I asked, "Dad, who were our ancestors?" he paused for thought before replying, "We come from a very distinguished family. We're related to Adam and Eve."

II

Apart from the awfulness of school lessons and the occasional bust-up at home, I wasn't having too bad a time. I was fair and open-faced, no matter how earnestly I tried to affect a tough exterior, and attracted the attention of girls. I had adventurous pals. I liked a fight now and then. It was mostly a version of the boxing-match workout recommended for centuries by teachers and superior officers to absorb adolescent energy, but in my case outside the ring. One Saturday evening, after a lager-and-lime session in a Buchanan Street pub (sixteen-year-olds had no trouble getting served back then), my drinking companion and I walked up one of the alleys that connect the main thoroughfares in the center of town and had an exhilarating three-minute scrap, before heading downhill to Central Station to catch the 10:10 pm Blue Train back to King's Park, where we parted as the best of pals. The parents of friends seemed to think I was bright, in a way that my own parents did not, blinded by the smoke rising from the scorched wasteland I left behind in almost every classroom. My knowledge of progressive popular music was becoming as wide-ranging as my knowledge of Scottish football had been at an earlier age. I could reel off Rangers teams through the ages, and can do so now—Niven, Shearer, Caldow; McCall, McKinnon, Baxter; Scott, McMillan, Miller, Brand, and Wilson—and could give you most of their club histories and places of birth into the bargain. The problem was school. I hated it. In return, it produced ample evidence—the evidence of the report card—that it could barely tolerate me.

Here are the figures from the last report card to be issued, May 1966: French 29 percent; History 22 percent; Maths 12 percent; Geography 8 percent. These are the ones I remember. In English I passed capably and in Art hovered around the midway mark, as usual. The science subjects I would drop on moving out of third year. The threat of a repeat had been avoided last time, but only just. Instead, I was shunted downstream to float among the Cs, where I sat next to Bruce in whatever subjects we shared. We used our jotters to exchange a concoction of *MAD* jokes and drawings and, from my side—a new thing—poems.

There could be no question of exhibiting these exam results at Kingshill Drive. The summer holidays were coming up: two months of open air, the feel of clean jeans on loose limbs, the annual trip to the Highlands and Portmahomack, to stay on the nearby farm at Rockfield where Mum had done her joyful service in the Women's Land Army during the war.

These once-enchanted holidays were starting to overlap with new-generation adventures, arriving too soon and too quickly and in too great a profusion to fit my parents' understanding: going on the road to Edinburgh, for example, with Bruce, to seek the sight, perhaps even the company, of beatniks; reckless bicycle rides on busy roads to places as far away as Saltcoats; the mingled scents and touch of neck and hair and flimsy nylon raincoat in a dingy tenement close; drawing more meaning, more intensely, from music than ever.

It was the nearest I would come to the freedom I had known in my blissful pre-Croftfoot Primary life, before the Fall. The expulsion from Eden arrived with the bitter fruit of knowledge: that school attendance and study (so-called) was a fact of life, destined to endure into the distant era of double figures—the ages of ten, eleven, twelve—carrying on through the teens: a daily, purgatorial stretch of classroom confinement. Dad explained to me that school would be followed by university, where studies would become even harder. I couldn't make sense of it. After all, I hadn't asked to bite the apple.

As those exam results came in, I was about to turn fifteen. Bob Dylan had replaced the Rolling Stones as my cultural amulet. The sounds of the American anti-war protest movement

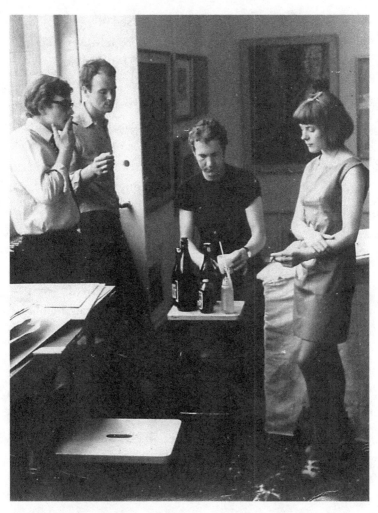

Jean, with fellow students, at her Diploma Show, Glasgow School of Art, 1968. Phyllis would have her show the year after. *Courtesy of the Carey family.*

were now heard across the world, expressed in folk music with intriguing lyrics, and the vibrations were felt even at King's Park Secondary: "Oh deep in my heart, I do believe, that we shall overcome some day . . ." How beautiful it sounded—more beautiful, perhaps, than anything I had heard up until then—in the Joan Baez vibrato. The music took up residence in the body. "Last night there were four Marys, Tonight there'll be but three . . ." The sounds now came into our home in the form of LPs in interesting covers with long essays on the back, which my sisters bought or borrowed from their with-it—how Dad enjoyed using that expression—art school friends.

Everything about Dylan's songs attracted me from first hearing: the yearning in the voice, the melodies, the protest against racial injustice in some, the seductive American vernacular of others, the jokes in something called a "talking blues," direct addresses to the president of the United States, place names right, left and center—"I'm going ba-a-a-ack . . . to Co-lo-rado"—dazzling imagery through it all. Unlike poetry that existed only on the page, the kind that Ducky Donald strove to interest us in, Dylan's poetry was transmitted to memory automatically, by melody and rhythm. I consoled myself on the road up to school in the morning by singing my way through one or two of his songs, just as literary folk of an earlier generation might have inwardly recited "Ode to a Nightingale" or a Shakespeare sonnet.

The key note was freedom, freedom. "How many years can some people exist," before freedom's embrace will welcome them? It didn't matter that Dylan had in mind whole subjugated peoples—an understanding gradually dawning. For now, the question applied to me.

During an English period, while Mr. Donald promised

delights in store between the covers of *Great Expectations* as he handed out class readers, I copied into my school jotter the words of an anti-war poem I had written after our weekend in Edinburgh, when I had met a little beatnik fellow with long dark hair from Castlemilk: John Cochrane, known as Coakie. He and I had ended up hitch-hiking home to Glasgow in the back of an open truck, while Bruce returned by bus. It left me with a new feeling—it went very deep—of "something I want to do."

Coakie was a member of the Young Communist League and wrote ban-the-bomb poetry. I didn't join the YCL, as he encouraged me to do—"A dustman's goanie make the same money as a doacter"—but I picked up on the poetry.

At the back of my school English jotter, the one with the fateful identity written in block letters on the front, the identity which had betrayed me at St Andrew's Square—"Jim Campbell, 42 Kingshill Drive"—I began writing lines on big subjects borrowed from the new, meaningful music that was suddenly all around, on the radio, on 7-inch singles, at parties. Freedom. Travel. Peace. War. It had evolved from Frankie Vaughan singing, "Honey Bunny Baby" to "We Shall Overcome" in just a few years.

One of my anti-war poems opened with the lines, "Death creeps slowly o'er the hill, / God's armies mass before the kill." With a bit of time, I might have ironed out that irregular beat. At the end, as a sort of coda, I appended the final stanza of Dylan's magisterial "Masters of War," a song addressed to cowardly politicians who shelter in offices behind desks while blood spreads and stains the field of battle.

Dylan had taken the melody for "Masters of War" from the English folk song "Nottamun Town," in the way that he appropriated many traditional tunes for modern purposes, and now I was borrowing Dylan's lyrics and folding them into my own protest poem. I tore the portmanteau work from the jotter and, without revealing the source of the final lines, passed it to Bruce, who read it as Ducky Donald ingenuously declaimed the opening words of Pip's narrative, in hope of hooking our attention.

We lingered together in the corridor during the brief interval before our next period. He liked the first part, my part, Bruce told me, but he mocked the ending, which I had pinched from Dylan. As we headed down the stairs to the first floor and Mr. Howard's Maths class, he spoke aloud the words of the song, until then unfamiliar to him, before landing on a laugh. "'Stand over . . .' What?" Then he came on with the strong Scottish voice, as he sometimes did: "Till ah ken ye're deid? Come off it, Campbell!"

Bruce loved the Beatles, as he had loved our *MAD* comics and the James Bond novels. His elder brother had got the Beatles album *Rubber Soul* for Christmas in 1965, and I listened to it in the New Year while lying on the shaggy cream rug before the electric fire in their TV-sitcom house in Toryglen. I was growing out of the comics but had not grown into the novels, and never would. On Coakie's recommendation, I was trying to read Wordsworth—in the park, while doggin' off—without much understanding but conscious that the words transmitted some odd feeling, nevertheless. It took you away for a few moments, and when you returned something had altered, as the light was altered by a cloud melting.

In class, Mr. Boyd the long-nosed History teacher—Beaky Boyd—asked each of us what he or she would like to do when the moment came to step out of whatever college we had chosen for our further education and go forth into the world. We had played this game in primary school in a composition, "What I want to be when I grow up." The boy sitting next to me, Andrew Miller, son of a postman, wrote that he wanted to be prime minister. I said I wanted to be a lollipop man. My inspiration was the white-coated figure at the top of our crescent, who saw us safely across the busy road each morning on the way to school with his red-and-white "children crossing" lollipop.

Now, when Mr. Boyd's question came round, I told the class I wanted to be a tramp. The teacher, no doubt expecting something of the sort from the disruptive boy, "the twins' younger brother," showed his exasperation and his scorn. He had never heard of Jack Kerouac and neither had I, but there was something in the air that only I was capable of picking up—something screened from Mr. Boyd and the rest of the class—a new kind of hip vagabondage. Dylan and Joan Baez were spinning a web of song lines all round the world and I was ready to follow the threads.

> All my life the blues has come and gone.
> I'm only getting started, it's time for movin' on,
> Honey, you won't see me here by dawn.

It was a new language, expressing a new spirit of adventure, and if it shunted old Beaky Boyd aside . . . well, he was just a History teacher anyway, a man of the past.

I was acting the smart alec, trying to deflect attention from my paltriness in the academic department, and he could see this but didn't know what to do about it. If there were an opportunity for a retrospective apology, I would send one to

The twins, Phyllis and Jean, Christmas, 1953, in our living room at Castlemilk Crescent, Croftfoot.

him without hesitation. But there was some truth in the ambition that I myself could not have made articulate, and in a few years' time I would set out to fulfil it.

Dylan brought his voice, his hairstyle, his shades, his cunning—the message was in the hairstyle and the cunning as much as in the lyrics—to the Glasgow Odeon in May 1966 on the famous tour with the Hawks, and I went to see him. The concert took the form of a sublime first-half solo acoustic performance, followed by a plugged-in electric set with the

Hawks, the Band in all but name. People called out from the stalls, "Give us the real Bob Dylan," as Robbie Robertson and the Hawks kicked up an unprecedented racket in folkie ears. In the middle of one song, Dylan extended a hand to silence the musicians behind him. "Bob couldn't make it tonight," he said, addressing the hecklers in the near rows. "I'm here in his place. My name's Donovan."

The crowd laughed and clapped, even though they still felt that the man in Cuban heels with the Fender Telecaster wasn't the real Bob Dylan. To others, he satisfied all present needs, with a smidgen of our native Donovan thrown in. Joan Baez, also part-Scottish, by ancestry and by art, was more to my sisters' taste, and I liked her, too. How could anyone not like her? "I'm having a good time tonight," we heard her say on the album *Joan Baez in Concert*, "and if nobody objects I'm going to take off my shoes." The whole family sat round the small black-and-white television in the living room, to watch a two-part concert on the BBC, one of the two channels available.

The face itself is a good enough reason for watching it now. Joan Baez's magnificent voice, by which, she said, she was simply possessed, is often spoken of; but her face is almost equally captivating. As she leans towards the microphone between songs, testing her pitch, the sound takes control of her features. Her heart becomes visible. The world would be a different place without the faces of that era: the face of Baez itself is a work of genius. So is Dylan's—a face that will change twenty times in twenty separate photographs, taken over a period of five or six years. It goes without saying that the 1960s would have been different without the music of the Rolling Stones, but we can also say it would have been different without Mick Jagger's face.

Jean was in the second year of study at Glasgow School of Art now—Phyllis had followed a year later—and brought home records by Bert Jansch and Davey Graham: new songs, new ways of singing, scintillating twists of scarcely credible virtuosity on a six-string guitar. It was music for youthful intellectuals, and it spoke directly and forcefully to me. Something was stirring in that old A stream inclination, without me knowing much about it.

<h2 style="text-align:center">III</h2>

Here is the story the report card told, as it approached 42 Kingshill Drive, shuddering nervously in my canvas haversack, one late afternoon in May, 1966: French 49 percent; History 42; Maths 42—Dad would never have believed anything higher—Geography probably a miserable 38 percent, but what else could I say? The single-digit results were easiest to forge, and therefore welcome in that respect. In English and Art I had passed without distinction. I didn't find it necessary to tell myself not to get carried away in making the latest improvements. I wasn't doing this to gain approval: that would have fitted my haphazard conception of dishonesty. I simply didn't want there to be a scene. It was to no one's advantage.

The card walked up the garden path, entered by the front door, never locked in daytime when Mum was at home, and presented itself to Dad when he returned from work by the Blue Train, from Glasgow Central to King's Park station, at 5:40 pm, as he did almost invariably. Meanwhile I stood to the side in mute apprehensiveness.

There was a fuss, but not too much of one. I had to give myself a shake, pull up my socks, get stuck in. I said I would—

of course I would—convincing no one, certainly not me. Then I went upstairs to play the Davey Graham album *Folk, Blues and Beyond*, which Jean or Phyllis had borrowed from some suitably with-it fellow art student. The sleeve notes, which I read with a degree of attentiveness never squandered on classroom lessons, mentioned Big Bill Broonzy, Reverend Gary Davis and Blind Willie Johnson—the constructions themselves rich with suggestion and the promise of other worlds, other place names—beyond Colorado and states hymned by Dylan—other folk and other colors, other ways of seeing things and being in life.

I was already addicted to the sweet taste of Ray Charles singing "Take These Chains From My Heart" and "I Can't Stop Loving You," and I played the 45 rpm singles—again borrowed from friends by Jean and Phyllis—over and over. They had bargaining power, those twin sisters: looks, talent, common sense, all-round feminine good nature. They could have got away with a lot, but had no need to try. The lot came to them. Life liked them, as it liked our mother, who had passed on these qualities to her daughters.

The next day I went back up the hill to school ("How many roads must a man . . .") with the signed report card and returned it to the teacher, as directed. By now it was getting to be an old trick, and I was a jaded conjuror, blasé about his magic. The ink eraser was set aside. My ingenious performance no longer required the presence of a rubber assistant. The card entered the historical archive at King's Park Secondary in its fictional state—not good, not even *not bad*, but not kept-in-at-night awful—never to be retrieved.

Or that's what I assumed would happen. One day near the end of term, in a French class—"The past historic is formed by taking the root of the present indicative . . . Bruce, tell us when to use the past historic . . ."—the deputy headmaster Mr. Crawford entered and spoke to the lovely Miss Christie in low tones. She always wore a black, flowing academic gown over a blouse and skirt, setting off her blonde hair which she pinned up. She had only to shrug off that gown at the end of the teaching day to appear to be undressing in front of us. The way she walked into the room at the start of a lesson when we were all seated, pointer in hand. The way she looked at you with a young woman's maternal fondness—no matter what— that I was capable of comprehending only later, in memory. Children of her own lay in the future; in the meantime, she had us. She had lately married, but was still Miss Christie.

When someone higher up came through the door and interrupted a lesson, everyone in the class assumed it must be about me, and it was. Summoned from my refuge at the back of the room—French was actually something I was working up an interest in—I traipsed along the corridor behind Mr. Crawford, followed him sheepishly down the stairs to his office at playground level and sat on a chair, as instructed, while he tucked himself in comfortably behind his desk.

Ah, yes, now. How were we getting on?

Not bad, thanks.

People said I had a nice speaking voice. Deep down, much deeper than the words the voice itself could call on, I knew that, despite everything, it projected a better self, a me that one day I would become familiar with. Some of the boys and girls at the new school since it had moved from King's Park up to Simshill (though it remained King's Park Secondary) wouldn't feel that. They were different from my sisters and me. Their coarse, untrainable voices were, in many cases, their nature and their future.

How were things at home?

Shrug. Grunt. Gaze at the wall. "OK."

A pause. A look, half-concerned, obviously false, not even intended to convince. It was all stagey. He was leading up to something and I thought I knew what it was.

And the evenings—what did I do in the evenings? Played football, mostly. Better not to mention girls and "getting somewhere"—not far—and the odd harmless fight to work off energy and stealing apples from gardens after dark in the autumn, and Bounty bars and Cadbury's Flakes from corner shops in daylight. Bruce and I sometimes went to see what he had been told, by his brother or by Big George, were risqué films, including *Yesterday, Today and Tomorrow* with Sophia Loren. At the end, Bruce promised, she removes her bra during the striptease she is performing in a bedroom for Marcello Mastroianni. I can recall our excited approach on the top deck of a bus to the Toledo cinema in Clarkston Road, the odorous, faded blue-velvet seats on which we sat throughout two hours of Italian romantic comedy dubbed into English, only to discover during the crucial scene, a few minutes from the end, that she has an attack of Catholic conscience and keeps it on.

So mainly football, yeah. That was about it. I hadn't made it into the school team, though I had been a goal-scoring inside-left in the last year at primary—Ralph Brand's position at Ibrox—and had fancied myself at the secondary school trials. Instead, I was playing for the Boys' Brigade on Saturday mornings, for which "everyone gets a game," as someone who was selected for the school First XI was tactless enough to tell me. That had been a great disappointment. The old King's Park was smaller, the pupils more aspirational in their sums and sentences. I would definitely have been selected there. Here, the boys from rougher areas kept me out. They were always the best at sports like football. The teacher in charge of the teams, Mr. Howard, had promised me a second trial—"You look like more of a player than some of them," he had said with kindly world-weariness—but it had never come about.

"What about homework?" Mr. Crawford asked, coming to the point. He was still doing the genial act, though now with a dollop of obligatory sternness. "Do you spend much time on that?"

A bit. Not as much as I should, probably.

A look of mock surprise. His tone changed again, becoming avuncular. He couldn't fool me and he was barely trying to.

"How are the lessons going?"

"Uh . . . Not so good . . ."

"What about the exams just past? How did you get on in the exams?"

"Not very well, if I'm honest."

I had to be honest, obviously. It was a great inconvenience, but the other thing—dishonesty, which had served me well until now—had run out.

"Maths, for example." Mr. Crawford was himself a Maths teacher, though I had never been in his class. "How did you do in Maths?"

". . . Not very well . . . I think . . . twelve percent."

"Twelve!"

He was taking it all the way. Enjoying it? Not really. Maybe he thought it was easier on me to go through this pantomime. He slid open the drawer of his desk and withdrew a repulsive-looking thing, my report card. "It says here forty-two percent." Our eyes met for a second. "How about Geography?"

"Only eight."

"Eight percent!" He extended his arm across the desk with the pamphlet-shaped report card open at the latest exams, Spring term, 1966. "What does it say there?"

It said thirty-eight percent. My modesty in making the changes was surely some kind of accomplishment in itself, but not enough of one to win him over. He went through the others, then flicked back to previous tables of exam figures, where the grubby evidence of the ink rubber—not such a miracle worker, after all—suggested historical tampering.

Mr. Crawford didn't rant and rave. He wanted to show as much patience as was available to him. They were decent people, the teachers at King's Park Secondary, and they wanted their pupils to be good and decent, too. "I see and aim for better things." That was what we were all there for, with a few vicious Castlemilk exceptions. We were in it together. It was just that, in my case, the togetherness had fallen apart. Other than being belted earnestly from time to time by Mr. Forgie, which hurt, and reluctantly by a few others such as Ducky Donald and Beaky Boyd, which didn't, I can recall little unkindness from teachers. It was we who were unkind to them. Lies and insolence and ignorance: that's what they got in return for aiming for better things.

"Butter wouldn't melt in your mouth, Jim," Miss Christie had said with a kindly smile on presenting me with one of the card-framed portrait photographs we all sat for. Her good nature wanted to like me, and I would have liked being liked by her. Other teachers liked me, too, when I put myself up for affection, which wasn't often. But something had stood in the way of my being liked, and of my learning, and there didn't seem to be any way of removing the obstacle other than by removing myself from the school.

My twin sisters wanted their troublesome wee brother to prosper, but there was an element in their solidarity with one another and their with-it, pretty friends, their twin-ness in the face of the world and the immediate society surrounding our family, all linked to their small but real and forward-looking successes, that cast me into an intimate solitariness. It was mine, in the way that little else was, besides the music and the jeans and the elusive fragrance of some Toryglen infatuation in a glistening raincoat. I had no choice—I wasn't even aware of the possibility of "choice," acting by instinct alone—but to extricate myself from the predicament on my own terms. It sounds trite to say the "existential predicament," but that's what it was. I could *choose* something else, but first I had to identify the nature of the choice, to recognize that there was a choice. Pulling my socks up wasn't going to do it.

Mr. Crawford let me know that he was not going to punish me. The case was beyond the reach of routine school punishment. He would have to write to my father, which even he seemed to realize was far worse from my point of view than a few strokes of the silly old belt. Then we would see what could be done, before the summer holidays came along. The most likely outcome would be to repeat third year, this time with little room for negotiation. I was immature. Time would take care of it. Academic performance would improve along with everything else, if we gave it time. After I had repeated third year, I would be set fair for O Grades at the end of fourth.

"You're good at some things," he said sympathetically. "What happened?"

Everyone knew I was good at English, though they also said that if I tried harder and paid attention, I could be much better. "Careless" was a word often used. Miss Christie, with permissive fondness, called me a dreamer, and it's true I preferred the classroom window beyond which lay mountains and seas and the lonesome road down which a man must walk many times, to the blackboard with its ugly words like "imperfect" and "subjunctive."

"You used to do quite well at Latin," Mr. Crawford said, flicking back to marks he could tell at a glance were authentic. I could count and do long division. The Arithmetic side of Maths wasn't the problem; it was Algebra, the cryptogrammatic language of the Devil, together with the confounding theorems of Geometry, that made my head spin and took malign possession of my will. I had learned my multiplication tables at primary school and would never forget them, as pupils at neighboring Catholic schools were not allowed to forget their catechisms and classical scholars their Virgil. "What happened?" Nobody knew.

I left his office. This was no time for dreaming. I had to pull up my socks and give myself a shake. There was a job to be done: the letter that Mr. Crawford was about to write and send to my father would have to be intercepted before it dropped through the letterbox at 42 Kingshill Drive.

4

THE LAND GIRL AND THE PETTY OFFICER: AN INTERLUDE

I

The war demanded service from both the school janitor's daughter from Moss Side Road and the range fitter's son from Quentin Street, as they emerged from their teens. He was called up for the Navy in late 1942, posted first to Plymouth, then to Invergordon in the Scottish Highlands and later Ceylon, in readiness for the battle on the Eastern Front. She went into the Land Army, the "replacement agricultural force" from which women stepped willingly into the fields to stand in for men on military duty. Seeking a Highland position, so as to be not far removed from his Navy call-up, she was taken on at Rockfield Farm in Easter Ross, near the seaside village of Portmahomack—always spoken of among familiars as "the Port."

It was Mum's great good luck to be billeted with the shepherd and his wife at Rockfield. To her and the young man courting her, they were Mr. and Mrs. Young, and remained so when the newly married couple went back up north for family summer holidays, three years out of four, for two decades and more after the war had ended. To the twins and me, and later Julie, they were always Uncle Willie and Aunt Mary. Out of hearing, Dad called him the Big Man.

Originally from Cromarty in the Black Isle, south of Portmahomack, Willie Young was a Highland shepherd in a manner unchanged by the passing of centuries. The world he and Aunt Mary inhabited was a different world to the one we lived in, preferable in many ways. It was a folkloric home from home, where the green fields, the dry-stone dykes, the sand and the sea came up to the door, just as schools and shops, cars and buses, busy roads and lollipop men to help you cross them were at ours. You spent the entire day under the sky, half of it on the shore, all of it in the gladness of imagination. When Uncle Willie and his mysteriously authoritative dogs, Fly and Glen, shepherded the baaa-ing flock to market, from Rockfield Farm to the burgh of Tain, twelve miles by farm track and tarmac road, it was no less fascinating an adventure than a Chaucerian pilgrimage would have seemed, had I happened to witness one on the way to the sea.

Each time I made the journey from the shepherd's cottage to the Port on my own, aged nine, ten, twelve, Aunt Mary would say, "Just go down to the road, Jim. You'll get a lift." Sure enough, the first approaching vehicle would pull up alongside the fair-haired boy, and the driver would scoot him to Portmahomack in exchange for two miles' worth of jetty-fishing and rockpool-dabbling conversation. No raised hand or thumb was needed. The drivers always seemed to know that we were lodged with Mrs. Young. Sometimes they even knew my name.

On the first day of the holiday, Dad and I would go together to the jetty at the Port, but not before making an excursion to the all-purpose Co-operative on the front to buy a net, a hook and a line. On the wet sands we would use my spade and pail to dig for lugworms. The line needed a weight, however—what Dad called "a sinker"—to take the baited hook to the depths where fishes lurked.

Once, as we came out of the shop, Dad spotted a scrap merchant's horse and cart on the main street of the Port. Horses were not so far from having been regular farm workers. As

I admired this one, Dad quickened his step to catch up with the driver.

"Hello there, Jimmy!"

The carter tugged the reins to bring the horse to a halt.

"Have you got a wee bit of lead for a sinker for the boy's fishing line?"

The Highlander was happy to oblige. Then he shuffled the reins and muttered something to his four-legged companion.

"Thanks a lot, Jimmy!" Dad shouted after them.

He fixed the weight to the line and we headed to the sandbanks, where orphaned ancient tarry anchors bit massively into the sands.

"How did you know that man's name was Jimmy?"

A pause. A gaze over placid waters.

"I met him in the Navy during the war."

In the evenings, if we happened to be in the Port and not at the farm, Mum would ask one of the wise fishermen loitering near the harbor to read the sky and foretell tomorrow's weather. "I doot it'll be fine, Ina," he would say, rubbing his hands together and smiling warmly. These fishermen returned from the Dornoch Firth with herring and mackerel by the box and bucketful, to be shared widely among villagers and visitors like us. Sometimes a silent salmon would make the journey back to Glasgow in Dad's golf bag.

The closest neighbors to us at Rockfield Farm were chickens. Two horses stood loyally in the field, Prince and Silver Eye, the latter named for his left-side blindness. Milk from the cow, cream from the milk, butter from the churn, oatcakes and crowdie, honey from the comb, peas from the pod, berries from the thorn, eggs from the henhouse, and on special days a chicken on the table. Laughin' tatties were floury potatoes whose skin split on the cool dinner plate when removed from the pan, letting the steam rise up. The front porch at the cottage was peopled by giants' boots, tweed jackets, waterproofs matt and glossy at the same time, varied hats, shepherds' crooks worn smooth by shepherd's grip, curiosities such as a lobster creel and conch shells through which you could listen to the sea. Like that sound, "creel" was a word that came into play only on holiday, and precious for that alone. The same went for items of new knowledge. I learned for example that, as companions, sheepdogs could never be compromised.

The Youngs had a daughter, Ishbel, born in the late 1920s, a teenager in wartime, who became my mother's lifelong friend. Their two younger sons were Malcolm and Derek, and the infant Malcolm served as a stand-in for my mother until her own son came along.

The Land Girl's work was not unpleasant. "I spent the day today planting potatoes and sewing peas," Mum wrote in a letter to her Navy sweetheart. Throughout the remainder of her long life, she felt blessed by this posting, and as the war drew to a close thought of taking a job and staying up North, hoping to lure her husband-to-be into agreement. She was popular with the local people, as she was everywhere she went. When Mum and Dad celebrated their Golden Wedding in Portmahomack in 1996, the folk I encountered in the seaside street still asked after her by her maiden name, Ina Beveridge. One former farm worker from Rockfield mistook me for my father. "By Jove, but you're lookin' well, Harry!" At the party after the anniversary dinner, as at many parties before and later, she played the piano in the bar at the Castle Hotel, while Dad grasped the microphone with life-and-soul assurance and sang "Bye-bye Blackbird."

Above: The shepherd, Willie Young, and his wife Mary (center), at Rockfield Farm, Easter Ross, 1949. Mum is to the left, with the twins in front. The two boys are the Youngs' sons. At right, their daughter Ishbel, Mum's lifelong friend, with her baby son. *Below*: Mum at Rockfield during the war.

My mother had taken piano lessons in Shawlands, but her most remarkable talent was her ability to play by ear. She could play practically any song a party-goer wished to sing—"Give me a key . . . just start . . ."—and never declined to do so. As a girl at home next to the school, she used to listen to the latest pop songs on the wireless in the evenings. "Then I would go through to the room with the piano and pick out the melody," she told me. We were sitting on a bench at Newport, looking towards Dundee and the Tay Railway Bridge which spans the Firth of Tay. She had just entered her nineties and had recently given up playing the piano in the residential home in which she now lived, named after St Serf, the mentor of Glasgow's patron, St Mungo. "Once you had the tune, it was easy enough to fit it together with the harmony."

A written record of Mum and Dad's service came to light unexpectedly at about that time: a small leather suitcase packed to bursting point with letters exchanged during wartime. When he was stationed at Invergordon, they wrote to each other practically every day, and went on doing so when his ship sailed for the Far East, and later when he was again at Plymouth, awaiting demob. For over three years, news, messages, declarations, recollections—sometimes twice daily—created a continuous back and forth between a primitive Highland cottage, where drinking water had to be pumped from the well in the yard, and Royal Navy ships in Invergordon, then Devon, then Ceylon. "This is my second letter to you tonight," she wrote in one, "as I am playing at a dance in Nigg. It is in the Norwegian refugee camp."

"I received no less than three letters from you today," he wrote back from SS Empire Spearhead in Plymouth, "and I feel good. I could have made an announcement on the BBC."

Delays in delivery would be compensated by the arrival of older letters that had been bobbing on the perilous seas for weeks. "I don't want you to be annoyed with yourself because you miss one day of writing," she told him as she sat down to convey the news from the Scottish Highlands. The letters, most of them carefully replaced in their envelopes, many with oriental stamps at top right, number about a thousand. Almost every one begins, "My Dearest Darling . . . ," followed by a promise of everlasting love, an expression of impatience for the war to be over, the explicit longing for the climax of marriage and the beginning of family life in Glasgow. At one point, he predicts three boys and a girl. Instead, they got twin daughters, one boy and, ten years later when Mum was nearly forty, a surprise third girl.

It was a love affair dependent not only on the post—and the piquant feelings of separation it helped to soothe—but on a bicycle. The road between Invergordon and Portmahomack to the north was a rural road, about twenty miles long, and my father relied on two wheels to pursue his courtship, cycling from the ship up to Rockfield Farm, or perhaps for a rendezvous in Tain—"Outside the Post Office at 4"—whenever he wanted to see the janitor's daughter, now the shepherd's ward. Not forgetting the Highland weather. This was written on November 29, 1943:

I had quite a pleasant run back on Saturday, apart from the fact that I got drenched. However after the rain had soaked through to my skin and I got used to it, I felt quite comfortable. I was fairly soaked by the time I got here. The rain started when I was about a mile away from your place, it started as a drizzle and gradually got

worse till I got to Fearn where it really did rain. By the
time I reached InverG. you would have thought I had
been for a swim in the Dornoch Firth.

He wasn't to be put off, however. In another letter, he reported:

I had a lovely run home on Saturday and never felt the
time drag at all. It got a lot lighter later on and I had no
difficulty in finding my way. The bike will soon be able
to do the road riderless so if it ever comes up that way
without me, just send it back by rail.

It wasn't long before rumors of her musical ability circulated
through the scattered burghs and villages of Easter Ross, and
she began to receive invitations to play at dances for farm workers, servicemen on leave, local women, and other Land Girls.
"I am going to be very busy next week, Darling. I am playing
every night except Tuesday night at dances . . . We won't be
very late Monday and Thursday as they will stop at 12."

There are many mentions of a call out of the blue to the girl
from Glasgow to provide entertainment. A messenger arrives
by bicycle at the shepherd's cottage at Rockfield Farm on a
Saturday afternoon, to ask if Ina Beveridge can stand in for an
absent pianist that night—in Fearn, where the nearest railway
station was, or Balintore, just down the coast from the Port but
not half as pretty, or perhaps in Portmahomack itself, where
the dances were held in the Carnegie Hall, opened in 1902 by
Mrs. Andrew Carnegie. (Twenty years after the end of the war,
I would be there when Mum was playing, dancing with girls
named Cathie Ross and Margaret Duff, and trying out the chat-
up line, "My mother's in the band.") In her letters to Plym-

outh or Ceylon, she doubtless thought it more tactful to leave out other attributes of the "smashing players" she sat down with night after night, but those of the twenty-two-year-old at the piano—self-assured, humorous, lacking airs and graces—would not have gone unremarked by the boys on leave.

Their penmanship is good, the grammar and spelling more or less faultless—Harry's punctuation occasionally stumbles—their command of the formalities of correspondence easygoing. In the Navy, he tried to learn touch-typing, and crumbling exercise books show that he engaged in a correspondence course in German—motivated, I suspect, by his love of music more than by a wish to communicate with the enemy. He was proud of his own musical taste, which drew him to the stern Romantics: Beethoven, Mendelssohn, Tchaikovsky. Mozart was just too much in the Classical mode to please him. Haydn squeezed in. He thrilled to the drama of the Beethoven symphonies and piano concertos, in particular.

There is no doubting the sincerity of his love, nor her loyalty, but in his letters I often catch a note that makes me cringe, mostly for her, a little for him, and just a tiny bit for the boy whose existence lay seven years in the future, but who would hear it frequently in the awkward age to come. It strikes with a heavy sound in a letter written from Glasgow to Easter Ross on March 13, 1944, at the beginning of her dance-band career, in which he invokes his own efforts to play the piano:

> How did you fare? No doubt you felt pretty strange at first, however as time goes on you will acquire more confidence, and it will at least be a hobby for you. Too bad you haven't a piano to practice on. Maybe if you speak to the lady next door she'll let you have the use

of hers. I'll send you up a few Beethoven sonatas just to impress her. As long as you don't try to play them you'll be alright. I don't think there's any chance of you doing that anyway. It's a band pianist you are, not a soloist. After the war we'll both go to a really good teacher and learn from the beginning again, the competitive spirit will make us keen and although I say it myself, I think I'll win, as my style (what there is of it) hasn't been polluted with boogie-woogie and repetitional bumping, call it jazz if you like.

He wasn't inclined to be severe all the time. Ten days later, now based in the south of England, he succumbed to the charms of "repetitional" music and the associations it held:

Are you still bumping out that Rhythm with the Fearn band? Do you still play "I'm thinking tonight of my blue eyes" and the other regulars which, on hearing, I immediately think of Fearn. I was listening to the radio today and all the tunes put me in mind of you. It's funny how music or popular tunes do that more than anything else. They played that tune "Put your arms around me honey" and it just put me in mind of our very first night together in Portmahomack, you were singing it as we walked down the road, and we were both very happy.

He was present at the evacuation from Dunkirk. In a letter dated June 8, 1944, two days after the assault on Normandy began, he described "a run over to France on Tuesday morning" where he saw "everything that was going on." The Tuesday referred to was D-Day. The mission was to monitor early developments at Gold Beach, on the south-western edge of the Cotentin. But the view of Operation Overlord from on board SS *Empire Spearhead* that morning was evidently a restricted one. "Things were just starting there, there really wasn't much to see, as the enemy put up very little resistance to our sea forces." He might well have been conscious of the censor looking over his shoulder. "Our shipping losses were very slight, the biggest relief was the absence of the Luftwaffe."

She lost three cousins in the war, but compared to many people, including friends, they had a relatively uneventful campaign. When his ship was directed to the Far East (with no advance warning, according to procedure), the enemy was boredom. "Of the 8 weeks I have been on this ship, I could have been on leave 7 of them, as I haven't done a day's work the whole time."

They were married in Glasgow, in May 1946, but still he had to return to Plymouth to await demob. The wedding photographs show a good-looking young man in his petty officer's uniform and a pretty girl in a veiled mini top hat with a lovely smile. They found a tenement flat in Dennistoun, and the twins were born in August 1947.

"I have no idea what a good secure job is going to be after the war," he had written in April 1944. The grandeur of the Clyde shipyards that had made a legend of Glasgow in the years leading up to and after the First World War was already fading. In any case, Ina was not set on being a range fitter's wife. Soon my father had a job as a clerk in the London, Midland and Scottish Railway, the start of a career that lasted the rest of his working life. After the LMSR was integrated into British Rail in 1948, he stepped up the career ladder one rung at a time, eventually attaining a position of seniority in what

Mum and Dad on their wedding day, Glasgow, May 1946.

became the Scottish Region, and later in the Western Region in the South of England.

II

Within three years of being married, they were able to move into a ground-floor cottage house in Castlemilk Crescent, Croftfoot, with tidy gardens fore and aft, as the ex-petty officer was apt to say. I was born in the front room, their bedroom, at dawn on June 5, 1951.

Few people in the crescent had cars and other drivers had no reason to pass through, unless to visit. It was a perfect arena for children's play. At different times of the day and on different days of the week, this or that "man" would come round the crescent, proclaiming his wares in sonorous tones: even when the words themselves were incomprehensible, the sound of the voice identified the arrival. There was the lemonade man, to whom we returned empty screwtop bottles from the week before, for a penny off the latest purchase; the roll man—morning and evening—whose powdered products cost three farthings each, five fresh rolls totalling threepence three farthings; the fish man, whose haddock and cod were economical purchases, compared to meat. If we had fish on a Friday, Mum would say, "People will think we're Catholics." Which, in some distant, secreted gene in the family body, we were.

A less regular visitor was the knife man, with his fierce and shining machine for sharpening kitchen implements. The rag man, often accompanied by a ragged woman, collected old clothes, to be sold at Paddy's Market, near Glasgow Cross. The first Sikh I ever saw was standing at our front door with an open suitcase full of useful things such as dusters—dusting was Dad's regular task—and dishwashing brushes and towels. This was the twins' job, one washing, the other drying.

My chore was to "clear the table" after the family had finished their tea, a more or less endurable event that lasted from about six o'clock till half-past. I liked to dart in from whatever post-school activity I had been pursuing, then shoot out again as soon as possible. Football, rounders, improvised children's games of every sort took place at the "recs," our word for the immense recreation grounds, two minutes' sprint from the living room with its dining-room table now hastily cleared. These glorious grounds were covered by four football pitches, where our school matches and later Boys' Brigade games were played, in organized leagues, come rain, come wind, come frost and ice, to an assembly of parents, local boys and girls whose turn in this or some other sport had just been or was yet to come, and assorted idlers.

The recs hosted a gymkhana, with colorful and proudly costumed riders and handsome horses, and had a pavilion with changing rooms and a gymnasium which was furnished with good equipment. On late Saturday afternoons, as rumors of the professional football results reached us through the grapevine—occasionally the shocking news: "Rangers got beat"— we were free to roam around the gym, clambering on to the vaulting horse and trying to lift 50 lb weights. The wide spaces rang to the happy voices of hairy men stripping off, showering and getting dressed—grown-up men, it seemed to us, though only a few would have been out of their teens.

The recs (always singular) was a stone's throw from the high-up platform of Croftfoot railway station, from which Dad would watch games while waiting for a train. He had his first sight from the Central Station-bound platform of Jean's boyfriend Millar Hay, a stylish and soon to be locally famous player. The last time I passed the space where the recs had been, the pitches and pavilion had disappeared and the ground had been given up to a housing project with an absurd pastoral title.

Nine years and eleven months after me, Julie was born in the same room at 45 Castlemilk Crescent, at a similar time of the day. In the most tender awakening I ever had from Dad, he touched my shoulder and said, "Come on through. You've got a wee sister." How it had happened I really wasn't sure, but there she was, in a tiny cot, an hour or two old. There was Mum sitting up in bed and smiling. And there was the midwife, also happy, clearing up and preparing to leave.

5

THE APPRENTICE: WASHIE'S

I

At 7.30 in the morning of Monday, October 3, 1966, I boarded a number 13 bus at the stop on Aikenhead Road, a few minutes' walk from our front door. The bus rolled past Hampden Park stadium, nosing into the lightening day via Govanhill and the Gorbals, setting me down with others at Glasgow Cross, the entrance to the district known as Townhead, never spoken of by any familiar or resident as anything other than Toonheid.

To me, until now, it was a foreign country, known only as the base camp of the fearful sounding gang called the Calton Tongs, arch-rivals of the teenage Gorbals tribe, the Young Young Cumbie. Tongs ya bass. YYC ya bass.

From the Cross, a five-minute walk up the High Street led to Ingram Street, opposite the site of the Old College, the city's first university and the fourth-oldest in the English-speaking world. Far to the west along Ingram Street, towards George Square, was Stirling's Library, and less than halfway down, at a sharp juncture, Albion Street, the location over time of various Scottish newspapers. Each of those institutions, in different ways, would come to have a shaping influence on my life, but at the time I lived in ignorance of their existence.

At the corner of Ingram Street and Shuttle Street stood a formidable gray, three-story warehouse with an angled balustrade fringing the top. The surrounding streets housed the Glasgow Fruit Market, where Dad had pushed a barrow as a school-leaver before the war. Mum's instinctive, forward-looking respectability discouraged discussion of it, as it did of the Roman Catholicism deep, but satisfyingly distant, in his background. Now here I was, back on native territory. By 8 o'clock in the morning the gutters were clogged with cabbage leaves, grubby green sprouts, crushed apples, squelched oranges and bruised banana skin.

The entrance to the printing factory was through the close at No. 48 and up one flight to the first floor. There, at eight precisely, I coincided with Mary McIlwham emerging from the cludgie on the stair, already reeking of smoke and gin. Or perhaps it was what Glasgow drinkers at the lower end called "the wine," a sweet sherry such as Lanliq—Lang's Liqueur—Four Crown or Eldorado, relished without exception for price over taste. Mary would have known the new boy was due to start

Washington Irvine, printers and stationers, occupied the first and second floors of this building, at the heart of the normally bustling Fruit Market. The factory entrance was through the close visible to the right of the Morris Minor.

that morning. She smiled in a guileless way that I was to grow familiar with, and spoke a few words of kindly greeting as she continued towards the shop floor in an elegant feminine step, with me at the rear. She had gray hair pulled back in a bun and a face blushed and lined with "the wine."

It was the first day of my apprenticeship at Washington Irvine's, printers, paper rulers, bookbinders, and stationers. Four months earlier, I had turned fifteen. On the days after my interview with Mr. Crawford, I had contrived to meet the postman as he came towards the house in the morning. With a shifty hello, I would ask if he had "anything for Campbell." He would hand me a bill or a postcard or other things that I could tell by the postmarks had come from somewhere other than the school. I had a paper round at a local newsagent and during those dangerous days I timed its completion to coincide with the postman making his regular approach. After several turns of mooching about with no result between 8:15 and 8:30, I dared to hope that Mr. Crawford had decided to let it go.

One morning, a week or more after the report-card meeting, I arrived back from delivering the papers to find my father still at home. This was unusual—I never knew him to stay off work even because of illness—but the reason was immediately apparent. Mr. Crawford's letter lay open on the table. My mother stood in the background, a handkerchief pressed to her face. My father picked me up, threw me on to the settee, whacked me across the side of the head with the back of his hand—the favored side—and continued with what I suppose has to be called a beating, though I don't remember that it hurt at all. Mere blows seldom did.

It was decreed that I would be kept in for a month. I would copy out two pages of my school history book each day, which

I would then read aloud to him when he got back from the office in the evening. I protested: "But Dad, it's the summer holidays," gifting him one of his good lines: "Holidays? Holidays are for boys who've been working. You've been on holiday *all year*."

At the end of August (the cruel sentence was soon commuted, thanks to the intervention of Grandpa), I had returned to school to face the humiliating prospect of repeating third year. There could be no starker evidence of my lack of academic aptitude. My contemporaries, beginning fourth year, were taking the first steps on the path leading to O Grades, the Scottish equivalent of O Levels, the following spring. I wouldn't have stood a chance. Repeat appeared to be the only option.

There was, however, another option: leave.

One day after school in early September, my mother raised the subject tentatively. Our next-door neighbor, Mr. Wells, a stationer, was the client of a small printing firm in Ingram Street. He had mentioned to Mum that the company had a vacancy for an apprentice paper ruler, and she had discussed it with Dad.

It was only a suggestion, she said . . . we just thought you might be happier . . . you know, school and all . . . since you don't seem to be really suited . . . maybe this is . . .

Her modest dreams for my future had turned against her with almost daily displays of blatant mockery. Neither discipline nor indulgence had worked. Mr. Crawford's letter was the final confirmation. One of her hopes was that her son might become a dentist. A chartered surveyor was another profession she spoke of with admiration, though I had no idea what either "chartered" or "surveyor" referred to. My father had offered to get me a start behind a desk in the railways, just as he himself had launched a successful career there twenty years earlier. The lure of "ten pounds a week" was set before me.

He was a thinking man who had never had the opportunity to refine and shape his intelligence with the quality essential to its development: curiosity. He would have loved to go to "the university," as he always phrased it—there could only be one—caressing the words as he spoke them. Such a move was economically out of the question for any member of a family like his in the 1930s, and anyway history stepped in: the Royal Navy had given him his education. He had trained as a medical orderly on board ship in the Far East, and devoured works on the long voyages by Dickens, Dostoevsky, and Hugo. One of the great reading experiences of his life was *Les Misérables*, which he pronounced "Lez Mizer-*a*-bulls." Another was *A Tale of Two Cities*. My father was one of only two people I've ever met who referred to "the Brothers Singer," Isaac Bashevis and his less well-known sibling Israel Joshua; the other person being Clive Sinclair, the author of a book on the two writers. For my sisters' benefit, he looked hard into Rembrandt and van Gogh, visited the Tate and the National Gallery when in London, but his abiding passion was the music of Beethoven. It must have spoken to him of other worlds than the stone-tenement world in which he was brought up, other expressions of emotion, in ways that the names of Big Bill Broonzy and Blind Boy Fuller—the names as much as the music—were beginning to suggest different realities to me.

Now that the benefits of learning had been extended by a victorious society to embrace all deserving younger citizens, he imagined that he might enjoy by proxy the days of study and comradeship amid the quadrangles at the university that he had once longed for, through me. Both twins were established at Glasgow School of Art—the first in the entire extended family to make the leap into higher education. Their talent had shone through early, and Dad had encouraged them, after some initial resistance, up to the happy moment of their acceptance. They wore their paint-smeared artists' smocks at every chance, facing down the light protests voiced by Mum at the dinner table. Her vain hope had been that the two girls would go to the Dough School in the West End, properly called the College of Domestic Science.

I was to be next. If not a surveyor or a dentist, then maybe a teacher. No one had foreseen a humble trade, an apprenticeship projected to occupy the next six years, a square brown wage packet handed over on a Friday at 3 pm (the timing being a safety measure, allowing the pubs to close for the afternoon), a dilapidated factory sunk in the moldy Fruit Market, its entrance next to our wide-open "pen" where vans backed in for the unloading of paper and card. Batches were carried up to the second floor in the hoist—another new noun—to be cut to manageable size and trimmed by Gilbert, the cutter (yet another), on his manually operated guillotine. Two fingers on his left hand were shorter than the others.

Maybe it would be a solution of a sort to the outer disturbances my inner turbulence had caused, and seemed likely to go on causing. At the completion of my training I would be a certified journeyman, a master paper ruler, with a job for life.

I accepted the proposal without hesitation. There was a final interview at school with Mr. Crawford, who in his time had doubtless taken leave of boys more troubled than this one. "So you're going where the big money is!" he said—the printing trade had that reputation—before I walked out of the school gates on to Fetlar Drive for the last time.

The big money Mr. Crawford was referring to belonged to the world of newspaper printing. It had nothing to do with the sort of jobbing work undertaken by Washington Irvine. The firm received its own orders from regular clients, and in addition undertook tasks contracted out from famous Glasgow companies such as McCormick's and Collins the publishers. Both were situated within walking distance of Ingram Street, and in my first year at Washie's I did part-time duty as a messenger boy, delivering and collecting parcels to and from various addresses in town, something I was always pleased to be asked to do. Now and then I was given a few pennies for bus fares, which of course I kept, walking quickly—sometimes not so quickly—there and back. A common mission was to be dispatched with a sturdy plastic container through the old Townhead streets—their inhabitants existing not so much in a different place from the people of King's Park, as in a different century—to the slaughterhouse and Meat Market near the Gallowgate, where Dad's maternal grandparents had lived and were married—in the flat which they shared, apparently, at 543 Gallowgate—on May 7, 1875. There I had to ask for "a quart" (never two pints) of ox gall.

I enjoyed the adventure of meeting muscular workers in bloodied aprons and wellington boots, dodging the lorries maneuvering into place at the entrance to disgorge their bellowing cargoes, glimpsing the bespectacled men dressed in incongruous suits and ties doing the accounts in glass-fronted offices, neat secretaries by their sides, seemingly oblivious to the echoing shouts and the clatter and grind of overhead trolleys from which hung rows of massive carcasses. The slaughterhouse was made the setting for Archie Hind's novel *The Dear Green Place*, published in that year, 1966, one of only a few works of its time to embrace the noise and air and color of Glasgow. But I knew nothing of that yet. Later, I would come to admire Hind's novel. "In the middle of the pass, barrows were being pushed up and down as the labourers collected the offal: tripes, livers, hearts, lungs, heads"—and somewhere in among it my quart of ox gall.

The job to which I had committed my future was putting lines on paper. The foul-smelling gall was added in tablespoonfuls to large porcelain bowls containing the inks that created the lines, to keep them fast. Starting pay for a first-year apprentice was £4 12s 6d a week, rising in increments of between £100 and £150 per annum, to settle at around £16 per week for a journeyman, about the same wage as might be earned at the time by a first-level schoolteacher. "And with overtime," people on the shop floor were always quick to add, "you can make a lot more . . ."

There were opportunities on Tuesday and Thursday evenings, 5:30 to 7:30, and on Saturday mornings, from 8 am till midday, all paid at the rate of time and a half. If you clocked in more than five minutes after eight in the morning, your pay would be docked a quarter of an hour, in my case amounting to about ninepence. There were two weeks' holiday in the summer—the Fair Fortnight, starting mid-July, during which the factory closed its doors—and a further holiday to be taken during the months of January or February, the "winter week." Membership of the union SOGAT (Society of Graphical and Allied Trades), which had negotiated these benefits, was obligatory. I was invited to join the menodge. This meant contributing two shillings (10 pence) a week to a general fund, with nine others—there was more than one menodge in operation on the shop floor—resulting in a sum which would be paid out to each member in turn. In this way, I would be poorer by two shillings for nine weeks in a row, but a rich man—a whole pound was mine—on the tenth.

The factory floor was dominated by three paper-ruling machines, one of which I would in time be given charge of. Two of them were neat modern apparatuses, known as disc machines, or just "the discs," both operated by the journeyman; the third was a quaint old edifice made largely out of wood, on which I was to learn my trade. This was a Shaw Pen Ruling Machine.

In the first stage of every job, the Shaw was operated manually, using a crank handle to cause a sheet of paper to advance slowly over the moleskin canvas, allowing necessary adjustments to be made to the spacing and balance of the pens, and

A Shaw Pen Ruling Machine, similar to the one on which I served my apprenticeship at Washie's in the late 1960s. This one was probably made around 1930.

to the density of the lines they were about to draw. When everything was set up and ready to go, a green button was pressed to power the machine by electricity, heralded by a low grumble. Paper was introduced by a feeder, always a woman or girl, dressed in a nylon overall. Mary McIlwham was the most experienced paper feeder on the floor. The first model of the Shaw Pen Ruling Machine was produced in Huddersfield in 1890, and development continued until the early 1930s. At a guess, mine was made somewhere in between.

It looked like a small four-poster bed, with a solid wooden frame. The slowly rolling blanket carried the paper through to the delivery box at the end opposite to the feeder. An upright frame supported threads, which went round on their own smaller rollers, keeping the paper firmly in position on the blanket. As the large sheets of crown passed along—more than 1,000 an hour at the top rate—the brass pens which had been slotted into crosswise wooden carriages rose and fell according to a regulated scheme. It was the paper ruler's job to fit the pens into the carriages and to slot cams into the timing wheel which caused the carriages to lift when one sheet of paper was ruled, then to come down on to the next sheet at the proper moment, leaving lines of a desired color and pattern—the basic being the universally familiar page of horizontally lined writing paper.

It was the ruler's job, too, to spread flannels neatly across the tops of the carriages above the bracket which secured the pens in place, and to ensure that the flannels were refreshed by regular applications of ink to flow into the pens—but not so regular that the downward flow would cause the pens to flood. The standard color of ink was "feint"; there were also shades of blue, red and green.

Each job came with its own ruling specifications. Some were quite complex, requiring a perfectly timed drop of vertically running single-line pens on to hitherto ruled horizontal double-line bars, with perhaps a thick single line or two underneath. This might be for the pages of what would be cut, folded with a flat "bone," and then bound on the second floor at Washie's into an account book or ledger. For some patterns, the paper was fed into the machine two or three times, front and back. The lines on one side ought to correspond perfectly with those on the other, and the "show-through" should be minimal.

The ink was contained in a bowl near the ruler's right hand and added to the flannels on the carriages by means of a small brush. If the ink dried up, through the ruler's negligence, the lines became scratchy. Too sudden a reapplication of ink would vary the density of the lines and cause too much show-through. Achieving a uniform density was among the paper ruler's principal tasks. At the end of a run, the paper was emptied from the wooden holder at the machine's rear end, counted into quires of twenty-five sheets and stacked, each sheet ready to be folded and cut according to the appropriate size: folio, quarto, octavo.

This was the labor that filled each of my working days, once I had acquired a basic mastery of the machine.

Long before then, when my first pay packet arrived, I was surprised to discover that nine shillings (45 pence) had been deducted in advance by the Inland Revenue, leaving £4 3s 6d. Union dues meant a further reduction. My mother took £3 for my keep—a concept apparently inseparable from my new status as a working man. Out of what was left, I was expected to pay my own bus fares from King's Park to Glasgow Cross and back again, leaving less than a pound as spending money after a forty-hour week, not much more than I had been earning on my morning paper round. Sometimes I managed to skip my fare on the bus, or else I walked home from work in order to save a few pence.

II

The owners of the firm were two brothers, David Irvine and Washington Irvine, known to the workforce as Mr. David and Mr. Washie. It was said that they didn't get on well. The third director, Mr. David's son Alister, acted as the main liaison between management and workers. Just over thirty at the time of my arrival in Ingram Street, he was addressed by us as Mr. Alister.

My journeyman and immediate boss was John Pollock, a thin-faced, dirty-minded man who made it known to everyone that he could never bring himself to work with a Catholic. It was not a policy held to by the management—there were several Catholics among the sixty-strong staff, but John Pollock didn't like to mix with them, and wouldn't have taken me on if I'd been a left-footer, a Fenian, a Pape, an RC, a Tim Malloy, a Mick or a Dan. Rangers fans from the Bridgeton area, who included John Pollock, were Blue Noses or Billy Boys, and before we became acquainted in person, John would certainly have made inquiries as to the name of the school I had attended. The likes of Saint Bonaventure's or Saint Aloysius in the reply would have made my employment in the paper-ruling department at Washie's impossible. John found it painful even to enunciate the names of certain central Glasgow streets, such as Saint Vincent Street. They reminded him too forcefully of the sickening accoutrements of the Roman Catholic Church.

Just as important as John Pollock to my early training at Washie's was Jeanette McGowan, the principal feeder after Mary. She wore an elegant, fitted, yellow nylon overall with white pinstripes and turned-up white collar—I seldom saw her in anything else—and the resident expression on her face throughout the course of a day was in equal parts humorous, sexy, intelligent, and hard. She was a type common in Glasgow and its satellite towns—Jeanette lived in Shotts, about fifteen miles away by bus—both feminine and inviolable. Not even John Pollock, who bullied Mary McIlwham mercilessly and teased his fifteen-year-old apprentice with innuendo barely understood, would have spoken out of turn to Jeanette. She took me in hand in a way that made me feel I could rely on her.

I was teased by one and all for speaking "polite" and regarded with mild suspicion by some for emerging from a bought house in King's Park, with sisters in higher education and a general background more commonly associated with the middle classes and management, a pairing that would have charmed my mother. But any sardonic, over-the-shoulder remarks from Jeanette—her eyes closing languidly, then opening halfway to gauge the reaction—were meant kindly, unless my behavior didn't merit kindness, in which case she addressed it directly. She was twenty-one at the time of our meeting, and the dynamic was elder sister to younger brother, one I was quite accustomed to. Jeanette was effectively second-in-command on the floor. She was engaged to Michael Heaney, who worked in lithography and—his name told me before John Pollock went out of his way to do so—was a Catholic.

Other feeders were nice to be around, too. Jesse, for example, aged fifteen, gauche, good-humored and with the gift of being totally natural. Nancy was older, pleasantly plump, and married to a "man"—the only word she or the other women ever used for their own or anyone's husband—she always spoke of warmly. She and Jesse reached almost daily for a word I had never heard until now: badness. "That's pure *badness*," they would say of some speech or action of mine or someone else. It could be either trivial or truly wicked.

When a round-faced, red-haired fifteen-year-old also called Nancy joined the team, the first became Big Nancy while the new girl was Wee Nancy, even though she was already taller than Big Nancy. Wee Nancy didn't have to wait long before she became the target of several of the boys from the printing and stationery departments on the second floor, though Big Nancy tried to protect her from dubious predators. Pregnancy outside of marriage was the greatest personal catastrophe and deepest social shame that could befall any of these girls. But the romantic kidology and horseplay in the air throughout the day was welcome, softening the harshness of the regime: 8 am till 12:30 pm, and 1:30 till 5 pm. On overtime nights, add two hours. The reams of paper in their waxed brown wrapping were stored in the basement, stacked in great, head-high piles with corridors in between, to create an underground maze, a likely place for smooching or, as we said, winchin'. Once Mr. Alister caught me at it with yet another Nancy, and sent us both upstairs, after a dressing down, to get back to work.

Even so, you snatched at consolation where you spotted it. If the union, SOGAT, bargained with management to guarantee our holidays and annual pay increases, it had little influence on working conditions at 48 Ingram Street. When it rained heavily, as it often did, the floor around our feet was covered in water. A complaint about cold in winter—John Pollock and Mary McIlwham wore fingerless gloves—was answered by Mr. David with the suggestion to turn on more lights and profit from the electric heat generated by the bulbs. It was forbidden to make or receive telephone calls during working hours— there was one black Bakelite telephone with a silver dial on the windowsill not far from John's disc machines—except in dire emergencies. Each morning my mother would prepare my "piece," which, if it contained bacon or sausage, perhaps topped by a well-fried egg, could be heated in its greaseproof paper on one of the radiators that was fitted under the Shaw to help the ink dry. After five minutes the mildly toasted white bread would be warm and deliciously saturated with butter and bacon fat.

III

One day, about a year after I began working at Washington Irvine's, I looked into the face of a guitar for the first time. It belonged to Áine Carey, a folk singer who would go on to record an LP—a rare thing in those days—of Scottish folk songs, as part of the Gleanna Four. Áine (pronounced as Anne) was an art school friend of one of the twins, Jean. The vision remains: burnished orange-red maple top; elegant neck with mother-of-pearl inlay and crosswise silver frets; bronze strings stretched along the neck from ivory bridge to gleaming brass keys. The prospect was erotic.

For the family group, Áine played Bert Jansch's famous instrumental "Angie" (adapted from Davey Graham's original "Anji"), with its thudding descending bass, while the index and

Áine Carey, at about the time she came to the house in King's Park and played "Angie." Here she holds a Spanish guitar, not the burnished steel string I fell in love with. *Courtesy of the Carey family.*

middle fingers gave the sparkling suggestion of a melody on the treble strings. Jean bought Bert Jansch's first LP—just *Bert Jansch*, already the object of widespread wonder—and I was allowed to listen to it.

According to the sleeve notes, Bert, born in Glasgow, was "raised 'in the field' in Edinburgh." What on earth did that mean? At the time of making these miraculous recordings, at the age of twenty-one, he didn't own a guitar. How was this possible?

Not long after I had fallen under the spell, first of the instrument and then the album, Jean offered to teach me the rudiments of guitar playing, which she herself had learned from Áine Carey. My first chord—everyone's first chord—was a C at the first position. The G chord was also playable, though forcing the joints of index, middle, and little fingers to do the work was a mighty task. Nothing on the fret board was comfortable for those untrained digits. For the F chord, the index finger of the left hand had to hold down the first and second strings at the first fret at the same time, a next to impossible feat. My tender fingertips ached. But with practice, Jean promised, it will come.

She told me that finger-picking was the thing to do with the right hand, more sophisticated than strumming, and gave me a basic 4/4 pattern that Áine had taught her: thumb for the bass note . . . now the ring, middle and index fingers—one at a time—on each of the treble strings . . . Same thing now on G7 . . . no, try again . . . now on the F . . . OK, it'll come. Now back to—that's it—C!

Equipped with just those three chords to play, one was initiated into a rare fellowship. Stir an easy E7 into that progression—"I'm going up the country, through the sleet and snow"—and it opened up the prospect of a whole new life.

Scottish, Irish, and English traditional folk songs told beguiling stories, occasionally cruel, but the Mississippi country blues led the singer down the road to a luminous underworld, even if that singer was sixteen years old and living in a respectable suburb on the Southside of Glasgow. Early Rolling Stones and Beatles records had pointed the way, but it was the real thing only for me from now on. The country blues, which borrowed fragments of the ancient traditions, was the living, continually changing folk music of the present day. These black and blue hobo troubadours still walked Big Bill's highway and rode Robert Johnson's railroad blinds, hanging on for rides from state to state between the carriages to the sound of a lonesome whistle. White people met them, talked to them, listened to them, took down their stories and wrote books about them.

By means of the magic carpet of music, the blue mood of the old South—of cotton-picking and "plantation," of "trouble in mind," a mind that reached back to slavery—could be felt in the room I shared with our little sister Julie in Kingshill Drive. The first African American people I encountered lived in places like Greenwood, Mississippi, in the 1920s, 30s and 40s. It would not be accurate to say that I met them only on the page or on disc; they lived in the strings and frets and bridge and tuning keys of my guitar, too; they lived in the sounds that emerged from it, however inadequately I might have attempted the songs.

The feeling I got from those meetings was vivid and transformative. It entered into me then like a form of religious instruction, or a program of military discipline, and has never gone away. I bought a record on which Big Bill Broonzy not only played and sang but talked to the Chicago journalist Studs Terkel, his fingers running up and down the neck of his guitar with golden touch as he spoke. I found Big Bill's speaking voice, full of honeyed light and shadow, almost as thrilling to listen to as his singing.

"Bill, tell me about the blues. What *is* the blues?"

"Well, the blues really came from the way people *live*, and the *way* . . . some of them . . . the way they're treated . . . and from the *places* where they live and the *work* they do."

We had our native singers, who were just as exciting. Jean borrowed records from fellow students: *Midnight Man* and *Hat* by Davey Graham, the Incredible String Band's self-titled first album, *London Conversation* by John Martyn. Both he and the Incredible duo, Robin Williamson and Mike Heron, were Scots, like Bert Jansch (Davey Graham had a Scottish father, so we were told) and even Donovan, whose early years were spent in Glasgow. John Martyn belonged to us more than most, because he, like Mum, was a former pupil at Shawlands Academy. Grandpa, the janitor, must have known him. His real name was Iain McGeachy and he had lived in a smart tenement building at the top of Tantallon Road, past which we walked every time we went to visit Grandma and Grandpa at the house attached to the school.

All communicated thrillingly in this new musical language—a blend of old-world and modernist folk, just as the songs that Big Bill learned as a teenager ("reels" he called them in the interview, not "blues") were a blend of British and Irish folksong and Southern woe, bound together by African rhythm. All were magically talented. John Martyn's first album was recorded when he was seventeen and released just after his eighteenth birthday. On it he played "Cocaine Blues (Traditional, arr. Martyn)," its clean notes woven tight with seductive expertise, cushioning his still boyish voice. The photograph on the sleeve showed him sitting outdoors, barefoot, cradling a guitar. Somehow or other, he had been born with that guitar in his arms, the way certain footballers were born with a ball at their feet. Even so, it was possible to attempt "Cocaine Blues" in a primitive version in the living room at Kingshill Drive.

Keep doing it, Jean would say, as no doubt Áine had said to her. It'll come.

IV

One day, while acting as the feeder for my Shaw Pen Ruling Machine, which I had long since mastered—I was scheduled to move on to the discs in my fourth year of training—Jeanette surprised me by saying she had told John Pollock that I wouldn't see my apprenticeship through to its full term, and that he had agreed with her.

"How not?"

"I just said to him. I told him. I said he's too clever f'rit." Jeanette let her eyelids close, in that familiar way, eyebrows arching as they did so.

It was as if someone had set off a controlled explosion on a chosen site, in order to clear away unwanted detritus, before a new work of building could begin. It wasn't that no one had ever told me I was "clever," now that I was free of school and had dumped "If you had 20 percent more brains you'd be an idiot" behind; but Jeanette was at the present center of my world. If people are shaped by how other people see them, then I was, day to day, being moulded into other forms.

My circle of friends was widening, and some people on its outer reaches had had a sort of education. Some passing pal had said I was a "philosopher" and I took it as a compliment, though I wasn't sure what it meant. Jean gave me William Golding's novel *Lord of the Flies* to read. I enjoyed the tale of civilized schoolboys stranded on an island, being sucked down towards an innate savagery. But the important thing about this first mature reading experience was my understanding that a story can be about something other than what the story appears to be: there could exist another story hovering above the realistic events recounted on the surface. Story No. 1 might be "an allegory"—an interesting new concept, which applied to the stories told in songs as well—of story No. 2. The second story—the story that wasn't really there, or not visibly—could turn out to be the more important one. Incidents that are described could be "symbolic"—another new thing—of events that are not. It was up to the reader be an active participant. Reader and book were in a relationship.

This was an aesthetic revelation every bit as momentous as hearing Áine Carey play "Angie" in our living room. Jean's suggestion was that *Lord of the Flies* was an allegory of Christ's agony on the cross. I failed to see it that way. But here was another aesthetic revelation: we could disagree.

For a while after that, I regarded every novel and poem I read and every play I saw in the theater—when at last I began attending the theater—as operating on a level above the visible story. Of even the most realistic work (*The Importance of Being Earnest* or Brendan Behan's *Borstal Boy*, both of which I saw at the great Citizens' Theatre in the Gorbals), I would ask myself: but what does it symbolize? What's the real story? In later years, I found this habit hard to kick.

At Mum's urging, I enrolled in a night class at Langside College and studied for the O Grade English exam, which I passed. I introduced some of my friends to the songs of Bert Jansch and the Incredible String Band. Without intending to, I began to see my intimate circle divided into those who were capable of connecting with Big Bill Broonzy's protest song "White, Brown and Black," with the psychedelic sounds of the Incredibles' *5000 Spirits or the Layers of the Onion*, and those who were not, for all they might have tried. This comprehension or lack of it separated me from boys and girls who up until then had been my good friends.

A button had been pushed inside my head and from now on I responded to a call at some hitherto undetected frequency. My feelings after reading Golding's novel projected me into another atmosphere, made by art. As I counted out chords and finger-picking arpeggios over the weekend, in the bedroom I shared with Julie, I was counting myself not only into new melodies but far-reaching myths:

I'll sing you this October song,
Oh, there is no song before it.
The words and tune are none of my own,
For my joys and sorrows bore it.

Robin Williamson, whose song this is, also sang: "Birds fly out behind the sun, / And with them I'll be leaving." Why "behind" the sun? Because he was bound for another hemisphere. He spoke of "fallen leaves that jewel the ground"; of meeting a man "whose name was Time / He said 'I must be going.'"

It was bewitching. It cast an inescapable spell. The language sounded familiar, as if it had long lain in wait, in expectation of my hearing it. But at 8 o'clock on a dark October Monday morning, I had to leave those weekend fancies behind—not to hitch-hike to Morocco, where it was rumored Robin had gone immediately after singing with a blend of weirdness and lyricism on the Incredible String Band's first album, playing guitar, fiddle and penny whistle, too—but to return to Glasgow Cross on the No. 13 bus and walk up the High Street to Washie's.

I had "October Song" to console me, and I sang it to myself as I turned into the close at No. 48, having braved the early-morning West of Scotland autumn weather, meeting red-faced, smiling Mary emerging from the cludgie on the stair, nodding a good morning to John, putting on my stiff gray flannel overall and preparing to give my hands up to ox gall and ink stains all over again. I liked Jeanette—and Big Nancy and Wee Nancy and trusting Jesse—but Jeanette had looked into the Ingram Street future and had failed to see me there.

6

THE SCOTIA BAR

I

I had been at Washie's for two and a half years when my mother made an announcement: Dad had been offered a high-up job in the Western Region of British Rail. It would mean Mum, Dad, Julie and me leaving Glasgow, to live in the south-east of England. He would have his office at Paddington Station, but the likely outcome would be to seek a house in a green outer suburb or somewhere further afield. Mum didn't want to live in London.

After some searching, a pleasant house was found in Booker, a leafy outpost of High Wycombe in Buckinghamshire, no more than a hundred yards from a wood, from which large hedgehogs came up at night to munch the garden plants. A traditional neighborhood pub, The Squirrel, was a few minutes' walk away. Dad took up the role of Stores Controller for the Western Region. Every morning, Monday to Friday, he got on the train at High Wycombe Station and made the thirty-minute journey to Marylebone. From there it was a short walk to his office.

In the spring of 1969, Jean and Phyllis, still at Glasgow School of Art, were on the brink of leaving home anyway. Julie, turning eight and a pupil at King's Park Primary, would go to a new school "down south"—a phrase now heard often in the living room. As usual, a question mark hung over me.

On hearing the news, John Pollock suggested that the union might find a way to insinuate me into an English firm, in the town or its environs, where my apprenticeship could be completed, enabling me in due course to enter the world as a journeyman. "You don't want to lose your trade." It was SOGAT's duty to fix it. What were we paying our weekly union dues for, after all? Surely not just an extra light bulb burning through the cold weather on the first floor at Ingram Street.

But I saw the change in my parents' lives—they were in their mid-forties at the time—as an opportunity to change my own. At home, I was sparing with the advice and assurances John had put out. I might even have hinted that such a move would be difficult to bring about—which I believe it would have been. There was unlikely to be a sheaf of paper-ruling firms in High Wycombe willing to adopt an unsettled apprentice in his third year, without interview or trustworthy reference.

The decision was made that I would rent a bedsit in the West End of Glasgow—people of the post-war generation still called it "digs"—and continue to manage my Shaw machine at Washington Irvine's.

I was nearly eighteen, the age at which many people left home, in most cases to study, and I was entitled to my own choice. It must have made my parents, in particular my mother, unhappy and relieved at the same time. I would visit them down south. Things were gradually improving between us, and when I walked out of Kingshill Drive and all its strife, most of it caused by me, setting up in a place by myself in the West End, they would get better still.

I found a spacious room on the top floor of a massive tenement in Saltoun Street, facing Ruthven Street, at the entrance to which was Byres Road. Next to me were other bohemian bedsit dwellers, all of whom were welcoming and helpful. I had a guitar, a record player, albums by Robert Johnson, Bert

Jansch and Lightnin' Hopkins. It was the first room of my own I had ever occupied. I had cast myself adrift from one society and had washed up safely on the shores of another.

II

I am happy to have spent the years I did working at Washington Irvine's. It was a kind of growing up. Planetary navigation is required to get from the dark side of fifteen to the brighter surfaces of eighteen, nineteen. The people I met in Ingram Street helped speed my evolution into a different sort of animal from the one that had lashed out dumbly against restraints on all sides at King's Park, causing so much whispered kitchen discussion and sleeplessness in my parents' bedroom, next to the one I shared with Julie.

What was the problem? It wasn't that particular school—though my mother was right to worry about bad company, in the shift from the smaller, local senior secondary to the socially comprehensive institution in Simshill—or the teachers. It was my reaction to being obliged to go to school in the first place. Only once I was free of it, and able to travel according to my own compass, did I begin to get over the sense of living under occupation.

The West End was yet another territory, with its student population and liberal customs. I fitted in right away, but I wouldn't want to have got there free of charge—that is to say, without having made the hazardous journey through Glasgow Cross, High Street, Shuttle Street, the hoist and the dank, worn steps up to the first floor at No.48 Ingram Street, from there to the Meat Market and beyond without paying my dues: literally, union dues. My mother and father had hoped that their children would be spared the bad air of Townhead, Calton and the Gorbals. It was the old Glasgow, a place with old-town diseases and hungers, ill-fitting hand-me-downs and deprivation of even hand-me-downs, a place that had been consigned to the fading pages of a history book while it still existed. The atmosphere that Mum and Dad breathed now was fragrant with fitted carpets, central heating, sliding doors, "all-electric," a family car, a separate dining room and good crockery and cutlery, for occasions when relatives came to visit.

Mum and Dad were familiar with the smells of the old city, however, as were, more so, their own parents: its poverty and filth, the single-end flat, the jawbox—a large kitchen sink, in which everything could be scrubbed, including manky infants—the jeely piece flung from the tenement window. They knew it all, even the barefoot weans glimpsed in the distance in black-and-white photographs, innocent fringes dependent on and fated to be victim of the low-level criminality of their parents. It was a life that came with its corresponding old-world thrills: pay-day drunkenness, loose love and Saturday-night singsongs in cider-only pubs. The folk I worked among at Washie's were more akin to the type of people Mum and Dad themselves had grown up with than those we lived next door to in Kingshill Drive. They were people Mum and Dad wished to steer me away from. My choice of company—a choice I didn't have to make—was a return to older territories, an instinctive seeking-out of West of Scotland first-nation peoples.

The free mixing of young men and women at Washie's, most of them older than me, the suggestive chat of the boys and the witty backchat of the girls, led by Jeanette, was civilizing. The stratum of working-class Glasgow from which they emerged, with very few exceptions, was decent and law-abiding. Dear, decrepit Mary, alternately giggling at John's hearty jokes and girning at his heartless chastisement, belonged to a different class, but her good nature, her fags, her secreted miniature bottle for a mid-morning slug in the cludgie, enabled endurance. John told me that she prostituted herself at weekends to get money for drink. He made jokes in her hearing on Monday mornings about her leaving her knickers up a close in the Gallowgate. Mary tittered in embarrassment and said, "Oh John," with an isn't-he-awful look, as she adjusted herself with professional poise and prepared to feed the large crown sheets into one of the disc machines.

Mary's Saturday night pub was the Saracen's Head in the Gallowgate—the Sarry Heid—rumored to be the oldest in Glasgow. It was licensed to sell only cider and "wine," meaning cheap sherry of the Eldorado variety. The Sarry made its own wine: White Tornado, sold by the gill. The liquid was clear or, as Mary and others said, "white." The pub sign showed a swarthy, turbaned man. People said that Samuel Johnson had once lodged there, whoever he was.

I was introduced to alcohol in the Gallowgate by the firm's bright young stationer, Ian McCalister. Some lunchtimes, Ian took me to drink a pint of cider at the Sarry Heid or a lager and lime at the Red House in Ingram Street or a pint of McEwan's heavy at the Old College Bar up the hill behind Washie's on the High Street. John looked disapproving when he heard about our midday trips to the Sarry—he was moderate in his drink—and advised me to avoid the place after dark. Maybe on a Saturday night with the fire of White Tornado in her pitiful belly, Mary was a different sort of person, but as far as I could see she had no badness in her.

That old Glasgow was disappearing, acre by acre. Districts like Townhead, neighboring Dennistoun, the Gorbals, and surrounding areas on the south side of the Clyde—Tradeston, Hutchesontown, Kinning Park, and by the end of the 1970s our King's Park neighbor Govanhill—were being bulldozed. In the haze of tumbling bricks and mortar, people saw phantoms of their lives pass before them. The resulting mushroom clouds dissolved, leaving swathes of desolate wasteland. These outer changes caused inner bewilderment—the ground was literally disappearing beneath people's feet. The shattered walls of the houses exposed fitments, surprised shadows on the walls, as in a public display of dirty underwear. They stood in the street and looked up at what had been their living rooms, fireplaces ripped out like bad teeth, severed piping in plastered relief, flame-like patterned wallpaper stubbornly clinging on to shredded memories. It turned out that a house, until last year, last summer, last month, last week, the embodiment of security and shelter, was just an assemblage of rotten brick and stained mortar. Anything that remained would disintegrate or be bulldozed tomorrow or the next day. The words "oor close," suggestive of an entire plan of existence, embodying courtship, coupling, procreation, child-raising, daily nourishment and weekend intoxication, sickness and health, were laid off, the lived life swept away in the swat of a wrecker's ball in the space of a miserable midweek Gorbals afternoon. What's "the Gorbals" anyway, if it has just been demolished? So where am I? And if I don't know where I am, then who am I? Folk took to saying that the Luftwaffe, which had bombed outlying areas of the city during the war, didn't do half as good a job.

When these neighborhoods went, their binding spirits, which make people quarrel and occasionally injure to the same

degree to which they act on the instinct to shelter and protect, went with them. Tenement flats housing several families, a curtained-off bed at one end of the living room and
the jawbox at the other, would exist only in recollection. No.
48 Ingram Street is no exception. The stairs leading up to the
cludgie, with the Fire Station across the road and the leftover
products of early-morning business at the Fruit Market lit-
tered all around, has ceased to be a built place, designed for
life and work, and has been spirited into memory. Without my
immersion in factory life at Washie's, among Jeanette and John
and all the Nancys, they wouldn't belong in my memory at
all. That old Glasgow is now a parallel world, and an invisible
one. Thanks to my paper-ruler's apprenticeship, albeit broken,
I had a last-minute chance to live in it.

The times were changing in other ways, and I was an
early herald of the shift in mood at Ingram Street. One day,
Mr. David, dressed in full-length management beige overall
as always (the male workers on the factory floor wore gray;
the women's nylon overalls were mostly blue, Jeanette being
a colorful exception), hirpled down the interior staircase—he
walked with a bad limp—and handed me half a crown. I was
surprised by his approach, as he had seldom spoken to me
before.

"Take this," he said in his cloudy, withheld voice, pressing
the coin into my palm and peering at me through filmy spectacles with his one good eye, "and get a haircut."

With a mixture of bafflement, defiance, and politeness—
instinctive reactions, in that order—I declined.

It became a talking-point. "What did he *say?*" The younger
girl feeders were impressed. Big Nancy shook her head: it
could only lead to trouble. Jeanette raised her eyebrows, folded

her arms across her chest and fixed me with an expression blending loyalty and severity that said: *I saw it coming.* John's thin lips—thinner now than ever—maintained their silence. He knew what was coming anyway. Mary took it as an opportunity to make her way to the cludgie, patting the side pockets of her overall as she went, making sure of fags and flask.

III

In the evenings, after completing my overtime shift, happy in the knowledge of extra cash at time-and-a-half to come in the following week's wage packet, I cut down Candleriggs to Argyle Street, then turned left at Stockwell Street and walked towards the Clyde. The Scotia Bar was the center of gravity of the Glasgow folk scene. Dublin was on top—the Merseyside of the folk-music revival—with the cosmopolitan magnet of London not far behind. In joint third place were Glasgow and Edinburgh. There were folk clubs scattered all around Glasgow, and the standard was high. Hopefuls in the audience—"floor singers"—could come up and try out a couple of numbers, with the possibility of being asked to return for a paid engagement. The Scotia Bar was one continuous folk club. From Thursday evening, when some people received their wages, through Fridays, Saturday lunchtimes and on into Saturday night, the sounds of fiddles, penny whistles, squeeze-boxes, pipes, guitars, and quavering human voices filled the smoky corner rooms, each of them a cell in a living folk tradition. Billy Connolly was often seen there, already a local star. Soon he would bring Gerry Rafferty with him. But at the center of all Scotia action was a bearded bear called Mick Broderick, leader of the Whistlebinkies.

Big Mick Broderick, leader of the Whistlebinkies and king of the Scotia.

Standing tall and broad in the back room, his apparently self-replenishing pint glass never far away, he held an 18-inch diameter bodhran (usually pronounced b'-*ran*) with his left hand at chest height, while he drummed a routine with the right on the goatskin surface, using a twin-ended "tipper." Mick could sing with just his bodhran as accompaniment, or else keep time for other musicians. His first group, the Jacobites, included Billy Connolly, an elementary but capable banjo player, and Tam Harvey, a fine plectrum guitarist. When Billy and Tam paired off to form the Humblebums, Big Mick, as he was known, gathered a more traditional set around him, with fiddle, pipes, and concertina. The pipes were not Scottish bagpipes—seldom an accoutrement to any folk ensemble—but Northumbrian pipes, emitting a milder sound. They were attached to the waist by a belt, the sound powered by the player squeezing a bag under one arm while fingering a low-down melody on the chanter.

My modest guitar playing dared make only the most furtive of appearances at the Scotia. But you could watch, listen, occasionally ask. "Show me again what you did there . . ." The better players were generous, as the higher-ups had been kind to them: a folk tradition in itself. The same songs were pulled out with different titles. "Fennario," "Pretty Peggy-o," "The Bonny Lass o' Fyvie-o"—all the same song with varying words and contested origins. An Appalachian ballad with a lamentable civil war history—"If ever I return, Pretty Peggy-o, / If ever I return, all your cities I will burn"—or the tale of an Aberdeenshire soldier and his lass? The answer is it is both. Guitars were tuned this way and that to produce different modalities. Someone showed me how to pick Bert Jansch's classic "Strolling down the Highway," a British Beat Generation blues. Even the canonical "Angie," with its thumping descending bass, yielded to repeated persuasion.

Accomplished players blew in from Edinburgh to the east, or from down south or across the Irish Sea. These fiddlers and squeeze-box players seemed to move with enviable ease from one ensemble to another, halting only to place an order at the bar on the way, as if they were members of an elect and this battery of vibrating single syllables and silvery phrases and long melodious paragraphs was their native language. How did they come to be on first-name terms with such a wide array of whistle tunes and battle songs and love laments with memorable poetry?

O the winter it has passed
And the summer's come at last,
  The small birds they are singing in the trees.
Their little hearts are glad,

The dead center of the Glasgow folk scene. You could watch, listen, learn . . .

> O but mine is very sad
>> For my true love is far away from me.

There were modern folksongs, too, often making strident political gestures—commemorating a strike, a sit-in, a march, a Clydeside disruption. Big Mick, a committed socialist, always seemed to be on his way to a protest somewhere, beret on his head, or was marching under a slogan-bearing banner from one historic site of oppression to another.

Some of the modern songs were the work of Matt McGinn, whose appearance at the Scotia was likely to cause a stir, or one of the Hamishes—Hamish Imlach, the most famous person on the Glasgow scene until Billy Connolly took over, or Hamish Henderson, based in Edinburgh at the School of Scottish Studies and more academic in his aims than most of the crowd. A few members of the core brigade were students; others worked at humble jobs; yet others strove to find a way of living by music and song.

The mundane folk style of Matt McGinn and Hamish Imlach did not attract me, strong performers though they were. It lived side by side at the Scotia with the exciting new "folk baroque," characterized by virtuoso guitar playing and a blue mood. Robin and Clive, as some fortunate people referred to them—Clive Palmer being the third member of the Incredible String Band for its first and most folksy record, though it was still gloriously avant-garde—had been at the Scotia before my time. Their very names, like certain place names, held out promises of pleasure and wonder. Was it possible, just maybe, to sing Robin's "October Song" at the Scotia on a quiet night and not be laughed at? Clive's "Empty Pocket Blues" was a join-in favorite and virtually foolproof, even with a fool at the helm of my Harmony Sovereign steel string.

There were Saturday night parties after closing time (10 pm), fueled by beer and singalong music, to which a runt could sneak in under the door. An address would be mentioned, some hangover-ensuring cans bought, and off we would go along Howard Street. Or else we would head towards George Square and the Glasgow Folk Centre housed in a tenement building in nearby Montrose Street, run by Drew Moyes. I saw the Humblebums there several times. Billy Connolly was comedian, banjo player, guitarist and West of Scotland chronicler, all at once. He took the current pop hit "Everyone's Gone to the Moon" and turned it into "Why Don't They Come Back to Dunoon?", a comic defense of the declining Firth of Clyde resort. Tam Harvey filled in with clever phrasing on a cutaway Fender acoustic. He had long blond hair, parted on the side, and a handlebar moustache, Wild Bill Hickock-style. In my memory, he is always trying not to laugh at Billy's deadpan patter.

The stage cleared, the laughter and applause died down, and John Martyn came on, curly-haired and barefoot, a creature from a different part of the forest, though he and Billy had grown up in Glasgow within a few miles of one another. There was a touch of adolescent narcissism about his manner, and the more traditionally minded members of the audience were impatient with his over-excited self-presentation. Some of them disliked progressive folk music altogether. But when John Martyn played "Seven Black Roses," a virtuoso tune of his own devising which involved moving the capo up the fretboard midstream, passing from one section of the tune to the next without stopping, raising the key by a full tone or semitone while maintaining the melody, increasing the headlong pace as he went, even the skeptics had to clap in wonder.

Drew Moyes's hero was Doc Watson, the blind country singer from North Carolina, one of the great bluegrass guitar pickers of the era. His music proved, as if proof were needed, that the quilt of country music was sewn using patches of the blues, that the blues borrowed from country, which was made of Scottish, English, and Irish folk. To elaborate the pattern further, there was nineteenth-century music hall and minstrelsy and "reels," to use Big Bill Broonzy's word. In the early part of his musical life, Big Bill told Studs Terkel on the record I played over and over at Saltoun Street, he hadn't known that he was playing "the blues." This music drew us all into a delicious melting pot.

It was said that Drew had been willing to pawn his Gibson in order to pay for Doc Watson's flight from the Carolinas to Glasgow, though I don't think Doc Watson ever came. Davey Graham, however, traveled from Notting Hill to the Folk Centre and on a Saturday night the small top-floor room in the Montrose Street tenement was packed with expectant cognoscenti. Davey clambered on to the stage, smartly dressed in black-and-white concert attire, eyes opaque, staring deep into his own self's numerous tribulations and exaltations. The lights went down, a hush descended, and he proceeded to chant and moan for forty-five minutes: "Nnnnawwawww, nnnnnaaaaaaahh-awwwo-o-o-o, nnnnnawwwwawwwwiio-o, a-a-a-a-aahhhhh, nnnnhhhhwww," running up and down mock-oriental scales all the while.

The Folk Centre crowd were unimpressed, not to say angry. Drew Moyes might have had to return some admission money, which had been increased for the occasion, to pay for Davey's fee and expenses. The evening took on a legendary status at the Scotia. Davey's veins shimmered satisfyingly with heroin, and the inward harmonies sounded sublime to his soul, which was pathetically unharmonious in everyday life when deprived of the narcotic; but what he sang was simply rubbish to the ears of the Folk Centre faithful. Nevertheless, I was sorry I missed him.

Every now and then, a group would set off for London in a packed van, barrelling down the A74 on to the A6, over Shap Fell, through the night, in search of work or a music gig. A single train ticket cost £6—not far short of a week's wages for me at Washie's by that time. Or there would be an expedition to the Highlands, to pass a weekend in Glencoe among climbers and noisy students—anyone who seemed more posh than us was called a "student"—at the Clachaig Inn. I read the sign on the door: "No Hawkers or Campbells," which seemed to everyone a terrific joke. There was usually a tent to sleep in or, in winter, a caravan. At bedtime (there were no beds), we filled thick glass lemonade or screwtop beer bottles with boiled water to warm our feet. Once, I removed the bottle in the middle of the night when it had cooled, and in the morning found it frozen solid next to my head.

The Scotia had its resident poet, Freddie Anderson, an Irishman from County Monaghan, who sold his poems in broadsheets and pamphlets, placing the coins he received immediately on the bar for liquid exchange. We thought of diminutive, bearded Freddie as an elderly and odd chap, though he was friendly to all, but I realize now that his age at the time was around forty. His subject matter was socialist in intent. In his play, *Krassivy*, about the Scottish communist John MacLean, Freddie took the role of Lenin to whom he bore a shriveled resemblance.

People at the Scotia seemed more knowledgeable about politics and more engaged with all manner of social affairs than I could possibly be. I didn't even know the name of the Prime Minister. My politics were intensely personal: they involved a lengthy domestic struggle, an industrial dispute in nineteenth-century working conditions, a property grab in the West End of Glasgow, and the price of bread and beer. Liberation came in the form of a wisp of a beatnik chick with a bewitching nonchalance, long black hair, and heavy eye-makeup. Everyone knew her as Wee Jeannie. The nonchalance, it didn't take long to discover, was only a style.

There were other poets, with more romantic subject matter than Freddie, and a little later I would present myself as one of them. I also played for the Scotia football team on nearby Glasgow Green, and on a Saturday afternoon, in between lunchtime and evening sessions at the pub, scored a goal while Wee Jeannie looked coolly on from beneath her fringe. There were other girls at the Scotia: careful girls and careless girls, nice and not so nice girls—one I remember acted as a honey trap for punters, who would follow her up a close where they were beaten and robbed by her accomplices—

girls who couldn't be persuaded and girls who couldn't persuade me.

And there were nice guys and not so nice guys. One of the latter asked one day: "You've got your own pad. Can we use it to fix up?" Before I could reply—probably in the affirmative—one of the nice guys stepped in. This was Coakie, whom I had first met in Edinburgh with Bruce some four years earlier, and who had introduced me not to heroin but to ban-the-bomb poetry and the perfect society envisaged by the Young Communist League. We had shared a brief friendship after our pioneering hitch-hiking trip home to Glasgow in the back of an open lorry. Until that moment I hadn't known, even since I had begun to see him again at the Scotia, that he was doing hard drugs. Now he scolded the one who had tried to enlist me, by association, into the junkie fellowship. "Shut yer mooth. Ye cannae ask the boy t'dae that."

IV

No one from Washie's ever accompanied me to the Scotia after work. They were separate worlds. I was being drawn from one, and pulled towards the other. Jeanette was right when she predicted that I wouldn't see it through to the end. It was in the summer of 1969 that I started going down that long lonesome road, nearly three years into my apprenticeship. A persistent cough and tightness in the chest led to a trip to the doctor's surgery in Hyndland, where I came across Billy Connolly sitting shyly in the waiting room. The doctor gave me two weeks off work, which led to another two and then another. I had not achieved the level of seniority that would entitle me to paid leave, so I applied for sickness benefit at the dole office—the burroo—the first of many encounters with one or other of those places.

After a month or two I was finding a way to live with my bronchitis, while becoming accustomed to a new style of life, perhaps the style I had always been aiming for: not idle—I never wanted that—but as master of my own time. The guitar was one part of my occupation, travel another—hitch-hiking to London with Wee Jeannie at my side, finding a day's work here or there; then to Dublin in the same way. In the July Fair Fortnight holiday, before my sick leave began, Jeannie and I had hitched up to Portmahomack, the great Campbell family holiday destination, and spread our tent out in a field, with the clear and thrilling sound of the North Sea in our night-time ears. We heated meals on a Primus stove and lay together in a sleeping bag on the ground, each dependent on the other's teenage softness for comfort.

There were firsts: we watched the first moon landing on July 20, 1969—that is, we watched the moon as the astronauts were said to be landing, while we sauntered along the front at the Port, in sight of the massive tarry anchors and the jetty where Dad had once upon a time taken me fishing for floun-ders; it was my first visit to the Port without my parents and sisters; Jeannie and I made love for the first time in the tent in Inverness on the way home.

Taking sick leave was a way of prolonging this idyll. Life was more meaningful than it had ever been, with new discov-eries at every flick of the calendar. I was getting used to being a state-sponsored pioneer. And who would dare to say I wasn't paying my own way? Hadn't I paid tax, as none of my student acquaintances had—starting at nine shillings a week (45 pence) and increasing—since October 3, 1966?

One day I went to the doctor's surgery to pick up my benefit note and saw a strange face behind the desk. Not the kindly, biddable female doctor, as usual, but a man I had never set eyes on before, bearded, bespectacled, brisk. What's the trouble here then? OK, let's have a listen to you. Pull your shirt up . . . Right . . . breathe in . . . now out . . . Right then . . . OK, shirt down. Everything sounds fine to me—*a little smirk*—you'll be glad to hear. Dressing a bit more warmly might help. Your present note runs out at the end of next week, and you can start back at work the following Monday.

Sitting down, head bent over the desk, silently scornful of my discomfiture.

"Tell me again the name and address of the place. Irvine or Irving, like the author?"

Other people I knew were being prescribed drugs by their GP: Mandies and black bombers. Yet others were said to receive forged prescriptions for methadone and even heroin. I didn't ask for anything like that. I wanted the doctor to prescribe Freedom. So far she would—women were usually on my side—and now he wouldn't.

I let Mr. Alister know that I would be coming back to work, after some ten weeks away, ten weeks' worth of even longer hair than Mr. David had been willing to tolerate, ten of the best weeks of my so-called adult life, a return to the primary-school holidays of the earliest years, which had been crowned by untethered adventures at the shepherd's cottage on Rockfield Farm and on the harbor and shore at the Port.

Mr. Alister appeared unimpressed when I outlined the respiratory ailment and what my (original) doctor had told me about it, that it was likely to be the result of prolonged exposure to damp. My top-floor flat in Saltoun Street was water-tight; at Washie's, rainwater sloshed around our feet when the skies opened. Upstairs on the second floor, under the roof, above the three-fingered cutter's head, there were tarpaulins in some places and broad brown swathes in others, as if someone had swept them on to the ceiling with a broom dipped in damp. In winter you could trace your breath indoors, while standing next to the moleskin blanket and cloth-covered pen carriages on the Shaw Pen Ruling Machine.

It was a pleasure to see Jesse and both Big and Wee Nancy again, to deflect Jeanette's sardonic remarks, as before, but a distance had already opened between us. I had left the back-to-front alphabet of the upstairs compositors' benches, to spell out a different life. I had found my present tense. No matter how brief my departure had been, it must have seemed to them pre-ordained: they knew from my way of speaking polite and from the sight of my father, who had turned up at the factory in his impressive hat and raincoat more than once, that I was only tarrying at this ancient contraption, in another century, with the smell of ox gall in the air. Sooner or later I would book my time-travel and go.

There was a dim whispering around Jeanette now, always involving Big Nancy, and it wasn't long before I discovered that it concerned the rupture of Jeanette's engagement to Michael Heaney. John closed his thin lips to it and turned his narrow, gray-overalled back. Mixed marriages were destined to go wrong. Even John could see that Michael had no badness in him, but a pape was still a pape.

Mary was more of a genial simpleton than ever, walking in her elegant step to the cludgie with greater regularity, but John's lips grew yet thinner as he understood that his apprentice was on his way out.

The tightness and wheezing in my chest came back a few days after my return to work. Jeannie sent me to the surgery again, where to my relief I found the woman doctor, who willingly signed another sick note. It couldn't go on. I told Mr. Alister that I would have to quit Washie's and renounce my paper ruler's apprenticeship. His response was just the same: the ailment I complained of had nothing to do with the damp which was visible on the ceilings and the floors of 48 Ingram Street.

I saw John Pollock only once after I had left Washington Irvine's. He was walking at a rapid pace down Buchanan Street in the direction of Central Station, as if in pursuit of some Catholic misspirit, or else in flight from a demon that was sucking nourishment from his insides at every step. He was too preoccupied to take notice of me.

One day in 1982, close to George Square, not far from Ingram Street, I saw Mary McIlwham at the center of a company of convivial winos. She was half-dancing and asking selected passers-by for money, while the bottle passed from hand to hand—Lanliq or Four Crown—then from mouth to hand and back again. When it came my turn to stump up a few coins, I made a remark about Washie's, but Mary didn't catch it. She had voyaged too deeply into the land of Lanliq to recognize anyone from outside, including me. A dozen years had passed since my departure. In the battle raging in Mary's life between wine and Washie's, even in my day, there could only be one winner. A song started up and another joke caused waves of joviality as I turned away.

7

LIFE IN THE UNDERGROUND

I

My dad's university had been the Navy. Mine was the Scotia Bar. Tutors included a new friend, Jimmy Dunn, who arrived in my life trailing a legend behind him: he had hitch-hiked to Morocco and back, had eaten maajun with djellaba-draped nomads on the fringe of the Sahara—the hotter it gets, the heavier the clothes they wear, Jimmy said—and returned with tales of camels blocking the road, goats in trees, snake charmers enchanting the market square, and prostrate donkeys hypnotized by storytellers.

Jimmy had long fair hair, a soft, pointed beard, and laughter lines darting from his eyes. He bore a passing resemblance to Robin Williamson, as much a style icon for us as Elvis Presley had been for a previous generation. Around his neck were strung odd beads and amulets bartered for on his travels. Others did the same, but Jimmy paced the track with an original gait. Only a year or two older than me, he was the first in a sequence of friends from whom I would absorb all the "learning" I could.

It wasn't street learning. It certainly wasn't academic, though Jimmy, who had left school at the same age as me, similarly unqualified, was knowledgeable about a surprising range of things. It was the kind of intimate education in which the teacher is unaware that the pupil is under his spell. After those mid-teen years of being closed off, I was suddenly open. The switch in direction was as rapid as a change of scenery in the theater. The narrative development was classic and the outcome was the happy one. Here was the landlocked student. Over there, the instructive navigator. For me, there was homework aplenty. I was already in the elementary music class, trying to gain knowledge from elders such as the great West End guitar player Alan Tall. And now something else, a harbinger of benign climate change on planet Me: reading.

Jimmy gave me a library copy of *Of Mice and Men* and I read it over the course of an afternoon in my bedsit at Saltoun Street. After that, he passed on *Cannery Row*, *Sweet Thursday*, and *Tortilla Flat*, fondly outlining the personalities I would find in Steinbeck's pages, and setting me off on an affair with American literature that has endured to the present day. Jimmy said that Mack and the boys in Cannery Row were bums, a bit like us. Anyone at the Scotia could have made that remark. What set Jimmy apart was that his favorite character in the novel wasn't a bum at all: it was Doc, the scientist and owner of Western Biological Laboratories. Jimmy saw himself in Doc, who reflected his own interests.

Doc's speciality was marine life; Jimmy's was the secret society of the Highland gateway woods near his home in Balloch, not far from Loch Lomond. As we walked there on different days, he identified bird calls and named wild flowers; he collected owl pellets and took them home, to his mother's affected disgust, to anatomize the feathery, bony, vomited contents. I was learning new words all the time, and that day I added "regurgitate" to the lexicon. He used advanced geographical terms to try to explain tides and winds, chronology and latitude, tropics and hemispheres. On other occasions I went to his parents' house in Balloch, which was connected by rail to Glasgow Queen Street, and we would hitch-hike up to Luss on the banks of the loch, passing the night in sleeping bags on the sandy shore.

Jimmy had a sister, Lorraine, younger than him but still too advanced for me—in maturity more than in years—who nevertheless accepted me. I was drawn to these big sister relationships. They confirmed me in a role which felt familiar: the younger brother. Lorraine was studying English and French at Glasgow University. It was a revelation—I was open to revelations—that her close friend Kate Reader had such a thing as a "favorite writer": Graham Greene. Since I was also open to influences, there was every chance that he might become my favorite writer, too.

Kate collected photographs of T. S. Eliot—another strange but alluring habit—and gave me a Faber paperback copy of his *Selected Poems*, which I still have. Its pages were full of mysteries, of a stimulating kind. She lived a little way outside Glasgow, in Eaglesham, and sometimes stayed over in my bedsit, sleeping next to me like another sister. On more than one occasion, the three of us, Kate, Lorraine, and me, slept in my single bed—those two at the top, me at the foot—giggling our way into a sound sleep. Kate took away my T-shirts and jumpers to wash—one favorite green sweater, she let me know, had to be done twice over—and gave me firm instructions how to make my way to the nearest public baths. The three of us hitch-hiked up to Portmahomack during the Easter holidays—Kate and Lorraine, as "the twins," going ahead, me following on behind—and stayed in a tent by the North Sea, as Jeannie and I had done before.

On arrival, I learned that Uncle Willie had died. Although he lived at Rockfield Farm, two or three miles away, not in the Port itself, the place felt empty without him. He had told me he never took a holiday and as a child I had thought that logical. Why would he, living here, where he was on holiday all the time? I walked up the farm track to the shepherd's cottage to visit Aunt Mary, now blind. She put a hand against my cheek and felt my long hair. "Oh, you've got a beard, Jim!" There were tears as she recalled how I used to sit on his knee and go with him at dawn across the fields with Fly and Glen to tend the sheep. "He was a good man, Jim."

Eventually, I left to return to the Port.

Just go down to the road, Jim. You'll get a lift.

On this occasion, though, I didn't. My long hair and strange clothes had drawn a barrier between modern me and the reliable old Port customs. When the fishermen in the bar of the Castle Hotel were reminded that I was Ina Beveridge's boy, the faces brightened again.

Back in Glasgow, we occupied "The Room" of Jean Cocteau's novel *Les Enfants terribles*, sometimes staying up all night and sleeping until five in the afternoon. Cocteau: "The Room prolonged its rites into the small hours. This made for late awakenings." Elizabeth was the sister of Paul in the Room of Cocteau's novel, and Lorraine and Kate were the sisters of Jim in the mini-Room we created in the West End. It was the first stirring of a feeling that one could live in literature—not exclusively but in a parallel fashion; be bodily in a flat somewhere off Byres Road, yet inhabit another realm—not Paris itself, but the Paris of the story—in imagination. It was a prelude to, training for, the travels I was about to embark on.

Reading to oneself and out loud to others, talking about the ideas discovered there, could become a way of life. Sartre's plays, Camus's novels, Cocteau all over, as well as Eliot and Greene, were as much the currency of Kate and Lorraine's conversation as the lyrics of Neil Young and Jefferson Airplane made up that of others. In that life, I reckoned, I could glimpse a small space for me. Just a corner: but it was a corner of The Room.

If the ideas of these great writers were half-understood, at best, no matter. There were a lot of things I didn't understand. Had I been familiar with it at the time, I would have identified with the comment made by Robert Graves to Ava Gardner. According to the actress, she said, "You know, Robert, I really don't understand poetry." To which Graves replied: "My darling, you're not supposed to understand it, you're supposed to enjoy it."

It was a new language. It had to be learned, and I was in the act of learning it. Those who were fluent in the tongue were charmed at the efforts made by the outsider—*l'étranger*—to communicate. I had evidently not grown up in my family as a "literary type." In fact, I had been a shocking failure at everything concerning the life of the mind. I had had another life. But if the life of The Room could be transposed on to that one, without doing fatal damage to it, then I might find a way to live with myself, as myself.

Jimmy told me that before going to sleep at night he liked to read a little, and when he woke up in the morning, he read a little bit more, while still in bed. That way he got through a book in about a week.

I did as Jimmy did, and read every one of Steinbeck's novels—even the turgid tale of labor activism, *In Dubious Battle*—as well as his travel book, *Travels with Charley*, the companion being a dog. At Kate's urging, I plunged into D. H. Lawrence's novellas, then started on Graham Greene. Lorraine gave me *L'Etranger*, which I read in translation as *The Outsider*. She explained that it was Meursault's indifference to his mother's death that condemned him in the eyes of "society"—a concept that was quick currency in our conversations. From Camus to Cocteau is a giant step, yet they remain neighbors on my bookshelf, having entered my life in adjacent weeks and made similarly deep impressions.

From Stirling's Library in Royal Exchange Square—just down the road from Washie's—I borrowed books about the blues, in which rural singers talked about the music and about their lives: *Conversations with the Blues* by Paul Oliver and *The Country Blues* by Sam Charters. This opening up of cultural canals—to Greene's Africa, to Camus's Algeria, to Cocteau's Paris, to Big Bill's Mississippi Delta—was the most important event of my teenage life to date. It was enriching, and the cultural capital—counted in units of imaginative freedom—could only increase. Cultural wealth is a rare thing among investments: it is foolproof. It never decreases in value and it never lets you down.

II

I had officially left Washie's in September, 1969, three years into the six-year apprenticeship. I was still drawing sickness benefit, more or less commensurate with what my pay had been—in other words, very little. In one of our many pursuits of money, usually with the thought in mind of "going away," Jimmy and I fell in with a group of London-based freaks, of a seemingly superior tone to the native species. They were party to an aesthetic scam: mass-produced works of art, in acrylic or pastel, were taken round the houses in the middle-class suburbs of Glasgow and its environs. We posed as artists and the artworks posed as originals, by "members of our group."

It was a fiasco, as these things always were. (One evening, the door of a house on which I knocked was opened by Mr. Washie, Washington Irvine himself.) But the young English men and women we met, while failing miserably to raise any money worth counting, were better educated than we were, more hip to the latest fashion in awareness, to the newest way to "be here now," or so it seemed to us at the time.

I had moved to yet another pad, at 3 Thornwood Avenue, off Dumbarton Road, well west of the university district, and an associate of the English gang came to stay for a couple of weeks. He remained in the room when I went to Glencoe with Jimmy Dunn—as I remained in the caravan while Jimmy attached his crampons and climbed a mountain—and was waiting there when I got back. We grilled sausages and deep-fried chipped potatoes and heated baked beans. I was puzzled by the amount of time he spent sleeping. Only later did I understand what was wrong: he was a druggie, with an uppers and downers habit. One minute he was bouncing around on black bombers, the next he was dead to the world on Mandrax. He had hidden the fact, and I was too naive to notice. At the time, I knew nothing about it.

Before this realization dawned, he proposed an exchange which appealed to me: I could go and live for some weeks in his apartment in London; meanwhile, he would continue to sleep in my room in Partick. While I was gone, he would pay my rent, £3 a week, delivered in person to the Pakistani land-lord who lived a few streets away. As for the London place—no need. It was all taken care of.

I agreed enthusiastically.

It was no small event to go to London for a few weeks. People looked at you with new interest. So it was that Kate and Lorraine, Jimmy and others, assembled at the bus station one evening in early October to wish me luck, after a few rounds of drinks at the Scotia (my guest remained asleep in Thornwood Avenue). The bus left from the station at the top of Buchanan Street at 10 pm and rolled through the short Scottish night into the long English early morning, arriving at Victoria Coach Station at 8 am. In my pocket, the address: 11 Queensway, right next to the Tube station and close to Notting Hill, dead center of the counterculture. I don't remember receiving a single instruction about what to do once inside the flat—heating, bedding, towels, gadgets, gas, and electricity—but I could sort all that out by myself. There was only one thing I needed to know: fetch the key from the neighbor at No. 9. No name, no gender, no nationality, just "the neighbor."

After a cup of milky tea with some charcoaled toast in a café at Victoria railway station, I went down to the Tube platform, to make my way to Queensway. I had been in London recently with Wee Jeannie. We had worked for a few days moving stock from one boutique to another, near Carnaby Street, so I didn't feel altogether like a country bumpkin from the north. Afterwards, we had sat in the pub at the corner of Carnaby and Marlborough Streets, watching the people passing by in an extravagant ballet of frill and flower and flair, listening to the symphony of otherworldly accents—English, mostly—conducted in what seemed a chorus of alien assurance. On the wall of an underpass at Piccadilly Circus I saw the spray-painted graffito: "Clapton is God."

That was some months earlier. Now I emerged from the elevator at Queensway station on to the street itself, a boulevard running north from Bayswater Road to Westbourne Grove, happy to feel the wash of another adventure making its way through me like a dye, its hue only heightened by my apprehension about the key. The first thing I saw, on the left, was a large plate with "No. 1 Queensway." A good start.

But there was nothing in sequence with the figures 9 or 11. At street level, the buildings were mostly shops and, as is often the case, the numbers were missing. I walked down Queensway, then back up. The numbers lacked the plain logic of a Glasgow street, which would go: 19, 17, 15—skipping the unlucky 13—landing safely at 11. Next door to that would be No. 9. Inside would be "the key."

But there was no door with a No. 11 plate screwed on to it. Nor was there any No. 9, behind which lived a helpful neighbor, pleased to receive news of our mutual acquaintance, fast asleep in Glasgow. In fact, there weren't even any likely-looking residential buildings. The only possible one was a six- or seven-story modern apartment block, starting at first-floor level above the shops, which unfolded all the way down Queensway to Princess Court at the next corner. It was called Queen's Court, and the metal box to the side, with a battery of unfamiliar buzzers, told me that it contained flats numbered from 1 to 30. When a man of genial appearance emerged from the double doors, I asked what number of Queensway was Queen's Court.

"This is 15."

Together we looked to right and left. Logically, it should be two doors up, in the direction of the station entrance. But that was a baker's shop, helpfully open on Sunday morning. I inquired inside.

"*This* is No. 11."

"Eleven Queensway?"

The baker looked at me: just a bumpkin, after all. In a movie, he would have drawled, "What do you think, Fifth Avenue?" But we weren't in a movie, or not one that had any kind of comprehensible plot. Even the cast—the neighbor at No. 9—had failed to turn up.

The helpful extra of a moment ago had likewise disappeared. Outside, I went back and forth, towards the Tube station in one direction and Princess Court in the other, at the next corner down, towards Westbourne Grove, trying to figure out an answer to the numerological problem.

Eventually, I returned to stand before the entrance to the block. It surely held the clue. And it was up to me to pose the question in such a way as to elicit the answer. Systems of house sequencing often presented riddles which revealed their solutions with sudden clarity. When another resident exited, I held the door, deflected her questioning expression with a polite smile, and entered. Up in the lift to the second floor, directed by a sign. The lift opened on to a row of doors. Let's see: 7 . . . 7A . . . 8 . . . 8A . . . 9! My new home, 11, was evidently on the next floor up.

I knocked on the door of No. 9. There was no response. After another knock and a wait of a few moments, a woman's head appeared round the edge of the door. It sized me up, a foreigner, with a stranger's regard. I smiled and tried to explain the situation. I mentioned my sleepy friend's name.

"*Eh?*" I couldn't see more than some tangled hair and a dressing-gowned shoulder. It was Sunday morning. She had never heard of him.

And the flat at No. 11?—keeping up the smile—nice boy—from Scotland—not some outlaw region, after all—pointing in the direction of the upper floor—was it occupied?

"Eh?"

"Do you know if someone lives there?"

She hadn't a clue. She didn't care. Her husband would be home soon. Goodbye.

No. 11, on the third floor, was not unoccupied in expectation of my arrival. In it lived an elderly man, also not English— English people were foreign enough for me—but slightly more forthcoming. At least he was willing to reveal his full person in the doorway. It took a moment for him to grasp the nature of the problem. This wasn't 11 Queensway, he said. This was Queen's Court, No. 15. Eleven was just the number of the flat in the block. Queen's *Court*. Not 11 Queensway. Queen's Court. This was just his flat, with *that* number, in *this* block of flats. Not *way—court*. It wasn't 11 Queensway.

Where was 11 Queensway, then? A shrug, from foreigner to foreigner. He took a step out of the door into the corridor and looked at the floor, as if we might see the missing house there. To the left? Downstairs? Outside? No. I had looked everywhere. "There's a baker's shop there." This appeared to be news to him. My friend's name meant nothing. Should I try the door at No. 10? A hand gesture. As far as he was concerned the conversation was at an end. "Not this. This is not 11 Queensway."

I walked down the stairs and emerged into the street. After more searching, I had to conclude that the flat at No. 11 Queensway was a phantom. Had my friend—he was no longer my friend, obviously—chosen the number because he knew it belonged to a shop? It was 10.30 am on a Sunday in October. I had no return ticket and little money. I had had the intention of making my way in the capital, one way or another. What to do now?

There was a girl in Notting Hill, a member of the same group of English freaks that Jimmy and I had fallen in with, in the phony artworks affair. She, too, had found that there wasn't any money to be made from the ridiculous scam, and had returned to London. It was she who had put into my head the idea of coming to stay for a while. Over a late-night drink (for me) and joint (for everybody else), to the sound of some far-out rock on the record player. So in a way she was expecting me. I had been meaning to pay her a visit anyway, when I arrived, but it was going to be sooner than intended. She might not have anticipated the arrival of a new flatmate, but now there didn't seem much else I could do.

III

It wasn't far to Portobello Road. With the help of a few passers-by, I found my way to Powis Square and located a house number—one that actually existed. No one telephoned in those days. Her name was Allie. She opened the door to my ringing, with a cry of—what? pleasure? despair?—and listened to my tale.

"But it's obvious what to do. You must stay here!" Nice woman that she was, she managed to appear delighted to see me and welcomed me in. There was only one bed, a mattress on the floor, but that didn't appear to be a problem. I was used to sharing beds in Glasgow flats with Kate and other girls who were not my girlfriend. People sat around in rough circles drinking beer or tea or coffee, cracking jokes and singing songs, then crashed out. There weren't that many beds, so you took a cushioned surface wherever you found it, and sometimes the pillow next to you supported a friendly head, some-times female, as often as not partly or fully clothed.

The famous market at Portobello Road was nearby, and Allie and I went there to look for a job for me. But although Allie knew lots of stallholders and much joshing conversation was made with curly-haired cockney men and warm-cheeked women in a multiplicity of scarves, I had no success in find-ing work.

In the evenings, and often in daytime as well, a procession of friends would arrive at Allie's place, hanging around for hours, smoking dope, drinking herbal teas, discussing macro-biotic diets and the horrors of straight ways of living. To each one, Allie told my story, and all looked on me with condescen-sion and pity. What was he doing in London? "He's looking for a job," Allie answered.

People said—addressing Allie, mostly—that they liked my accent. "Scotland, yeah." Another drag on the joint. The word "beautiful" came into play. There would be some anecdote of driving in a rickety van to the Highlands where Gino from Camden or Lucy from Dorset had bought a beautiful cottage on a croft. Did I ever do crofting? No. I knew about share-crop-ping in the Deep South and picking cotton in the Mississippi Delta, but I had scarcely even heard of crofting. Did I wear a kilt? "Beautiful, man." I began to feel like a tartan doll. It was not the life of The Room.

One unforgettable event occurred when someone men-tioned Davey Graham. He lived close by, apparently. *Davey Gra-ham*—the very syllables had thrilling potential. I could hardly believe it. That would make it all worthwhile. If only I could pass Davey Graham in the street in Notting Hill, and return to tell the tale, my journey would be justified, my presence at

Davey Graham, "midnight man," the source of the great 1960s flowering of folk and blues guitar technique. *Courtesy of Brian Shuel/Getty Images.*

the Scotia transformed, for however brief a period, from black-and-white to full color. Allie pointed to one of her friends who had his arm crooked in anticipation of the circulating joint, and said that he knew Davey Graham well. The way they said "Davey Graham," in a certain tone, tailing off in the direction of the final sound, pronounced "Groy-im," made me feel that their respect did not match mine.

Still, here was someone who knew Davey Graham. "Really?"

A mouth opened. "Davey Graham owes me five bob." The mouth accepted the joint and sucked in a lungful.

Another voice: "Davey Graham's a fucking hopeless junkie." Dope was cool, but junk was not. Junk borrowed money and didn't pay it back. Junk let everybody down. My mention of him as the greatest guitar-playing genius alive—his seniority placed him above even Bert Jansch—got a shrug or a yeah or a used-to-be.

A few days after my arrival, Allie said she had to go and visit Joy Farren to deliver a parcel. Did I want to come? Of course I did. I was eager to meet the denizens of this new planet. "I don't know if Mick will be there."

I had heard of Mick Farren, rock star bizarre (later one of the many editors of *International Times*, and later still a prolific novelist). He led an iconoclastic group called the Deviants. At music festivals, Mick Farren gathered together a band of free-music subversives, the White Panthers. They were more political than most of those on the freak scene, trailing an aura of violence. People reached for the word "heavy," as they did with junkies. It wasn't my thing, but the White Panthers had been known to protest against admission charges at music festivals, and tear down the fences so that those without tickets could enter free of charge. This I would be quite happy to take advantage of the following year at the Isle of Wight, while leaving the gross act of subversion to someone else—to Mick Farren, in fact.

The proto-punk sound of the Deviants was not to my taste at all—"I take some pills and go to bed / I might get lucky and wind up dead"—but they had a reputation nevertheless. They were famous Underground people, or at least he was. It was for this that I had entered this new ecosystem, to seek out remedies and serums, study obscure documents and codes of communication known only through rumor in the remote north.

The promise of the key to a flat that didn't exist might just have been a rite of passage, one that would lead through a

Mick Farren of the Deviants and Joy, "high-up member of the reigning family of Notting Hill."

non-existent door to a back-to-front "knowledge." Here I was, after all, barely arrived, and already I was keeping watch for Davey Graham on the street. Maybe I could save up and pay off his five-bob debt? And now I was about to meet a rock star with mammoth shades and afro-style hair. That Queensway flat—perhaps it was a good thing? My fortunes had turned. This would make it three tales to tell when I returned to Glasgow: first the phantom, then Davey (another phantom, since I hadn't seen him yet), and now a visit to Mick Farren's pad.

Allie and I walked over to Colville Road, just a few hundred yards from her place in Powis Square. Joy admitted us at the first-floor, then returned to her chair in a large living room, like a high-up member of the reigning royal family of Notting Hill, which, in fact, she was. She was wrapped from head to toe in a dress of black crinoline that caught the light and sharpened the splendid effect, with high collar and an ivory pin brooch at the neck such as your grandmother might have chosen. She was wearing little round granny glasses, too, the ironic fashion of the time. She couldn't have been more than twenty-five.

The Farrens had covered the walls of the high-ceilinged room with silk and cotton hangings. A four-part oriental folding screen stood in one corner, creating a mini-room within the larger one, with teasing vintage slips tossed purposefully over the top. There was a mirror with an elaborate frame positioned at a tilt on the floor, and a handsome wooden fireplace. Even though she was married to a monster—a marvelous monster, Mick—Joy remained a gracious figure. Her style was natural and pleasing. For half an hour or so, I enjoyed her not unfriendly talk, and through it all held to the thought that the event might climax with a glimpse of the deviant star.

"The new album's arrived!" Joy announced to Allie. Her conversation, like that of most people I had met so far, bypassed me, but on this occasion I didn't feel offended, as I had with the anti-Davey Graham lot. Mick would know Davey, surely. Inwardly, I overheard myself talking to him about the eclectic assemblage of tracks on Davey's great debut, *The Guitar Player*. He might invite me to come back to Colville Road to play a couple of Bert Jansch numbers.

Joy went to a pile on the floor that I had noticed from the corner of my eye but hadn't taken the measure of, and picked up an empty record sleeve. It was called simply *The Deviants 3*. On the cover was a lipsticked nun—a model, obviously—sucking an ice-lolly with a lascivious gleam in her eye. The title of the opening track was "Billy the Monster," which sounded just right. I could probably get to like the Deviants, even while ignoring their music. Photographs of Mick on the mantelpiece showed a man with Hendrix hair but a style of cockney stallholder menace in the face—I knew it was only a style and although it repelled me I was prepared at that moment to tolerate it—that Hendrix didn't have. He was wearing outrageous spectacles, a scowl, and of course flamboyant clothes.

Allie drew Joy's attention towards me for a moment and said: "He's a musician, too. His hero's Davey Graham."

"Davey owes Mick ten bob," Joy said.

After about an hour, we left, without seeing Mick.

IV

I stayed on at the Powis Square flat for another two weeks. As October looked towards November and bright autumn skies clouded over in preparation for winter, it became clear that Allie had had enough of me. I was broke. I had no desire to be her tartan-doll lover, as perhaps she had thought I would be. During my stay, she often expressed her horror of "straights," and although I didn't count myself as one I might have been seen that way after a fortnight's exposure under the glare of the far-out heads of Notting Hill. I had a Mum and Dad in High Wycombe. I had nice elder sisters now working as art teachers, and a little sister for whom I felt a deep protective love. Julie's own loves were ponies, children's television presenters with names like Wendy, and a boyish pop star called David something.

Where did all this fit into the deviant world that Mick and Joy and Allie were shaping? Not only had I not struggled free of the intolerable occident (another new word), emerging into the transcendental zones of India or Morocco, as several of Allie's friends had done, I had never even crossed the English Channel. I liked pubs and I bought my round. I venerated Davey Graham, but when it came my turn to bite into the maajun cake, I refused. Maybe I was a straight, too?

I moved out and went to stay at Blackheath where my sister Phyllis was living in a commune run on strict principles of equality and redistribution. Everyone's pay packet went into the pot and spending money was dispensed to each according to their needs. Under pressure from the communards to find a job, I started washing dishes in a café on Lewisham Road, at the foot of Blackheath Rise. The Turkish Cypriot manager wondered why the Scottish boy was in London and asked a question which pleased me as much as any compliment: "Police looking for you?" He paid me £9 a week, cash.

The words Mao and Maoist were spoken at the commune, which was mainly made up of Oxford and Cambridge graduates. There was a social-work element to it, too. They looked after drug addicts, ex-prisoners, malcontents of various kinds. Possessions belonging to the commune dwellers, such as cameras, were sometimes stolen from bedrooms—almost expected to be stolen, as no locks were permitted on the doors—and sold on the street or in rotten pubs for money to buy drugs. I attached myself to one of the less complicated figures, and he offered to give me a tattoo on my left wrist—an authentic prison tattoo, as I've happily told people ever since. No one could mistake me for a straight.

He had learned the art of tattooing while serving time in a borstal in Kent. First, sketch the desired pattern with a pen on the arm or other body part where it's wanted—the forehead was a favorite in the borstal, he told me—then take a decent-sized needle. Wrap thread around, close to the point, to create a tiny ball. Dip the threaded tip into a jar of Indian ink and jab hard into the skin of the tattooee, leaving a single black dot on the flesh. Repeat as necessary, until the pattern is complete.

In my case, it was some kind of fertility symbol or perhaps a letter from an ancient alphabet, a hieroglyph borrowed from the back sleeve of an Incredible String Band LP, or somewhere like that. I've never been quite sure. After several dozen painful stabs, we were done. Amazingly, I never suffered an infection or any other ill-effect. In mid-December, I returned to Glasgow with this and my various tales, souvenirs of a trip to London during the chilly autumn of love. Sharon Tate and four others had been murdered by members of the Charles Manson cult in August, three months before.

Word had got around that my flat-share friend had woken up, broken into the gas meter, taken all the money he could find, then departed with that and a few of my meager possessions—*Blonde on Blonde*, *The 5000 Spirits or the Layers of the Onion*—leaving the door ajar. Some pals from the Scotia went to Thornwood Avenue and tidied up. The police were summoned by the landlord and one evening after I was settled back in, two plain-clothes men arrived from Partick police station.

My lack of guilt must have spoken for itself and I never heard from them again, but the landlord had understandably had enough of my tenancy and before long I was on the move once more, this time to a pleasant, central room, with a nice address: 1001 Sauchiehall Street. It was here, without making the connection to *Arabian Nights*, that Jimmy and I would drop acid at midnight and spend the early morning hours in the enchanted groves of Kelvinside Park.

There was a party to celebrate New Year at a house outside Glasgow at which Big Mick Broderick and other members of the Scotia crowd roared, laughed, hugged, kissed—as the bells tolled—drank and drank and drank, then sang and sang. Good morning, 1970. It was no longer the 1960s.

PART TWO

THE LAND OF AWAY

8

ISTANBUL AND SPETSAI

I

Only a twist of fate brought me to Greece, where I had never intended to be. My compass pointed in the other direction, towards the East. I was on my way to India—so I told everyone in Glasgow. My friend Dudley and I talked endlessly about travel, referred to as "going away." This one was "away" in Spain, where things were as cheap as you dared to imagine; that one in Morocco, a more feasible destination than the subcontinent, exotic none the less, where the world would represent itself beguilingly back to front. Everyone wanted to be going away to India, which had a mythical status in our imaginations and in our conversations. We knew little of the reality, drawing half-nourishment from crumbs scraped from black-jacketed Penguin Classics of the *Bhagavad Gita* and the *Upanishads*. Those few who managed it returned gently bearded, adorned with amulets, jangling with bracelets, encrusted with parables and riddles, telling tales of holy cows in the street and unholy bathers in the Ganges. They kept us spellbound in our bedsits, as joss sticks smothered the northern chill and familiar West of Scotland rain pelted the windows.

Most people Dudley and I knew lived in a single room or a shared flat, where they draped oriental hangings on the wall and positioned fat cushions on the floor. People could go for months without sitting on a chair. Bricks and planks were modeled into bookcases, housing Timothy Leary, Richard Alpert (*Be Here Now*), Richard Brautigan, Jeff Nuttall, anything by Khalil Gibran—*The Prophet* was essential—the poems of Yevtushenko. No author was likely to outnumber Hermann Hesse: *Steppenwolf, Demian, Narcissus and Goldmund, Siddhartha*, and, of course, *Journey to the East*. Perennially smiling people encountered in these rooms introduced new words to the language, such as *futon, kilim, chillum, soya*. Brown rice mixed together with vegetables *sauté*—another one—with soya sauce, was stated with wistful certainty to satisfy most dietary requirements. Various sorts of brown bread were served, as foreign to our parents as green tea or Lebanese red. The word "uncool" was heard often, usually in reference to dress, bad temper, alcohol, meat, and people over twenty-five.

Just the act of saying that I was going away—"To India?" . . . "To India . . . yeah . . ."—gave me pleasure, as if it were somehow a credit to me. At last, I would step up into that vagabond elite, the Kings of Away, who roamed the East. I might not yet have reached the place itself, where an inner initiation would automatically occur—a vacuuming of industrial Glasgow unmindfulness—but I had stated my intention. The quest was begun. News circulated: Jim's going to India. Far out.

I sought the advice of some well-known hippie elders, and everyone assured me it was possible. "Go via Germany, then through Austria. The Alps. *Man!* Yugoslavia could be a wee bit of a problem . . . Big Tam got his hair cut off at the border—of all people! . . . but after that you'll be in Bulgaria. It's straight on for Istanbul. Simple enough."

More simple than one dared to imagine. "Stay in Istanbul for at least a week. There's lots of hostels for heads. Then take a bus through Iran and Afghanistan. Bonn voy adge." The thought of the journey produced a kind of fear which I succeeded in repressing, but which remained like a dormant ailment. I wasn't going on a journey so much as taking a test.

I traveled without a rucksack; just a shoulder bag, which contained a sweater, an extra T-shirt, a copy of *Cain's Book* by Alexander Trocchi, and another paperback or two. I had a towel, a toothbrush, and a pair of sandshoes, elsewhere known as plimsolls. I remember with fondness a crew-neck sweater knitted out of green wool. Each morning, on whatever patch of grass I rose, I would roll up the sleeping bag, secure it at each end with a rope, then loop the rope from one side to the other to make a strap and sling it across my shoulder with the bag. Somewhere I might find a cup of coffee or tea. Hot water for face and hands was a luxury. In public lavatories I washed my plentiful hair with soap. From time to time I even washed the T-shirt. Then I did what I did best, my proper skill, my living: I stuck out my thumb.

So: starting from the ferry port at Ostend, first drink a Belgian beer—shockingly expensive, with a sharp, lemony foreign flavor and a vexing inch of lather on top—then find a place to crash. In the morning, buy some bread, cheese, and ham. Next, seek out the right autoroute through Belgium, nudging past the Netherlands—though I found myself to my surprise one pleasant evening stranded in the border town of Arnheim—carrying on through Germany.

These were all good countries for hitch-hikers, and Germany was the best. Just keep traveling due south. After "east," "south" was the second most desirable direction. North and west you turned your back on. On my feet, the sandshoes or a pair of leather sandals of oriental design, with a hard coil for the big toe, a herald of India, bought in one of the incense-heavy head shops in Glasgow's university district. As a guide, a map of the most elementary kind (later I developed an obsession with maps and walking shoes). Most of the time, I depended on road signs: Cologne . . . Karlsruhe . . . Stuttgart . . . Salzburg . . . Zagreb . . . Sofia . . . Sometimes I overshot an *Ausfahrt* and had the driver to set me down at the next one, so as to hitch or walk back a few miles to pick up the proper connection. Whatever happened, I would find the way. Just go down to the road.

Occasionally, on this journey or another, a driver would ask: "Where are you going to sleep tonight?" and I would reply, "By the side of the road," and he would invite me to dine and to sleep at his home. By these acts of mostly disinterested kindness, on different journeys, I became more cosmopolitan. For three or four nights, I slept in a luxurious double bed at the home of a middle-aged couple at in the French foothills of the Pyrenees. Our consolation was mutual. Their son and daughter had recently left home and they were happy to pamper a Scottish boy who, for all his past delinquency, was ever-attentive to the ordinary courtesies instilled at home. In the daytime, I took the daughter's bicycle and explored high-hedged country roads.

Near Bologna, an American motorcyclist picked me up and positioned me on the pillion of his exciting machine, my arms around his waist, both of us unhelmeted. In the evening, after he had settled me in a small spare room with a single bed, he made a telephone call and then announced that we were going out to dinner at the home of an American friend, married to an Italian, "who looks rather well."

She was delightful and pleased to see this roadside straggler, but her beauty did not strike me as the sort that was generally advertised in advance. She served a pasta dish with an oil, garlic, tomato and anchovy sauce which I have tried unsuccessfully to emulate in the decades since. Then—just when I thought the meal was over—chicken drumsticks in their warm and crispy aromatic skin. Salad. Cheese. Dessert. Coffee. Nothing in the fabled East could be more exotic than this to a Glaswegian Southsider. I realized only when my American friend and I had parted the next day, after another thrilling bike ride to a convenient hitching place, that he had said of his compatriot's wife that she "cooks rather well."

When I was traveling through Germany with a girlfriend the year before, a muscular young man in a suave car brought the pair of us back to his flat in the center of Dortmund. He told us he was a footballer, working his way up through the ranks at the local team, Borussia Dortmund. That was interesting. Otherwise, he was not, but we were pleased to be sitting under a safe roof in comfortable armchairs, sipping the famous German beer and nibbling slices of fatty sausage. Were we married? No, we were not. He smiled. Not to worry. There were two spare bedrooms. In the middle of the night his hold on his strict moral code slipped and he tried to climb in with Linda, something she told me when we were out and free and on the road again.

It was one of only a few occasions on which the offer of hospitality, or just of a lift from one town to the next, came with unstated sexual complication. I could usually get the signal and take steps to avoid it. My fearlessness was a twin to my naivety. It wasn't deep in the bone but it was useful. Therefore everything was possible and everything, in the end, was easy. I had no ambitions of the other kind: study, career, marriage, property, money. They existed in another land of away, a lower-case country, in the direction opposite to the one I was taking: west not East.

I reached Istanbul in an off-duty tourist coach, driven through Bulgaria by a crew of Turks. They already had a young English-woman and her obnoxious blond South African boyfriend as passengers. His contemptuous remarks about peasants work-ing in the fields, as we zipped by, embarrassed her. The Turks took a dislike to me—perhaps because I didn't join in the back-slapping and pidgin-English jokery—and as we approached Istanbul the portly South African gave me to understand that while he and his girlfriend were being guided by the hosts to a hotel, I was expected to get down as soon as we were inside the city boundaries. I was glad to be rid of them. I felt sorry for the girl, who seemed uncomfortable among the flashing-eyed Turks and the over-ebullient blond man.

Istanbul struck me straightaway as belonging in different zones of time and space from any other city I had been in. So this was the East. In tiny booths along the road leading to the center, craftsmen of every imaginable kind—the micro kind—worked into the evening: cobblers tapping on their lasts, tai-lors stitching and sewing, barbers shaving, scribes attentive to dictation, watchmakers, metalworkers, heads looking up as I passed. Young men held hands in the street. A couple, two couples, three, surrounded me smilingly, as if greeting a sud-den arrival from an outer atmosphere. At corners, elderly musicians with faces charting ancient topographies played on curvaceous instruments. Once, I took a borrowed guitar to accompany one of them. There was a crowd and everyone applauded when the young European with the long hair and the old turbaned Turk reached the end, but I blush now to think how it must have sounded.

"Stay in Istanbul for a week or so," the sage adventurers of Glasgow had advised. "Then take a bus to Tehran. It's amazingly cheap." At the hostel near the Blue Mosque at which I found a bed, I made inquiries about schedules and fares. Amazingly cheap turned out to be quite a lot—things always cost more than the estimates you heard in advance. I could manage, but it would leave me little money with which to carry on through Iran and Afghanistan to the mythic destination.

Take another bus when you arrive in Tehran, they had said, to get to the border. What kind of bus? Starting from where? Which border, anyway? There was no such thing as preparation for a journey of this kind. No one I knew ever opened a guide book or looked at a detailed map. It was travel by grapevine, by rumor, by good tip (or bad tip), finally by faith. I never considered the need for visas which, when required—information received from other hitchers only as I got close to passport control—could be obtained at the frontier. There was only *the road* and the instinct to get *there*, wherever there happened to be. It was Away.

I had recently read a story in the newspaper of two hitchhikers disappearing in Afghanistan. My shallow-rooted fearlessness shuddered protestingly. The dormant ailment stirred. I would be completely broke by the time I got to India. I tried not to think about it—not thinking about things came naturally—and told myself that something would turn up.

And so something did, though not in the form expected.

II

One afternoon in Istanbul, at an orange-juice street stall, a middle-aged man in a short-sleeved shirt approached. He had the beak of a raptor and had eyed a long-haired young morsel. He was German. He said he was a lorry driver and he looked like one. "You are going to Tehran?" Yes. How did he know? "Because I made a guess. I see you with your friends in a café last evening. And I recognize the hair."

He put on a friendly look, but it failed to mask a shadow I can bring to mind even now. "If you want, I can take you to Tehran. I often help the young people." Hearing himself use the word "help" obliged him to smile. "I make the journey each two-week and I like the company. We are able, we can, to leave tomorrow."

This was captivating. The sound of it blotted out other sounds I ought to have paid attention to. A truck was preferable to a bus, any time. Faster, smoother, less crowded, more like hitching.

"You will have to pay me a little, but it will be less than the bus."

Pay? He named a sum, which he made me understand he wanted in advance.

Just then, I felt the fear again, but I banished it, to prevent other fears clustering round. Fear or fearlessness was a choice. Now was the moment: India or not? Do I commit myself in union to the person I claimed I wanted to be, a mariner of Away? Could I blend being and performance to create a single entity, emerging as "me"?

There could only be one answer. Already, at the orange-juice stall on that thronged but still half-Western street, on the near side of the Bosporus, I saw myself writing letters from an oriental café, curry smells on the heated air. I had heard that a café owner in Kabul or Delhi would pay a European to sit in the window, in order to attract other hip young folk. Imagine being paid just to be the person I was, or was becoming. "Dear (somebody-or-other), Yes, I've arrived in Delhi. It's something else, man. The food is far out . . . you can eat for just . . . the people are great . . . there's music tonight in a . . . did I tell you I played in the street in Istanbul? . . ." The script was being written even as I stood there facing my German.

People looked closely at us as they walked to and from the orange-juice stall. One man tried to engage us in a friendly manner—in Turkey people think it natural to talk to strangers—but the German kept his guard. Slightly hunched in his short sleeves, gray hair slicked back, gray face again unsmiling. I was a naïf, but my animal instincts sent messages urging me to attend to the vibration. The word "Tehran" exercised a pull in the other direction, the one to which I had pledged allegiance.

Yes, I said.

"You are going to need money in Iran. I can change for you on black market"—he pronounced it "on *black* market." Wasn't his main concern for my well-being, after all? We were traveling companions now. "The difference in value is—" he made a broadening gesture with two hands. "I get you good exchange." A shadow smile, a sage wink, a softening tone. "Don't worry."

The naïf went to the hostel to fetch his pitiful purse, then came back to the orange-juice stall to rejoin the driver, waiting patiently. Wasn't that a good sign? He took the money, then led me to an underground car park. Tomorrow—this was serious—nine. "Nine o' clock?" His head nodded once as his finger pointed to the concrete floor on which we stood. "You know where to come."

The next morning, I returned to the car park he had led me to—the precise spot—after taking custody of my banknotes. He stationed his truck there overnight, he said. I waited under the concrete structure, gray like him, for more than an hour. I had said farewell to my friends of the past ten days at the travelers' hostel, and accepted their blessings in English, American—that lonely guy I'd had a long conversation with about *The Dharma Bums*—Dutch, and probably German as well. Now I had no choice but to go back, admit that I had been had, and hope my bed wasn't already taken. Angry? Not really. Humiliated and bewildered. And relieved. I kept that part secret.

I could now add a new performance to my repertoire: the one in which I told the tale of how I was prevented from reaching the East. No one could say it was only the fear that had kept me back. Who would travel these dangerous roads with just a few pounds in his threadbare pocket? I had instead been initiated into another caste, lower than that to which the high priests of Away belonged, but not without honor: the travelers who had been Ripped Off. "Did you hear about Jim? . . . Turkey? . . . Poor guy."

I hung around Istanbul a bit longer. I felt strangely free now. The back alleys seemed to be lit all the way along by one continuous sizzling grill, and I ate there with a young man from a town reassuringly close to my parents' home in High Wycombe. In the streets near Agia Sofia I met a French freak called Pierre whom I knew from Glasgow—encounters like these were surprisingly common occurrences in the Land of Away. Pierre was a close ally of Dudley's: extravagant, untrustworthy, explicitly attached to drugs and the petty crime they brought with them. We exchanged news and he offered consolation, but we didn't waste time on each other.

Then I was safely seated on a bus at last: but in the unmystical direction, back to the European frontier, a jolting four-hour journey from Istanbul to the border town of Ipsala. I stood for the first time in sight of the light blue and white, horizontally striped flag and an overhead sign saying "HELLAS," with the crescent moon and twinkling star of Turkey already behind me. A customs officer on the Greek side rummaged through my little bag without conviction and motioned me forward with a backward switch of the head. My naivety was my shield, as much as my passport. Soon I was in a VW campervan with a bunch of genial Americans heading south to Athens.

III

The prospect of returning to Scotland after just two or three weeks away, when friends had seen me off on a voyage expected to last six months or more, was too shameful to contemplate. But what to do? The money I had kept back from the con man would see me through another fortnight, not far beyond. In Athens, you could sleep in a hostel for the equivalent of about fifty pence a night, and I loved the tavernas, which were a riot of Mediterranean light and smells and shouts and clattering cutlery. But the most inexpensive bed or meal was still expensive to me.

One afternoon I was crossing Syntagma Square when a fellow at an outdoor café table signaled from about thirty yards away for me to come over.

A cup of coffee, a cigarette, a sign. "Girl wanted, to work on island with horses." He was a confident type, older than me—even people my own age seemed older to my eyes—heavily bearded, recognizably American.

He squinted behind the glasses. "You're from Scotland, right? . . . Glaz-gow?" He pronounced the second syllable to rhyme with "cow."

What did I say? Had he heard me chattering and exchanging stories with fellow travelers in a café on the same square the night before, as the thief in Istanbul had claimed to do?

"Your name's Jim Campbell?" It was posed as a question but stated with certainty.

Jerry Robock and his traveling companion Richard had spent the night on the floor of my bedsit in the West End a year before. Dudley and I had met them one evening as we roamed Kelvingrove Park. Now, when I was seated at the table in a café on Syntagma Square, we calculated that the anniversary of that encounter must be practically to the day.

Jerry had told us then that he intended to make his way to Israel. Richard wanted to set up a poetry magazine, publishing work not only in English but in German, in which he was fluent. For the time being, they were both students, which in America seemed to mean living a flexible, free life, with plenty of time to work as a guard on a ski slope in Oregon, or somewhere geographically indeterminate, earning the kind of money we never even talked about. They seldom hitch-hiked, but traveled on student rail passes—another mystery. They clutched copies of *Europe on $10 a Day*, which was meant to suggest a tight budget but was about five times what I permitted myself. Americans were different from us: bigger, with more assurance, more good humor, more information on how things operated, more know-how. We shared a language; that was all. We were more fluent in their dialect— learned from Dustin Hoffman, Bob Dylan, William Burroughs—than they could possibly be in ours. We liked and admired them—likeability was one of their main features— but as much as we understood their ways and habits, they were ignorant of ours.

In the park, Jerry had looked at Dudley. "And you two? Also studying?" Dudley answered yes. "At the university of life." It was uttered so spontaneously and earnestly that the travelers didn't think to laugh. The conversation went on amiably, with some mutually amusing linguistic interventions. Not Edin-*burg*: Edinburgh. Not *Lok* Lomond: loch.

"Where are you going to sleep tonight?" I asked. They looked at one another, then at us.

"In the park." Jerry gave what was already his familiar shrug. "It's not against the law?"

I sensed that it was likely to rain later. I also felt an unburdensome obligation to invite them to crash at my place. It was the etiquette of the day. They would have invited me. At any rate, they would now invite the next unsheltered body they encountered. One small brick in the construction of the new world.

We walked towards my latest pad, a red sandstone tenement building high up on Wilton Street, near the Botanical Gardens, where first of all Dudley and I introduced them to the Scottish-oriental music that was our speciality—he as percussionist, me on my DADDAD-tuned Harmony steel string. A kind of Caledonian raga. Then Dudley left to go home—he lived with his parents—while the rest of us settled down to sleep: me in my bed, my two new friends in their sleeping bags on the floor. In the morning, I offered them muesli and some herbal concoction to drink before they left for Queen Street Station, still practising how to say *Loch* Lomond. They were nice guys. I didn't think much more about them.

And so it turned out that in Athens, twelve months later, Jerry was able to place his own new-world brick on top of mine, stabilizing it. I recounted the sad story of the theft in Istanbul. He listened impassively, then, without seeming to consider it at all, said, "You want to take this job?" He indicated the sign.

"But it says 'Girl wanted.'"

"Don't worry about that. We'll find a girl."

"I've never been on a horse."

The no-problem shrug. The squint. The half-smile. "We'll teach you."

For the next two and a half months, I became a horseman on Spetsai, an island grouped with others in the Saronic Gulf—Aegina, Poros, Hydra—about five hours by boat in those days from Piraeus. We did find "a girl" that afternoon, a pleasant young American, but she didn't take to the set-up and within a week had decided it wasn't for her. She was an experienced rider, however, and she offered me a couple of lessons. I mounted. I sat up straight. I held on. And throughout a summer's trotting, cantering, and galloping, I never fell off.

I thought then, and I have thought often since, of my German lorry driver (if he ever did such a thing as drive a lorry), of how much I owe him, and of how his actions must have punished him—I was certainly not the first of his petty victims. Recently I read, in a novel by Françoise Sagan, words given to a character who has been sacked unjustly from his job and reacts without bitterness. "I have never lost anything from what I have given. It is what you steal from others that costs you dearly." (*Un peu de soleil dans l'eau froide.*)

IV

We were employed by a local man, Takis Pareskevas: overfed, superficial, curt and arrogant in his dealings with the visitors from whom he made his living. He owned apartments on the island, which he rented to tourists, several sailing boats and speed boats, tennis courts I heard about but never saw, and the horses, of which we were the masters, Jerry and I. It was Takis who opened the discotheques on the island in idyllic places, where before there had only been tavernas; and Takis who closed down the old kafenia and put up neon signs saying "Bar." There is a Takis on every Greek island or resort to which foreigners are drawn, slowly spoiling the things the seekers claim to come in search of, and he is usually native born.

We were given a house in which to live, high up on the hill above the port, with a half-acre yard and five horses: Caesar and Romeo were Jerry's favorites. I chose Zorba to be mine, possibly because of Nikos Kazantzakis's novel, which was on sale at the harborside kiosks in the chunky Faber paperback and was being passed around in dog-eared form. The others were Oliver and the endearing chestnut Rufus, with a touch of the mule.

Spetsai is a small island, oval-shaped, about 7 km long at its greatest stretch. Private cars were forbidden. It has a port town (Dapia) and no other villages. Up above the port there is a pine forest, through which one walks to reach the opposite shore on the island's south coast, stumbling over tortoises (American friends called them "turtles"). Aghia Anargyri is now a tourist spot, but then it was a more or less deserted cove, with just a whitewashed chapel, some frayed straw sunshades, and a makeshift café for refreshments, if desired by riders.

Leading the little posse out of Spetsai port, one passed the imposing English school, built in 1927, where, Jerry told me, the "leaders of the Greece of the future are educated." I learned its name later: the Anargyrios and Korgialenios School, modeled, so they said, on Eton.

Takis did not pay us any wages, as such. He presumed that the two-story house on the hill, in full view of the Aegean and with a glimpse of neighboring Hydra, was the best part of our reward. From each circling of the island with a tourist group, we were granted a small commission. For a full tour of four people on horseback, for example, the fee might be 350 drachmas. To Takis, who seemed scarcely ever to shift from his seat in the office by the port, went 300; to us, the remainder. We were sometimes three- or four-strong up at "the ranch," as Jerry liked to call it, but the commission stayed the same and was shared among the company. I had looked forward to the opportunity to earn some money. No matter how hard I worked, however, I remained in the same parlous state throughout my stay.

The house on the hill was splendid in its way. It lacked basic plumbing and electricity but we had lamps with canisters, and candles in reserve. On a gas-powered cooking ring, large stew pots simmered. None of the rooms had much furniture, though there was a proper bed in the living room, in which I slept, Jerry in the hammock hitched to the ceiling beams not far from me. Others kipped down wherever they could, sometimes outdoors. Dawn broke through the unshuttered window to the buzz of persistent flies. I might wake to find a body beside me that hadn't been there when I had lain down the night before. There was no interior staircase: the upper floor was reached by an unsteady wooden ladder perched against the wall outside, leading to a gaping window. No glass in any of the windows and no flushing toilet. The house was a shell, a glorious shell, overlooking the cerulean sea studded with ships and vague humps in the distance, islands large and small, inhabited or abandoned.

The house on the hill on Spetsai, "a glorious shell." The stepladder used to access the upper floor is seen at left. *Courtesy of Jerry Robock.*

Each morning at about nine, we led the horses to the hay that was stored in an outbuilding, brushed them down, one after the other, then waxed the bridles and saddles. More than once I found a tick in my armpit, fattening itself on my blood. One of our gang at the time of the first discovery was brought up on a farm in the north of England and he knew straight away what to do: first sponge the armpit with vinegar, then pull out the capsule with tweezers. On the ground, the tick would dissolve in a red splotch: a blood brother.

Before leaving Glasgow, I had begun writing a novel and had brought the notes with me. In a café or in the sociable hostel in Istanbul, I continued with it, and now, in the more tranquil interior of the hilltop house, I covered a page or two every other day. It wasn't a novel in the ordinary sense, rather a series of experimental philosophical reflections. My lessons in The Room with Kate and Lorraine, or at the Scotia, or by the midnight shore of Loch Lomond on the way to Glencoe with Lorraine's brother Jimmy, had given me an education and a vocation.

The writings had not yet gained a title. There was, at this stage, no main character or anything of that sort, just a first-person truth-teller whose enigmatic parables were mixed together with naturalistic incident, some of it now based on life at the ranch. There was "the hangman" and there was "the deserter." Just as my imagination wished to draw my feet to the nebulous Land of Away, so my pen was guided by the gravitational pull of epigram and paradox.

The model for the work was *Cain's Book*. Alexander Trocchi's best-known novel—though it was only barely a novel—was originally published in New York in 1959. When a friend in Glasgow gave it to me to read, I was electrified. Even the title had something extra, some glow, that the titles of other books did not possess. "Cain's Book": the book left out of the Bible. The book of the Pariah dog, the un-Chosen. Trocchi lived on the extreme margin of society, and would have liked to go farther out than that. For me, the book itself became a kind of Bible, something to believe in, to adhere to and act by. Other books were measured against it, and found lacking.

—*What the hell am I doing here?*
At certain moments I find myself looking on my whole life as leading up to the present moment, the present being all I have to affirm. It's somehow undignified to speak of the past or to think about the future. I don't seriously occupy myself with the question in the "here-and-now," lying on my bunk and, under the influence

of heroin, inviolable . . . One is no longer grotesquely involved in the becoming. One simply is.

The author's hollow-cheeked face stared at you from beneath bushy brows on the cover of John Calder's Jupiter Books edition: an inverted prophet, a Glasgow hard man protesting against social constraints not of his making; wise, tough, *against*. It was the seduction I was ready for.

V

On Spetsai, we had several clients who came regularly to ride their favorite horses, including two Greek girls of about fifteen or sixteen. One, very pretty and already well groomed, always chose Romeo, perhaps because he flattered her self-image. The other, Lia, was not so pretty in the simple sense but full of humor and wit, with freckles and a thatch of straw-colored hair. We liked them both and treated both well. Lia had the eagerness of a girl from an adventure story. I wrote her into one of the more realistic sections of the book.

> "Tell me something happy," I said, "and then something sad." It was almost midnight. We clambered down the rocky path, touching our way with our feet, not wishing to walk too hurriedly or to leave one another's company but bound to fit her mother's deadline for return. It was her last night on the island, thus the permission to visit the farmhouse for dinner and the extended time limit.
>
> She sighed heavily. "I won't tell you about my parents—they are divorced, you see—that's much too complicated." Silence. "Well, there was a boy—"

"Ah," I said, lightly mocking.

"Yes, I know," she replied quietly, "there is always 'a boy.' Anyhow there was this boy—a Greek boy—I met him on another island. I wanted to make love to him but he wouldn't. He said I was too young and that we must wait."

We broke out of the maze of streets on to the seafront. Despite the lateness of the hour people were dining on balconies which overlook the sea. I watched the moonlight spin across the water.

Lia always wanted Caesar, the most wilful horse in the stable. Riding fast excited her, she told me in the earnest tone she adopted for almost everything she spoke about. Normally, the girls' parents paid us at the end of the week, or else the riders brought the cash themselves for each tour, but when they had passed their pocket-money limit and came up the hill to the ranch together with hopeful expressions on their golden faces, Jerry let them get up for free if business was slow. He was the boss around the farm, and an easy-going one.

At about seven o'clock each evening, we went down to Takis's office with the takings for the day. While we stood by his desk, he remained seated, counting the money and checking it carefully against the bookings. Then he would hand over our small commission. He didn't interfere with our lives otherwise, only repeating two things: "Don't touch Greek girls" and "Don't forget to feed the horses."

Jerry used the word "lecherous" about him, the first time I had heard it. There were many words and phrases I was hearing or reading for the first time, some of them in *Cain's Book*. Its diction was more exciting to me than its tender descriptions of drug-induced states. "The present being all I have to affirm." I could never have written a sentence like that, simple as it was. Or selected "inviolable" in the way that Trocchi did. A partial list from my increasing vocabulary might go: *propitious, adventitious, impracticable* (not impractical), *in abeyance, innate, perspicacious* . . . Sometimes I would write them down—*distaff, gimcrack, erstwhile*—checking in a dictionary when I found one, or else asking Jerry.

If we had arrived on horseback in Dapia straight from the final tour of the day, we would get back in the saddle after our duties with Takis were fulfilled, then ride uphill to the ranch in the gentling heat to feed the horses, drawing glances and greetings from locals and visitors. We were "a sight," and we enjoyed being figures in a romance of our own making. With the horses unsaddled and fed, we would sit on the plank-and-brick bench outside the door in the remaining light, trading tales of home or Away. Later in the evening, we might all walk downhill, through town and past the English school to the strip of beach where tavernas perched on stilts, around the ankles of which sea water lapped sweetly. It was easy to spend the meager commission from a day's work, in view of moussaka, fasolakia—the green beans in tomato sauce that I particularly liked—kalamari, and one orange tin jug after another of retsina, ordered by kilo or half-kilo, rather than by litre. As a result, in spite of all my efforts, I was no less broke than before.

When the end of August arrived, the holidaymakers thinned out and business slowed down. Our groups of friends moved on to other islands or began to talk about going back to college in the States, where it seemed they mostly studied subjects to do with sociology, business or film, seldom sat exams, and were already planning more time off to pursue adventures that were bound to be costly. Where did they get the money? Jerry shrugged. "They get loans. Their parents help them. They can get jobs and save." It was as much a foreign language to me as the language heard in the kitchen of the taverna when we went inside to relish the evening dishes before giving our order.

One day, Jerry announced his intention to leave. His friend Barbara had arrived by aeroplane from New York. She wanted to see some sites of antiquity, which Jerry named but which I hardly recognized. There was another American girl at the ranch—not my girl friend, nor a worker, just someone grateful for a roof above her head—who also wanted to leave. Who was going to do the work? What would happen with the horses? What was I going to do? I had been away from Scotland for so long that any nagging remnants of homesickness had evaporated. I had no definite desires. Anything positive would have demanded a budget. I would be what I always was,

Me on Zorba, leading a pair of riders into town after a tour of the island.
Courtesy of Jerry Robock.

Heading back to the ranch on Spetsai, with Carl (left), and Oliver, Romeo, Caesar and Zorba. *Courtesy of Jerry Robock.*

a mast leaning with the wind. Just as mild breezes had carried me safely from coast to heavenly coast, an ill wind like this one left me grounded.

We were having this conversation on the brick-and-plank bench outside the front door of the house. Jerry squinted behind his tinted glasses in the afternoon sunlight. His black hair was drawn back in a pony tail and he had kept his bushy beard all summer. He was only a year or two older than me, but seemed at times to belong to a different generation. In between our first encounter in Glasgow and the unexpected reunion in Syntagma Square, he had fulfilled his stated ambition of going to Israel, which he talked about with subdued pleasure in his characteristic, even tone.

"You could go to Kibbutz Mishmarot for the rest of the season and live there . . . work there. It's not autumn yet, but soon they'll want people to help bring in the avocado harvest.

They won't pay you anything, or not much, but you can live for free. Get all your food and a place to sleep. Interesting experience. Why not?"

Why? Because Israel is separated from Europe by the Mediterranean. I made that or some other petulant comment. "It's difficult to hitch-hike across the sea."

Jerry said nothing more about it. One of the horses needed a new shoe and we took him down to the port to be shod by a man in a Stetson hat and leather boots with decorative stitching, into which he tucked his trousers. We knew him as Black Bart. While Bart hammered in the nails, Jerry cupped the upright hoof in both hands, his back pressed against the horse's rear haunch, as if he had been doing this kind of thing all his life.

The next morning, after we had brushed down Caesar, Zorba, and the others, Jerry told me he had been thinking about my situation and was going to suggest something to help me get off the island and make my way to Israel.

"Quite a few people haven't settled their accounts for some days," he said. "That Greek girl, for example, Lia's friend, who rides Romeo, you know the one . . ." Of course I did: her beautiful face and bobbed hair consoled me during lonely nights at the shell. *Don't touch Greek girls.* ". . . her parents owe us," Jerry was saying, ". . . probably a decent sum. Then there's this one and that one. Friday's going to be a busy day, with several rides, starting early. Barbara wants us to split at the weekend—but I haven't said anything about it yet to Takis."

He looked at me for a moment fixedly in the silence before going on. "Saturday evening, we can ask a fisherman to take us in his boat to the other side." From the harbor in Spetsai to the mainland coast of Sparta was a short distance. "Then we

Jerry helping Black Bart, the local blacksmith. *Courtesy of Jerry Robock.*

can all hitch up to Athens the next morning. We travel in pairs and meet there. You can buy a ticket for Tel Aviv from one of the travel agencies."

I had been in every country in Europe and had placed a sandaled foot in Asia, but had never passed through the doorway of a travel agency.

"Don't worry about the price. You'll have enough."

At the end of the week, we collected the outstanding money. I remember the look of surprise on the Romeo girl's face when I told her that Takis wanted to bring the accounts up to date. Could she ask her father about it and let me have it by five? Her name has disappeared from my memory but not the puzzlement that shaded her features, before they lightened beautifully again and she said, "Of course" with the soft Greek "f" and "s" which added to her charm. My charm that day was of a different kind. I knew it but kept the knowledge hidden from myself, or tried to.

On Saturday evening, as the sun bedded down beyond the Peloponnese, we packed our bags—a task that took about ten minutes in my case—said goodbye to Romeo, Zorba, Oliver, Caesar and Rufus, and went to an apartment being rented (from Takis, of course) by some friends we had met at the harbor café. Jerry had arranged the evening voyage out with a local fisherman, who was naturally unaware of the nature of our scheme. We left a note behind at the house for Takis. "Don't forget to feed the horses." Someone suggested adding, "Don't touch Greek girls," but that would have been going too far. Jerry might have scribbled some kind of philosophical justification for our action.

It was already dark. At the smaller of the two jetties that defined the harbor, we climbed aboard the fishing boat, settling down as the leather-faced captain gave the engine cord a sharp tug. Half an hour later, we disembarked on the mainland, near a village called Kostas. After Jerry had settled up and we had thanked him individually, the fisherman made a 180 degree turn and bobbed back to Spetsai.

In my pocket there was enough money for a ticket to Tel Aviv; in my head, the excitement of a new adventure about to begin; in my breast, an unwelcome grumbling. Takis had exploited us, no doubt about it, and the money represented only a kind of tail-end grab-back of what we had earned and passed to him over many weeks. But we had accepted the job on the terms he offered, frankly and explicitly. Coarse as he was, he had never shown us any deliberate unkindness. Underneath the hilarity that rang around our evening table at the taverna on the Spartan coast flowed an uneasy current.

The next day, we set off for Athens, hitch-hiking in pairs. Once in the city, the young woman from LA who had been my traveling partner said goodbye. I had made a plan to rendezvous with Jerry and Barbara at the same café in Syntagma Square where I had met Jerry by accident almost three months before. "There would be a nice symmetry in that," Jerry had said. (I jotted down the word "symmetry.") At the travel agency, he talked to the woman at the counter in his worldly way and reserved a place for me on a flight to Tel Aviv that same evening—my first time in the air. Then he gave me what was left of the money, not a large sum. Maybe he even added a few bills from his own fold.

"You live for free on the kibbutz," he said. "After that . . . something will turn up."

He outlined directions on how to find the bus station in the center of Tel Aviv, told me which number of bus to take to Kibbutz Mishmarot, where to get off, to walk about a mile down the little road to the kibbutz and to ask for a woman called Tirza.

"She'll know my name. Give her my regards."

After saying goodbye to him and Barbara, I walked towards a park where I could sit and read while waiting for the bus to take me to the airport. The plane was scheduled to arrive in Tel Aviv in the early hours of the morning. When I turned again to give a last wave of the hand, Jerry and Barbara had vanished. A Greek policeman who had appeared at the corner paid me no heed.

9

KIBBUTZ PHILOSOPHY

I

The flight from Athens began its descent to Tel Aviv at just after three in the morning on September 4, 1972, my first trip at 33,000 feet. When all the passengers had disembarked and filed through passport control, I wandered out of Arrivals into a field, together with a French girl I had met on board. We slept together, soundly and chastely, in a single sleeping bag, without attracting the attention of police or military, until woken by the overhead roar of morning flights.

We parted at the bus station in the center of the city. Jerry's instructions were to seek a bus going to Haifa, which would drop me within walking distance of Kibbutz Mishmarot. Get off. Just go down to the road. Once there, ask for Tirza.

When the driver let me down, I obeyed a sign with the name of the kibbutz in both Hebrew and English and an arrow pointing towards a slight incline away from the main road. After half a mile, the parched red ground gave way to moist, green terrain, freshened by sprinklers. There were no guards in view as I approached the settlement, no protective fence, only a semi-circular row of neat houses and an assortment of farm and family vehicles. People were moving about in the distance. I asked a woman who regarded me quizzically about Tirza.

"I am Tirza," she said. I told her I had arrived overnight from Athens. The name Jerry Robock was mentioned. An unsmiling nod. I said I had come to work on the kibbutz.

Tirza's interested look changed into something I now suppose to have been restrained incredulity. New arrivals were required to apply through the agency in Tel Aviv, she said, which would assign them to kibbutzim that had registered requests for foreign workers. This one had not applied for any. Her English was practically faultless. "You can't just come out here."

A flesh-and-blood refutation of that statement stood before her.

"But now you're here." The magic word "Jerry" had charmed her, after all. I was accepted for volunteer duties, with the advice, somewhat sternly administered, that tomorrow I should find a job.

On the way to the volunteer quarters, Tirza stopped to speak to a tall, fair-haired Canadian, whom she asked to take me in hand. My fugitive status was outlined and she left me in his care. Where was I from? Where had I been? Was Scotland beautiful? Was I going back to school? The usual questions, no less congenial for that. I was assigned a bunk in a concrete row of two-bed rooms, shown the communal lavatories and showers, told where to find a towel and bedding, and given other bits of friendly advice.

My roommate was a stocky Italian who spouted jets of operatic melody at the end of every other sentence. The first Israeli food I tasted was a grape from a huge bunch he extended, of a richness unsuspected in the West of Scotland. The helpful Canadian, Gordon, pointed out the kibbutz office, told me to go there in the afternoon, say that Tirza had accepted me, and that I would like a job. I would be given cigarette coupons. If I didn't smoke, take them anyway and do an exchange with someone else for beer or candy coupons.

"If you're looking for an alibi this afternoon, you can help me dig this trench. Show willing and all that." He shrugged. "It's a job."

An unpaid job. A tiny financial recompense was dispensed at the end of each week. My two months and more of service on Kibbutz Mishmarot gave me sun, some expertise, such as driving a tractor and managing irrigation systems, bed and bread—but next to nothing of the other sort of bread. For visits to Jerusalem and Tel Aviv over the next ten weeks, I had to rely on coupon exchange and the good will of fellow volunteers, chiefly Dennis, a yellow cab driver from Flushing, New York, with the spirit of the city ripe in every friendly fake snarl and funky joke and gesture. Like me, he had no studies to return to at the end of September, and he planned to remain in Israel as long as he could. Eventually, he married a girl from the kibbutz and became a member.

Kibbutz Mishmarot was relatively small, with about eighty full-time inhabitants. Most were second- or third-generation Israelis, with some recent arrivals from Russia and South America. There were a few American members, and a group of black Moroccan Jews who lived a separate life and moved to the beat of another metronome.

Among the twenty or so volunteers were Olivier from just north of Paris, and Peter, a rock-music dropout from east London, the only Englishman. Most were North Americans. A sharp-talking woman from Chicago was called Blair. There was an angular Dutch girl and a couple from Argentina. Gordon was Scottish on his paternal grandfather's side, he said, which accounted for his Celtic features and fair hair, but felt fully Jewish. I was one of only two gentiles on the kibbutz, a detail never mentioned in my presence. Yet we were in Israel, sure enough. The bloody interlude of the Munich Olympics brought us together round a transistor radio during my first few days in the country. Eleven Israeli athletes were taken hostage and murdered by a group of Palestinian militants known as the Black September Organization. The atrocity bound the volunteers together, creating a bond between them (the Americans, especially) and the Israelis.

Among the kibbutzniks were many army veterans, women included, some of whom had been active in the Six-Day War in 1967. They had an aura, as if lit from a different angle. At intervals on the road stretching all the way from Tel Aviv to Haifa, male and female soldiers waited for lifts.

Maybe I could hitch-hike to Tel Aviv?

"Don't even think about it."

"Unless you're in uniform."

"Don't worry."

"Buses are cheap."

People always said that.

II

About three years before leaving Glasgow, I had seen Fleetwood Mac playing at Green's Playhouse in Glasgow, a roomy cinema in the center of the city that doubled as a concert hall. They were known as Peter Green's Fleetwood Mac at the time, after the founder. They were the leading proponents of the white electric blues, and Peter Green was one of the three recognized kings of the genre. Some connoisseurs elected him to the highest seat, ahead of Eric Clapton and Jeff Beck. "Clapton is God" said the graffiti, which is rather crude; Peter was "the Green God," which made some kind of pleasant sense.

I preferred the unamplified music that had formed the backing track to my post-King's Park Secondary life: country blues. My heroes were the black troubadours of the Mississippi Delta of the 1920s and 30s—I had only recently learned what "Delta" stood for—and the young virtuoso British folk-blues players. The supremacy of Bert Jansch remained, a youthful indoctrination. Neil Young had called him the Jimi Hendrix of the acoustic guitar. Not to me. Hendrix as the Bert Jansch of the electric, perhaps.

Even so, Peter Green was a star, and the concert at the Playhouse on Renfield Street stayed in my mind. I can still conjure up fragments of the spectacle: the lighting, the deep-lying pulse of the electrified blues, the yearning in the dark-hued voice of Green the singer. At the close, after an encore—maybe "Black Magic Woman," the rousing favorite kept till last—the black-haired, bearded Green embraced the second lead guitarist, Danny Kirwan, his opposite in looks, fair and soft-skinned. "My blues brother!" Green looked joyous. "You are the best audience *in the world!*" We were thrilled.

I had been on the kibbutz for about a month when Dennis approached me after lunch one day in the kitchen, where I was doing the washing-up for a hundred diners. He was in a state of excitement, as he often was, sometimes over something as trivial as receiving a packet of razor blades through the mail from his mother in Florida. This time, the current was so vivid it seemed it might lift him off the floor. A new girl had arrived. "A fox, Jimmy." Dennis rubbed his hands in uncontainable delight. "A FOX!" I remember the word because it was the first time I had heard it used like that.

Later in the afternoon, I caught sight of her from a distance: long black hair, beautiful in the beau-monde manner,

Dennis, left, and fellow volunteers at Kibbutz Mishmarot, with the cabins of
Desolation Row behind.

dressed in a stylish skirt, top, and heels. Just the thing for our
little company, I said to myself. Then, as usual, I took my guitar
and began to play my open-tuning Scottish-oriental raga, which
could last for half an hour or more. Evenings were long on the
kibbutz. A single television set served all, in a bleak community
viewing room to which I never wished to go, even when the
film being shown was in English. There was one gramophone,
locked away and requiring permission to listen to the scratchy
old discs in faded paper sleeves that were stored with it. There
was no such thing as a café or bar. I had bought this light and
wiry guitar in Athens for the equivalent of a few pounds. It had
given us some entertainment up at the ranch on Spetsai during
the summer, and now it amused me—if not all my fellow kibbutzniks—into the autumn.

In the middle of the night, after I saw the fox for the first and
only time, I was awakened by a grand commotion. When the
sun rose, she was already gone.

"What was that all about?" I asked Dennis on the tractor, as we bumped along towards the avocado fields.

"Who knows? Something to do with Peter, I think."

On first arriving, a short time after me, Peter had sat apart from the rest of the volunteers in the *heder ochel*, the dining room. He wasn't part of our doorstep congregations in the evenings, when we talked about the atrocity in Munich, the chances of Nixon's re-election in November, trips to Amsterdam or Florence or Rhodes that people had made before coming here. The lousy youth hostels. The great trains. Meat-eaters vs vegetarians. I read all the books that were lying around, and people were starting to use me as a library. Peter was clean-shaven with medium-length black curly hair and a long, sad face. For days on end, he might talk to no one, except Dennis, who found a way to talk to everyone. Dennis reported back, calling Peter a secretive type. "Kinda private."

Nevertheless, the kibbutz was a limited space, without much to do during the looming free hours after work, and soon Peter turned up to one of our groupings. Little by little, he grew more sociable. If you lasted long enough on the kibbutz, you could, when somebody left, take possession of one of the small cabins that stood on what we called Desolation Row, overlooking a line of eucalyptus trees. I had moved into one about a fortnight after arriving, and when the cabin next to it became vacant, Peter took up residence. They were good places, those cabins, and Peter was a good neighbor.

In the evenings, I would play my raga outside my door, as usual, and soon Peter took to accompanying me on a pair of Moroccan drums. We became an "act."

There was sadness all around him, even in his sense of humor. He had not expected or wanted to see the fox, who had followed him here from some other country. He told me that he hoped to meet a maternal woman on the kibbutz, "with big hips for child bearing," which was an unusual thing for someone to say.

One evening as we prepared for a party, Peter unfolded a new T-shirt. "We might meet our future wives tonight," he said in his east London voice—"moight" and "woives." The seven o'clock October air was sweet and caressing. Peter stood before the door of his cabin with a broad smile, showing off the crisp garment. No, not that particular night.

He had a sharpness of wit, and a strong intelligence without the interference of intellectualism. He never read books, never talked on the subjects of art or music, or about global politics, as the rest of us did in our evening parliaments. He expressed solidarity with the Palestinians, which took some volunteers aback, especially the Americans. He could be sardonic, if not unkind. One afternoon when we were in the shower, after our return from the fields, I sang a song in French. At the end Peter said, in a dry tone, "Very *good*, Jim." He had picked up on my showing off and didn't hesitate to let me know.

One lunchtime, a rumor circulated in the *heder ochel*. It was Dennis, naturally, who spoke the first word. Could it be possible? We were aware that Peter Green was the invisible man of rock and roll. The case was well known. "He was working as a grave digger," I said, a detail I had picked up from one of the music magazines at a time between the Green's Playhouse concert and the present. "After that? Who knows?" How to discover the truth? We could of course just ask, but no one wanted to be tactless.

It was me who came up with a way of finding out. I recalled another magazine article, which reported that Peter Green of

Peter Green when he was lead guitarist of Fleetwood Mac. In 1972 on Kibbutz Mishmarot, where he and I were next-door neighbors on Desolation Row, he was clean-shaven.

Fleetwood Mac had a small, handmade tattoo on his forearm, in the form of a cross. The fact stuck in my mind because of the similar tattoo on my left wrist, imprinted by the ex-borstal boy in my sister's Blackheath commune in 1969. I told Dennis about it, and said I would probably be able to confirm by breakfast.

So, next morning, we drove out to the avocado fields as usual, three or four kilometers from the cabins. On the way, if you were lucky, you caught the metallic blue of a kingfisher as it flashed over the surface of a canal, or you might grip an orange from a tree without needing to brake. We stepped down from the tractor and set about the task of reorganizing the irrigation pipes, unlocking the fifteen-foot-long aluminium sections, then moving them, piece by piece, to lie between adjacent rows of trees. There, they would be locked back together again. This was done every day or every other day. When the moment came to twist the tap and turn on the water, it was a joy to walk through an avenue of rainbow spray as the sun came up. By 7 am, it was already hot.

Right, Pete. Sleeves up. Let's get on with it.

And there it was: a small cross on the forearm.

Later in the day, while we were taking a walk around the kibbutz in the settling dusk, I put the question to him, and he replied simply, "Yeah." The rock industry had sickened him, he said. After distributing his money among various causes, including a charity for Biafran war orphans, saving only £80 for himself, he had given away his guitars to friends. He kept one: a favorite Fender Stratocaster, which was at his parents' home in Bethnal Green. He didn't want to receive royalties from his songs, some of which had been enormous hits: "Black Magic Woman," "Save Your Love for Me," "Albatross," "Man of the World." One member of the group, Jeremy Spencer, had simply walked out one day and disappeared—into a religious commune in Los Angeles, or into the jungle, or on to the moon. "Not surprising," Peter said.

His blues brother, Danny Kirwan, would later leave the group and be seen living as an addict on the London streets.

We had made a circuit of the kibbutz fringe and now were walking back in the direction of Desolation Row.

"Want to play a little bit?"

"Why not?"

"On the guitar?"

"No, thanks. I prefer to leave that to you." That dry tone, with an ironic twist. "I'm learning to play the drums."

Peter Green's electric guitar playing is admired by connoisseurs for its tone and feeling more than for speed or noise. Dazzling flurries of notes on the upper reaches of a Strat or a 1959 Les Paul were not his style. When his sound was lovingly characterized as "out-of-phase," Peter replied he didn't know what out-of-phase meant. "Bit messy," he was known to say when invited to comment on a treasured passage of his own playing.

He was generally tactful enough not to make comments on my droning DADDAD raga routine, for which he provided percussion, but one afternoon he let fall an unkind remark in front of a kibbutz visitor who was himself a decent guitarist. It stung, needless to say, and the sting persisted. Later, though, I read in a music magazine an interview with Christine McVie, of a subsequent Fleetwood Mac incarnation. "He was definitely in charge. He turned to Mick Fleetwood after a gig one night and said: 'I've got more swing in my left bollock than you do.'" If you must be the target of Peter Green's sharp tongue, it soothes the pain to know you're not the only one.

The sojourn ended with promises and an exchange of addresses. After I left, I heard from Dennis that Peter had gone south to Eilat with Blair. Like me, he had no place of his own in Britain, so we swapped the numbers of our parents' homes. When I called there one day from a telephone box in London, his mother said, "Peter is in Bermuda." Perhaps he had accepted some of those "Albatross" royalties, after all. It was the only time I tried to get in touch with him. We had re-entered our former lives.

On the kibbutz, after I had broken the news of the tattoo, Dennis was thrilled. "I remember I saw them at a concert in New York. It was great, man! They were fan-tas-tic. At the end, you know what he said? 'You are the best audience *in the world.*'"

III

When November arrived, people told me, the cold would begin to bite. Someone demonstrated the working of a tiny paraffin heater, which was supposed to keep my cabin warm. Only a handful of volunteers would be left. The harvests would be in. But who knows, my heating engineer said, "You might find something interesting to do." Once again, as on Spetsai at the end of August, I began to see myself as a left-behinder.

The problem—the only problem, really—was the Mediterranean. Once transported to Athens, I could make the journey by thumb to Ostend or Calais without much difficulty. It took five days. When the last car dropped me on the northern fringe of Belgium or France, I would find a way to get over the Channel. There, you could ask the solitary driver of a truck or car to take you as a non-paying passenger. From Dover, it was a day and a half's thumbing to reach Glasgow. When leaving in May, I had given up my bedsit in Wilton Street, where Jerry and Richard had crashed on the floor, but I didn't consider that to be a problem either. The Med was the problem. It required a boat. The boat demanded a ticket. The ticket wanted money.

I wrote to my father. He and I were not on good terms, largely because of my disinclination to study or look at regular employment. I had quit my six-year apprenticeship at Washington Irvine's three years in, and ever since I had been doing what I had always wanted to do, what all my friends were doing, what it seemed everyone ought to be doing—my own thing. Someone in Glasgow owed me money, I told Dad. It wasn't a lie. Not much money, but almost enough to get me on to a boat and over the sea to Piraeus. If Dad would advance me the sum . . .

It took about a week for a letter from Kibbutz Mishmarot to reach High Wycombe, and another week—assuming the recipient answered right away—for the reply to arrive. The mail for volunteers was distributed every lunchtime in front of Desolation Row. People waited in a group in anticipation of hearing their name called and being handed a letter, and sometimes it was my name. One morning an envelope was extended with my father's handsome handwriting on the front. I opened it carefully. There was no money. He used the occasion instead to deliver a lecture and remind me of "the family motto: No reward without effort." It was the first I had heard of a family motto.

I wrote to one of my sisters. She sent a pound sterling. I wrote to a girl I had been seeing in Glasgow before setting out for Turkey and then taking up with Jerry and the horses. I thought we had an on-again, off-again relationship, which had suited me fine. I thought it suited her, too. She took the opportunity to tell me it didn't, but she included another pound. I had about one-tenth of what I needed.

Dennis suggested looking for a job in Tel Aviv. He gave me a copy of the local English-language newspaper. I scrutinized the lists and found a likely one: "American Pizzeria. Help wanted. Dizengoff Street. Telephone . . ." I rang from the coin-operated kibbutz public telephone and—just like that—had a job.

"Can you be here Thursday at ten?" the voice asked.

It meant temporarily quitting the kibbutz, where by then I was in a position of some responsibility in the avocado fields, working with Dennis or Peter. My cabin on Desolation Row, overlooking the eucalyptus trees—their brittle leaves emitted an exotic perfume when crushed—was homely. I had books and a ruled pad for writing, on which I tried to add some recent Greek experience to the novel: the smell of horse and hay, the reassuring smack of leather, sun and sand, fun and flight.

In the long kibbutz evenings, I read or wrote or sat outside thrumming my open-tuning Scottish-oriental rag, with the former lead guitarist of John Mayall's Bluesbreakers beside me providing percussive accompaniment on Moroccan drums. (Peter had been Eric Clapton's replacement in the Bluesbreakers before forming Fleetwood Mac.) Now that I had to leave it, it seemed like just the life.

I packed a few things and caught the bus from the top of the road into Tel Aviv. The buses were always busy with soldiers who seemed to be treated by everyone as sons or brothers, Arabs excepted. As usual, there were uniformed figures along the road, hitch-hiking east and west. They never had to wait long. Sometimes a bus driver would stop for a pair of them, pushing back the fare. Female soldiers also got around by hitch-hiking. It was one big family, in every shade of skin and kink of hair and rhythmic gait imaginable; a once-in-a-millennium sense of belonging in a land that had been returned by providence and politics.

The words of an elderly kibbutznik who walked me round the limits of Mishmarot one afternoon never left me: when he came here from Russia, before the Second World War and the foundation of the State of Israel, it was "stone, dry, desert." We passed through orange groves and skirted the avocado fields. "The land was thirsty. Now look." I was touched by his pride. I didn't think a lot about the Arab passengers on the buses, who were themselves Israeli citizens. They didn't look defiant or benighted. They cultivated an atmosphere of neutrality.

The first thing to do in Tel Aviv was find a place to live. The choice was limited. I chose a space in a hostel, ten or twelve beds to a room. The next morning, I went to Dizengoff to meet the owner of American Pizzeria, my new boss. He was called Jim, like me, an open-faced American with a big smile. He repeated what he had said on the phone, that the pay was three Israeli pounds per hour, about 30 pence, the equivalent in today's spending power of—let's be generous—roughly

£3. (The Israeli currency changed from pounds to shekels in 1980.) I had known that before I arrived, but the meagerness had failed to impress itself on me. On the first day, I worked ten hours. I had to pay for my bed, naturally, and for something other than pizza to eat after work. It was still hot in the Middle Eastern October, and I was not in any case inclined to stay indoors in the evenings. It was easy to spend a day's wages before midnight.

In a bar near the hostel, I met a young Englishman who I was pleased to learn was a student of English Literature. Despite my lack of formal education, my Scottish autodidactic instinct had served me reasonably well. There was a Hip Bibliography: Hermann Hesse, of course, Camus and Cocteau, Sartre, Beckett, the Black Mountain poets (not the Beats), Dostoevsky before Tolstoy, the odd Penguin Classic from Ancient Greece or India tossed in for wisdom's sake. In my full callowness I was by now well versed in it. Kate, Lorraine, and others at Glasgow University had studied French and philosophy, and I adopted their opinions second hand and made simple use of them. I was able to make a pretty decent attempt at literary conversation while the saucers piled high.

One evening my new friend and I sat up late talking about Sartre, still the hero of the time. In the intervals, he listened to my story. Stranded in Israel, eh? A touch of drama to enliven the rendezvous. Let's have two more beers. He was sympathetic, yet blasé—"Cheers"—it needn't be a problem, all hangups were of your own devising. "You need to *act*," he said. "*Do* something. Don't hesitate."

I liked the sound of that. It made me feel at home, among the existentialists of Glasgow's West End. *Act. Do something.* "But what?"

Be authentic. Commit yourself. Don't be a victim of bad faith. Become engaged. He might have used the French pronunciation, as I certainly would have. There were philosophical solutions galore. "Choose freedom."

Together, we cooked up a plan—I remember the evening as if I were watching a film—shuffling the variations to increase the exactness of the execution. When it was too late to go further, we shook hands and arranged to get together again the following evening.

In the morning, I learned that I had been promoted. I hadn't been there long, but Jim said: "We are going to turn you into a pizza maker!" He gave me a humiliating paper hat, under which I had to tuck my hair. "You need to wear this." Jim also told me that I would be in receipt of a raise: from now on, I would be earning four Israeli pounds per hour (about 40 pence). When I told my English friend in the bar that evening, wondering if we should call off the plan, he raised his glass above his head and laughed. "You have to act. It is simply not possible to *live* otherwise."

The next day I approached Jim. "There's something I'd like to talk to you about in confidence, if you don't mind."

That big American smile. Jim had told me he was from California, which had associations with Joni Mitchell, Laurel Canyon, various writings with Big Sur in the title.

"Sure, Jim. Wait for me outside and I'll join you in a minute."

We seated ourselves on a bench on the boulevard, in front of American Pizzeria. It was a beautiful sunny day, like all the days. In Glasgow, it would be rainy and windy, people would be turning up their coat collars and raising fatalistic eyebrows as they passed each other on the street. Glasgow was another family. From inside the restaurant, the aroma of baking dough reached us on the bench. We specialized in thin crust, the house secret. Lunchtime rush hour was our best time.

"What's on your mind, Jim?"

"There's a little problem."

Suddenly, he was looking straight at me. "If I can help you, I will. You can be assured of that."

I explained that I was staying in a kind of a hallway—a dump, frankly, with nine other people, snoring, coughing, coming in late, getting up at all hours. "It's not exactly comfortable. So much noise. And kind of dirty." Jim offered a sympathetic nod. "I have the chance of a room—another dump, actually"—we laughed—"but at least a place of my own." I told Jim I was writing a novel in my free time.

"Really?" He looked interested. "What's it about?"

"It's kind of an existentialist thing. The landlady . . . she's asking for a deposit."

Jim was looking pensive, but not about my book. After a moment, he asked, "How much?"

My café-intellectual friend and I had calculated that it would cost 150 Israeli pounds to buy a ticket from Haifa to Piraeus. Then it would be necessary to live for five days while hitch-hiking to Ostend or Calais. I knew I could hop across the Channel for free, but there would be another twelve or fifteen hours on the road before reaching Glasgow. I had no concerns about surviving once I was there.

"She wants 300 pounds."

How long a pause? How searching a look from his eyes into mine? How sincere a gaze in return?

"I'm going to speak to my partner, Jim. But I can tell you that I like this plan. It's so difficult to find workers like you, who work hard and are willing to stick around in Tel Aviv. You're not a student?" Just for a moment, he seemed put out. "You're not going to disappear back to school in a month or something?"

Not at all. I was "free," in a sense that Jim was incapable of understanding.

"Let me speak to Jeff. We like you. I'll speak to Jeff and give you an answer this afternoon." His firm, friendly hand made a warm impression on my back. "Right, let's get to work. Pardner!"

The next day, a Friday, Jim brought 300 Israeli pounds in an envelope, for which I thanked him. I worked until five, then went back to the hostel, picked up my bag and checked out. At six, I was at the bus station, now familiar, and took my seat on a bus, surrounded by Israeli citizens of every kind. I patted my bag to assure myself of the security of the envelope. The bus would take me to Kibbutz Mishmarot.

All through the journey I looked out of the window at the soldiers, the women with children, the laborers who had finished a day's toil and were returning home to spend the evening with families. I was not in their world, nor in any world that felt real. I was a character in a film, made on a low budget—a budget of 300 Israeli pounds.

I stepped down as before at the stop nearest the kibbutz and walked along the sloping path leading from the main road to the entrance, where I had arrived full of anticipation about my new life two months earlier.

At first I thought I was alone, but soon realized I had company. For the entire length of the route, a small, scruffy dog followed me, barking constantly. I had walked up and down this path many times, but had never seen or heard that dog before. I never saw it again, and it must have died over forty years ago, but I have never forgotten it. It is by such characters that one's own character is formed.

Finally, I made it to the kibbutz, the philosophy of dogs still sounding in my ears, and entered my cabin for the first time in almost two weeks. Familiar things welcomed me: the guitar, the books (including *Being and Nothingness*, left behind by a previous occupant), the comfortable little bed by the small window, the smell of crushed eucalyptus leaves when you stepped outside. There was some kind of outdoor theatrical event going on that evening. Sitting on the grass in front of the stage, I recounted my adventure to Peter.

"Right," he said, and fixed me with the same look that I had seen on the face of Jim outside the pizzeria when I made my request. Peter, who had escaped a life of unwanted celebrity, had given away thousands, maybe millions, to poor people throughout the world. I was poor, too, but not like them. "You'll be free to leave now."

"I needed to do something. To act."

I had been looking forward to showing off a bit to Dennis, to setting off his vibrancy. We had spoken before of a ruse whereby one could pose as a victim of theft, claiming that one's Traveler's Checks had been stolen, then cashing them quickly. Or cashing them first, before reporting the "theft." I forget which. I had never had Travelers' Checks. American Express was apparently under obligation to reimburse the amount stolen.

But Dennis failed to congratulate me. He looked at his feet.

"Jimmy." Then his eyes creased and he peered at me with a fierce-friendly gaze. "Jimmy, you can't go round Europe rippin' people off. You gonna find yourself in prison, man." He raised a hand to shield his eyes from a kibbutz spotlight behind my head. I still see the hand and the squint. He had his own philosophy. "You ever heard of karma?"

The next day, Shabbat, I put the banknotes in an envelope.

On the front I wrote the address of American Pizzeria, Dizengoff Street, keeping back a little for the work I had done, as I explained to Jim in my covering letter. Honesty had not yet taken full possession of me and I made some flimsy excuse for my peculiar action. It seemed better not to mention existentialism.

The following morning, I returned to the avocado fields where the sun was welcoming and reassuring. We worked for two hours before climbing on to the tractor and heading back through the orange and banana groves for breakfast at nine. Then we set out for the fields again, shouting excitedly at the magic glimpse of the kingfisher along the way. I have never been so brown. My hair was yellow. When I told Peter about returning the money, he looked at me with the same expression. "You did the right thing."

I never discussed it with the dog.

★

A footnote: It was Dennis who gave me the money to help me leave Kibbutz Mishmarot and return to Europe. One day in the avocado fields, he put a stop to my complaining. "OK, Jimmy, I'll give you the money to get over to Greece. At least I'll get some fucking peace that way."

We went together to a shipping office in Haifa where he paid for an overnight voyage to Piraeus. Dennis then cashed a traveler's check and handed me twenty dollars.

On my first trip to New York, in 1981, I carried his telephone number with me, hoping to catch him by surprise and hand him the money. But there was no reply. In the White Horse Tavern in Greenwich Village, I had a drink with Jerry Robock, but he couldn't tell me where Dennis was. I made occasional efforts to locate him after that, and thought about him often. Arriving in New York, I could see that Dennis had introduced me to the city in advance, in his voice, his jokes, and gestures.

When the internet era arrived, I discovered that he had remained at Mishmarot, marrying a kibbutz girl, as he had hoped to do, but was no longer there. I still hoped to return the money—partly as a token souvenir of old times' sake. A clue came from someone who had been a Mishmarot volunteer after my time, overlapping with Dennis. She said he was living in Florida.

I tracked down the address—it mentioned "prior: Flushing, NY"—and sent a letter by mail, recalling our mornings in the avocado fields, Desolation Row, Peter Green, and the loan waiting to be repaid, but received no reply.

10

TROCCHI'S PAD

I

I arrived back in Glasgow from Israel in November 1972 with the pages of my *Cain's Book* pastiche stowed in the bag, so far untitled.

> The Hangman is mocking me again . . . My head is low-ered to the ground. I know I can rise and walk away, but only when the Hangman's smile is removed will I be able to stare into his eyes. That is the condition of my release. To leave now, while he still laughs, I would have to rearrange my terms. And that I refuse to do.

The editor of *Glasgow University Magazine*, known as *GUM*, heard through mutual friends that I had this and other writ-ings, and we arranged to meet. By the age of twenty-one, Jack Haggerty had a developed taste and a sense of literary style far in advance of his contemporaries. While others tricked them-selves out in Goulimine beads and amulets and embroidered tunics, Jack preferred to dress in a sober suit, sometimes with that truly exotic accessory, a tie. Everyone grew their hair long and parted it in the middle, while Jack's was usually tidy and properly cut.

Each Friday, he bought a new novel in hardback from John Smith's Bookshop in Saint Vincent Street, frequently by an unfashionable author, perhaps an English provincial such as Stanley Middleton, while the rest of us surfed over the Hip Bibliography, trusting in paperbacks, bought, bartered or borrowed. Other people mentioned pocketing the occasional volume from Smith's, sometimes justifying it as a species of revenge against "the system," which seemed to mean whatever was convenient to make it mean at the time. These acts of simple dishonesty fell under my judgement of *mauvaise foi*, translated in *Being and Nothingness* as "self-deception." Between them, Dennis and Jean-Paul Sartre had persuaded me that no act of dishonesty, however minor, could remain unexamined.

Jack read with attention to nuance and detail. Why this word and not another? Why "essential to" and not "integral to"? Short sentences create one mood; long, unbroken paragraphs something different. Adjectives and, particularly, adverbs—here Jack might invoke Graham Greene, his ultimate arbiter—should be handled with care. The backbone of every sentence is the verb, which must be made as strong as possible.

For a brief period, like most of those in our circle—I was an exception—Jack was a student at the university, but after a year he quit his courses in order to pursue a career as a journalist on a local newspaper. Nevertheless, he continued to act as editor of the university magazine. No one needed to know that he was no longer a student. Those who did know didn't seem to care. He was divided into two: Dr. Jack and Mr. Haggerty. During the day, he worked as a reporter in Clydebank, near Glasgow, a town that had gone into decline with the shipbuilding industry it had existed to serve. The opening of a new hospital, a school's annual sports day, a grandmother who gave chase to a thief while wielding her frying pan; Jack was there, notebook in hand. By night, he returned to the pubs and cafés and student bedsits in Byres Road, in the university district, and assumed the role of literary editor. His parents lived in a modest council flat on a housing estate on the western outskirts of Glasgow, and Jack continued to stay there, unlike most people we knew, who rented a bedsit or shared a head pad (not a "hippie flat") with others.

He had grand plans for the student journal. Jack was a devoted reader of the *New Statesman, Encounter,* the *TLS.* He would put on an amiably skeptical expression when *International Times* or *Rolling Stone* was mentioned. If someone was going to be in London, Jack would ask to be brought back *Esquire*—"*Esquire* magazine," he would say—or *Harper's,* with specific instructions as to where it could be bought on Charing Cross Road. When we arranged to meet in a café or one of the restaurants he liked to frequent, I might arrive to find him already at the table, pencil in hand, marking some well-turned phrase in a review, or underlining a word that was new to him. He would later slip those words into conversation. *Epicene,* he muttered once; Brando was epicene. Someone's literary comments were *sophomoric.* The criticism was administered gently. *Diaphanous*—referring to the light blue blouse on the pretty girl at the party. A decorous unbuttoning gesture. "Wouldn't it be marvelous to be the one . . . ?"

Physically, he could be seen walking through Glasgow or leaning on the bar in a pub with me at 6 o'clock, beginning a conversation that would last until after closing time. In his imagination, we were in New York, where he occupied the skin of Norman Mailer or Gore Vidal, writers who held the place in his esteem that rock musicians did in that of others. It was he who introduced me to the name of James Baldwin, a man who would come to figure importantly in my life; and to books by Truman Capote, F. Scott Fitzgerald, and others. To judge solely by his first-name conversation—"and you remember what Truman replied when Norman said . . ."—you might

Jack Haggerty (right) with Gerald Mangan (center) and others in Dublin, 1971. *Courtesy of Gerald Mangan.*

have thought they were intimate friends. Neither of us had been to America. Jack had never traveled outside Britain, except to go to Dublin for a wedding.

He was capable of quoting long passages of prose, verbatim, as others could reel off poetry, and he recounted anecdotes about modern writers as if he had heard them from someone who was there when the action took place. *He* was there, in every sense—in every sense but the real one—and *there* was a good place to be with Jack. To grant Vidal or Mailer a continuous speaking part in his imagination was to lend a glow to the dank West End of Glasgow night as 1972 crossed over into 1973: a glow of words, the right words in the right order, one of Jack's maxims.

All the while, he was keeping up with English provincial authors, who offered a more naturalistic reflection of his own experience, and whom he esteemed equally. Baldwin occupied no greater a place in his pantheon than Stan Barstow. Styron was not a grander figure than David Storey. Mailer was a prince, but there was an honorable place at the Court of King Jack for humble Stanley Middleton.

Jack read a sheaf of my stories—I held back my *Cain's Book* meanderings which, now that I was removed from sun and sea and sky, seemed to have lost course—and printed one of them in *GUM*, with an illustration. I began to assume the role of assistant editor. We had the right to use a small room in a university building on Gilmorehill, but Jack preferred to do most of the magazine business from a little café-restaurant called the Grosvenor, next to Hillhead Subway station in the dead center of Byres Road.

He ate there most evenings, the only person of my acquaintance who never hesitated to dine out, and who knew how to conduct himself when he did so. My introduction to the look and taste of spaghetti carbonara, even the sound of the words, took place in the Grosvenor Café. The sumptuous plate was followed by Black Forest gateau and then "un espresso"—splendors suggestive of the other world from which I had lately returned, the one beyond dark-at-4 pm, drookit Glasgow.

All the waitresses smiled on him, and he always left tips. Jack was a figment of Jack's imagination, with the leading role in a movie called *Jack*, directed not by Jack himself but by his brother. George Haggerty really was in that glamorous American world, though in his case it was Hollywood, where he was learning to be a film director. The cinema—or, to be more precise, the writing of realist drama for television: The Wednesday Play, Play of the Month, Armchair Theatre; David Mercer, Dennis Potter, Jeremy Sandford—featured among Jack's own furtive ambitions, and he talked often of the short film George was on the point of completing with the actor

Stacy Keach. Jack was disappointed to learn I hadn't heard of Keach. It was released in 1975 as *Hamburger Hamlet*. No one I knew had ever met George.

One evening, Jack summoned me to his office—that is to say, the café next to the station. He finished off his carbonara, lit a Gitane and hooked an arm over the back of his chair. He said that the editor of *Cosmopolitan* had once gathered all the staff together in the boardroom and announced that he wanted them to come up with feature ideas for a new magazine which the company was about to launch. Brilliant suggestions poured in, whereupon the boss revealed that there was no new magazine. So, he wanted to know, why had those ideas not been put forward for *Cosmopolitan*?

After that, Jack began to speak about his latest plans for *GUM*. First and most important, we had to find a new design and a new title. GUM? Bubble gum? There was a huge department store in Moscow called GUM. Did we want to be identified with that? What would Norman say if asked to write for a magazine with a name like *GUM*? Never mind the news about student associations, charity drives and so forth, which we also ought to get rid of.

For a title we settled on the *Moving Review*. I was the one who came up with the name, though it wasn't entirely original. There was an underground magazine run by Jeff Nuttall in the north of England called *the moving times*. Alexander Trocchi was associated with it, and William Burroughs was a contributor. I had never seen a copy, only knew that it was vaguely "underground" and the name had stuck in my mind. Jack thought about it for a few seconds, then murmured: "I like it . . . yes, I like it, my friend." At these moments, you were expected to feel proud, and you did.

There was an assistant editor called Brian Hannan, a student—so much the better—who was an energetic contributor to the magazine and the Grosvenor café meetings. He had another idea for the title. I forget what it was. I didn't have much in common with Brian, and he felt that I had usurped the place in Jack's kitchen cabinet that he had occupied himself. With good reason. Brian wore large black-framed spectacles and had a 1950s hair style. Not retro—that wasn't a concept in fashion yet—but straight (to say "square" was square). He was the link to the university. Jack chose my title anyway, and Brian was made to feel that he was part of the old regime.

Jack had the idea of placing at the center of the *Moving Review* interviews with celebrated writers, in this way satisfying his desire for big names. He would telephone somebody out of the blue—John Braine, for example, or Alan Sillitoe, two of his Angry Young Men idols—and would hold them in conversation for an hour. He had the knack of keeping up a pertinent line of questioning, at the same time sounding intimate, without being intrusive. The writers must have been flattered by his familiarity with their work, by his curiosity, his strange air of worldliness despite being so young. Some kind of future rendezvous would be provisionally agreed.

One Saturday afternoon, as we were coming out of a café of the superior kind in Buchanan Street, where I had chosen the cheapest thing on the menu and Jack the most expensive, he crooked his arm and looked at his wristwatch. "Oh dear. Three o'clock. I was supposed to be meeting Alan Sillitoe in London . . ."

"Today!?"

"Right now . . . at his house in Ladbroke something." It was the first time he had mentioned it.

Jack wanted those good ideas. In the café next to the Subway station I proposed an article on the subject of Trocchi. Why wasn't he talked about in the pubs and lecture theaters, or written about on the literary pages of the heavy Sundays or in *Encounter*? The novel was in a dire condition in Britain—it was a cliché even then to say that the novel was dead, a cliché steadfastly resisted by Jack—yet *Cain's Book*, a masterpiece, a *mastercrime*, was never mentioned. *And* he was Scottish. So much of contemporary Scottish writing was "stale porridge," Trocchi had once pronounced at an event in Edinburgh, at which Hugh MacDiarmid and others were present. "Of what is interesting in Scottish literature of the past twenty years, I myself have written it all."

In their ignorance, journalists, critics, the reading public, dismissed this majestic declaration. In my ignorance, I embraced it.

Jack rubbed a hand across his chin without at first giving a response. He had heard of Trocchi only from me, had never read his infamous book, which was not his kind of thing. *Cain's Book* was a minority taste—"a cult," and I was the most enthusiastic cultist of all. I knew few others.

Not only did Trocchi live outside society; he lived outside the law. He was a drug addict. He had devoted his life to the habit, in a literary fashion, in the tradition of Baudelaire and Cocteau. Opium was not necessarily a prison. On the contrary, with heroin in his veins he was free—super-free. "I would recommend that heroin be placed with lucid literature pertaining to use on the counters of all chemists (to think that a man should be allowed a gun and not a drug!) and sold openly to anyone over twenty-one."

Cain's Book revelled in the kind of literary tricks that excited me. For example, the anti-hero, Joe Necchi—Trocchi himself, in every pertinent particular—is in the middle of writing a novel, and the title of the novel is *Cain's Book*. One evening, after having shot up heroin in a New York pad with some derelict cronies, he reads aloud a passage from the work-in-progress by firelight. But the section in question does not exist elsewhere in *Cain's Book*—that is to say, in the novel you are holding in your hand. The reader has the teasing thought that there is another book of the same title, existing in an alternative zone—a hidden book, of which we are granted only a glimpse: a pair of hooves beneath the hem of the curtain. It was as if an actor in a film had halted the projector and stepped out of the screen to stand before the spectator. A film by Cocteau, the great modernist conjuror, in my eyes, from the fantasy country of France before and after the war. Trocchi was from Glasgow, not a fantasy land at all; it was the land in which I had first read his book.

Trocchi described with precision and some beauty the effects of narcotic drugs. I didn't feel the desire to emulate the author or his character. I was, rather, intoxicated by the effects of this writing, a species of magic, even when I could not fully understand it, as any form of magic remains at best partly understood. I carried *Cain's Book* with me to the pubs of Glasgow, the souks of Turkey, the ports of Greece . . . and preached its gospel like a downy, adolescent priest.

II

Finally, the editor showed his approval. But not a literary essay, *please*. He preferred the big projects. "Why not an interview? Do it long. We'll rediscover him."

I wouldn't have known how to go about finding the man whose face I had gazed at so often on the cover of the John Calder paperback. How to start, even?

Jack had no such hesitation. The next day he called the publisher in London and asked for the author's telephone number, explaining what it was we hoped to do. With his mysterious power of authority, he got straight through to Calder himself—like us, like Trocchi, a Scot, which might have helped—all done from the telephone box on the street outside our "office." Calder gave him the number and promised to send a copy of Trocchi's latest publication, *Man at Leisure*, a collection of poems. Jack then rang Trocchi and they talked for a quarter of an hour, as Jack pressed coins into the slot.

The great man was flattered by the proposal. He was himself a former student of Glasgow University, news which surprised and pleased Jack. He would welcome the reporter from *GUM* (we hadn't changed the title yet) whom Jack recommended, and asked that he—me—call to make arrangements.

How did Jack learn to do all this—to ring publishers and request review copies and telephone numbers with complete confidence? He had grown up in a typical Glasgow working-class family, attended the local school and still lived with his parents. He had met few people of literary accomplishment and probably only one or two who had actually written a book.

"If he invites me to shoot up heroin with him," I asked, "then what?" Jack didn't hesitate. "You must accept. Go ahead. It'll look great in the piece."

I took the night train to London—the cheapest—and arrived at Trocchi's place one wintry Sunday at noon, as per arrangement. He lived in a top-floor apartment at 4 Observatory Gardens, between Notting Hill Gate and High Street Kensington, in those days still a dowdy district, with his wife and two young sons. I can picture myself from outside my body, as if in yet another film, ringing the doorbell—the clench on the heart, the halt on the voice. Trocchi proved himself to be not just a tough face on the cover of a Calder Jupiter Book by responding on the intercom, the first of its kind I had ever encountered.

"Ah. It's you." The door opened with a metallic click and I began climbing the stairs to his apartment. He was waiting on the landing at the top floor, looking down at the figure below, a man of enormous frame in a black T-shirt, with a protruding stomach and a nose like the inverted horn of a rhino—a nose so large it was impossible not to focus on it. He smiled when he saw the long-haired emissary from his home town. I wrote: "One is immediately struck by his sallow complexion and the scars on his arms which are white like snow."

As I approached the landing where he stood, he said: "I was just about to give myself a fix. Can you wait?"

I had walked through the mirror, like an actor in a film by Cocteau, and entered into the pages of *Cain's Book*.

III

My girlfriend of the time, Pamela, was with me when I pressed that first intercom buzzer. Trocchi invited us to sit down in the living room and served tea together with muffins hot from the oven, which he recommended with a bafflingly un-outlaw-like enthusiasm. "Danish, I think they are." We met his wife Lyn, seated on the sofa behind dark glasses, though it was murky December, and two boys, one of whom obeyed a gentle command to lower the volume on the television. It all seemed disquietingly normal. He had the decorators in, and suggested that I return the next day, when he would be better organized and we would have more time in which to do "this thing," our interview. "Do it properly," he said.

I loved the sound of it. His voice was still strongly Scottish, and I was already planning to re-read *Cain's Book* through the filter of our native accent. In the meantime, he gave me a copy of *Helen and Desire*, the most mainstream of his six erotic novels written in Paris in the 1950s and published by the Olympia Press, and an American journal with an essay about him by the Black Mountain poet Edward Dorn. I suppose he hoped it might lend some seriousness to the article I was proposing to write.

The next day I returned alone and we settled ourselves— on the floor, of course—in his wide attic studio. There were books everywhere, as well as loose-leaf binders, a typewriter, letters unfolded from their nearby envelopes. A "comfortable shambles," I called it in the article.

"Like are you just going to fire questions at me?" His sentences were dependent on that word "like," the peculiar Scottishness of which has been overlooked. He apologized for the mess. "That's one thing about drugs, like they certainly make you disorganized."

The subject was not slow to arise. In *Cain's Book*, and in anything about him I laid my hands on to read, which wasn't much, Trocchi played the evangelist in promoting the salvational effects of heroin. It was one of his gimmicks, like asking you to wait while he gave himself a fix, a part of his grand outlaw persona. Drugs removed him from the mundane despond. Though I didn't want to share in it, the drug-taking nevertheless had an outsider aspect, and any hint of outsiderism was sure to appeal to me. Jack was more pragmatic and mature.

Before I left Glasgow, he had insisted that I read to Trocchi a few lines from an article by Cyril Connolly which had recently appeared in the *Sunday Times*.

A striking observation is the anti-intellectual climate that prevails in the networks. All who have known someone addicted to drugs . . . will have remarked on the increasing indifference to reality, whether to the time of day . . . or reading, or any of the pleasures and passions, food, drink, love, sex, places of art or the acquisition of knowledge, which make life worth living, friendship a joy or conversation a pleasure.

As soon as I read this aloud, I knew that it described better the context in which I aspired to live than the scenes of junkies hungrily seeking an uptown fix in *Cain's Book*, or in anything written by Burroughs or one of the other underground authors being passed around. I didn't even smoke dope. Yet I continued with my romance, for I enjoyed it. It was exactly that: a romance, a literary fantasy. It consoled me and provided a temporary rescue from my state of under-development. It occupied the place in my imagination that the works of Tolkien did in that of others. They didn't seriously think they were going to enter Middle Earth and meet the wizard Gandalf, but the fantasy consoled them.

Trocchi treated Connolly's eloquent objection seriously. In my 4,000 word profile which appeared in *GUM* several weeks later, in February 1973—probably the longest piece about Trocchi to have been published to date—I wrote: "Trocchi looked at me a little sadly. 'What is one going to say about that?'" He answered with reference to some great literary figures of the past. Here is what he said, transcribed from the recording I made of the interview on a borrowed tape machine the size of a small suitcase:

> I suppose up to a point it's true. But it's referring to a particular group of people who, whether they used drugs or not, would not be involved in this or that intellectual pursuit, would not be interested in reading. I think it's true that many people who use drugs do use them as armor against experience but I don't think that could have been said about Coleridge, for example, or de Quincey, who if nothing else were intellectuals.

He didn't wish to suggest that it was necessary for everyone, or anyone, to turn on to heroin. From the tape again: "I think that for me at a certain time it was necessary to take up this attitude and go far out—but it's something that can either enrich your experience or destroy you. It can destroy you very easily if you give way to all the social fictions about it. People tend to become what society believes they are."

What undermined and ultimately ridiculed the outsider stance was the difficulty of obtaining the drugs he wanted, and the penalties attached to doing so. One of the reasons Trocchi had returned to Britain from the United States was to be eligible for the prescription of narcotics on the National Health. In short, the great outlaw became more dependent than most others on the rules established by the society he wanted his readers and literary peers to think he was plotting to overthrow. Who ever heard of a state-subsidized outlaw? He had walked into a trap outlined in a passage in *Cain's Book* which had always delighted me:

For centuries we in the West have been dominated by the Aristotelian impulse to classify. It is no doubt because conventional classifications became part of the prevailing economic structure that all real revolt is hastily fixed like a bright butterfly on a classificatory pin; the anti-play, *Godot*, being from one point of view unanswerable, is with all speed acclaimed "best play of the year"; anti-literature is rendered innocuous by granting it a place in conventional histories of literature.

While I was thrilled at having laid eyes on my hero, Pamela, when she saw him that first day and sat on the sofa sipping tea beside dark-eyed Lyn, said she could "smell evil about his person." I was too much in awe for any such perception, but it chimed with the opening poem in *Man at Leisure*, which had arrived from Calder just in time for me to read it on the journey to London: "Where to begin / which sin / under what sun . . . ?"

Where to begin with sin? And where to end? It is well established now, though I was ignorant of it then, that Lyn had been forced into prostitution in the US by Trocchi, in order to raise money for drugs. She was a junkie herself, and died not long after our encounter in Observatory Gardens. Another of his gimmicks was to say things like, "I've no objection, if I myself am incapable for one reason or another, to finding some young bull for my wife . . ." I didn't put that into the piece.

It was the flipside of the charm, though charm there still was. And there was another sort of charm for me in hearing the names of Robert Creeley, R. D. Laing, William Burroughs, and others, let fall elegantly, without name-dropping clumsiness. Norman Mailer had referred to Trocchi as "the most bril-

image of profligate associated with the man. When I mentioned that an arts lab should be opening in this city shortly, he was pleased but sceptical. He said it was pitiful that the final say on sexual licence for such establishments rested more or less in the power of a few councillors. It is this attitude which has awarded his books their unfortunate reputation.

The three main distributors in this country will not handle *Cain's Book*, though that still sells and is shortly being made into a film from which he will profit. And at the time of that book's original publication in Britain it was banned and burned in Sheffield.

Lady Chatterley, Ulysses, Henry Miller, Cain. It is no secret that we are afraid over what we cannot assert ourselves; scared of the unrecognizable, or of what becomes uncomfortably familiar. *Cain* is honest and true and burned

> I always felt it was strange that the
> butcher Abel should be preferred to
> the agriculturist Cain.
> Abel waxed fat and rich breeding
> sheep for the slaughter while Cain
> tilled
> And soon Abel had vast herds and
> air-conditioned slaughterhouses
> and meat package plants, and there
> was a blight on Cain's crop. And
> that was called SIN ...
> And Abel saw his elder brother and
> he was thin and with a starved look
> and held the spade to no purpose in
> his hand.
> And Abel approached his brother,
> saying,
> Why don't you give up and come
> and work for me? I could use a good
> man in the slaughterhouse.
> And Cain slew him."

And so Cain was cast out. And Trocchi is cast out. And Cain wore a mark that he be protected against random homicide and he was the first city builder and he inaugurated the first civilised life.

Through his book (with respect to literature), through his habit (with respect to consciousness), through the political sigma project (with respect to a civilised society) and through himself Trocchi, wearing the mark, protected by himself and his ways against indiscriminate judgement, attempts to erect, assert himself, attempts to inaugurate something of what he, the man, and his ideas are the primogenitor.

His contemporaries have always eyed him nervously. In 1962, at the International Writers' Conference, organised by John Calder in Edinburgh, Scottish writers formed the mainstay of their crew with McDiarmid in power. He brushed roughly up against Trocchi and Burroughs, writing them off as nothing more than a couple of drug fiends. 'I've nothing against the man,' Trocchi says now with an apologetic grin, thinking back to the event. 'I mean, he is sane, in a relative fashion, isn't he? But he started attacking us, babbling on about matters he knows nothing about, and all that brigade were drunk out of their skulls with their drug while Burroughs and I were quite *compos mentus*.'

Trocchi became involved in a debate with McDiarmid and and that all Scottish writing over the last 20 years, his own apart, was a lot of 'stale porridge', and that only he had written a book which was living and would remain alive. *I am a cosmonaut of inner space.*

In *Cain's Book*, he states his view more plainly. 'I told him that the one urgency for literature was that it should once and for all accomplish its dying, that it wasn't that writing shouldn't be written, but that a man should annihilate prescriptions of all past form in his own soul refuse to consider what he wrote in terms of literature, judge it solely in terms of his living.'"

It was around the time when Trocchi landed in England from America that he began to channel his energies away from direct artistic out-put into some- thing which had occupied his thought since the Paris days, but in a far less serious manner than he now began to involve himself with it: project sigma.

The whole chapter of underground vicissitudes of that time — the sixties — is related and discussed at some length in Jeff Nuttal's *Bomb Culture*. It will suffice here to sketch in a few background relevancies. To put it roughly, the 'Underground' was just coming 'over', ie it was communicating itself, involving more than only the directly self-consciously involved. Tom McGrath launched *International Times*, beat-writing, having learned to walk with Kerouac, was starting to run with Ginsberg and Burroughs, and for many — impressed by its exuberance and lack of pedantic pretension — was running a deal faster than the slow-moving straight movement. The poetry reading at the Royal Albert Hall was a congregation, a success and proved to be a landmark. R. D. Laing, the psychiatrist, was involved with David Cooper and Esterson, in the Philadelphia Foundation; anti-psychiatry. Leary was telling us that LSD is where it's at, and Alpert was finding out that it wasn't.

But for all of these people, and others, rebels, sigma became a cause. Their centre was sigma and Trocchi was the centripetal force.

Trying to define sigma is like trying to define zen. The proof is not apparent. The physicality is not in evidence. Only the actuality exists.

'For myself, I think it is not so much a question of choosing to exist as of discovering oneself in and of the 'invisible insurrection' by virtue of one's practical posture. The (r)evolt is taking place at the level of symbols; there is no question of our ever meeting the forces head-on in a war on their terms. But it is happening. If you are aware of it, you are *ipso facto* involved.'

The fundamental ideal of sigma is to make intelligence self-conscious; to channel the new amounts of leisure time which are already on us and must inevitably grow in this future, into routes more creative, more self-conscious than civilisation has previously managed. Ostensibly, sigma (the word represents in mathematics any number between nothing and infinity) is an elitist theory using culture as the means of an insurrection — an insurrection of minds: more than anything else it is simply a new way of looking at things, a common viewpoint which would eventually involve everyone to a higher level of intelligence (but which must begin with the few conscious) — 'Only those who are able to comprehend those conditions and exploit them are responsible for their own biographies. It is to those we address ourselves — though they choose themselves, are not elected.'

Trocchi is humble without abjection. 'That may sound a little far-fetched. But it's all we can hope for. For man to learn to live with one another, to manipulate their energies toward something more creative, something other than ideas of how to destroy each other.'

The small group at the offset in the early sixties included R. D. Laing, David Cooper, William Burroughs, Ginsberg, Leary, Alpert, Tom McGrath, Jeff Nuttall and Trocchi himself whose part in the fundamental problem of communicating sigma was probably the largest. He had essays by himself and the others run off on Gestetner sheets and sold at cost price, and tried hard to get something concrete, something deliberate moving around sigma. Now he still has the ideas, the hopes, if not

A page from *Glasgow University Magazine* (*GUM*), February 1972, with my profile of Alexander Trocchi: a first extended appearance in print.

liant man I've met." Creeley had written a gnomic preface to a 1967 reissue of one of his pornographic novels. "In *Thongs*, as in other novels he has written in this genre, Trocchi defines the *isolation* of persons in sexual rapport . . ."

I carried the cassette tape home to Glasgow, a touching blend of callowness and diligence. In my Wilton Street room, which I had regained after returning from Israel, I wrote a report of the adventure in longhand and gave it to Jack, who printed it in *GUM*, without benefit of editing.

Among the other material I brought back from this first literary expedition was a short article in typescript by Burroughs, "M.O.B.," which in the Burroughs lexicon stood for "My Own Business." I had asked Trocchi for a piece of writing of his own for *GUM*, and he regretted not being able to offer something. But he held out "M.O.B." with one of his confidential smiles and said, "Why not publish this?" It consisted of three pages, in Gestetner duplicator form. "Just phone up Bill and say I suggested it."

He wrote down Burroughs's Mayfair telephone number: 01 839 5259. When I returned to Glasgow I dialed it, Jack-style, and sure enough Burroughs picked up the phone, listened to my stammered explanation and answered my polite inquiries.

Answered in his fashion, that is. To everything I said, Burroughs replied, "*Shu-ah!*," in an elasticated drawl. Or "*Yea-ah!*"

So, that's OK then?

"*Yea-ah.*"

Permission given?

"*Shu-ah!*"

William Burroughs could from then on be listed among the contributors to *Glasgow University Magazine*. Money wasn't mentioned (there was no such thing anyway). He became expansive only when I asked for his address, to which would be sent a copy when the piece appeared later in the year: "8 Dook Street Saint James," and put down the phone.

11

HITCH-HIKER'S PERSONALITY TEST

I

The state of original desire in the Land of Away was Morocco. Therefore, I had one more journey to undertake: through northern Europe to Sicily, over the Gulf of Tunis, then by land across North Africa, and down through the labyrinthine Moroccan roads to Marrakesh. It was a route of some 7,000 miles, though I would not have been able to tell anyone that then. A journey without maps. I decided to go when GUM/Moving Review was on lengthy sabbatical during the summer holidays.

My starting point was a squatters' community in North London. On an April Sunday evening in 1973, I emerged into light rain at Tufnell Park Tube station, looked around to take my bearings—this was as much a foreign turf as any I had trod so far—turned right along Junction Road and arrived at No.9 Poynings Road, almost midway between Tufnell Park and the Archway roundabout. The terrace houses, classic early-twentieth-century two-up, two-down, were earmarked for demolition and several had been abandoned to the elements. The most forceful elements here were young people in search of a place to live at a next-to-nothing price. Four or five of the houses in the upward sloping, acutely curving street—standing at the foot of it, you could not see past No. 7—had been taken over by a mixed assembly of Londoners, Irish, a number of Scottish guys whom I didn't know before and two Scottish sisters, former school friends of Dudley's, whom I did and who had offered me the introduction.

No one seemed to be expecting me; no one seemed surprised to see me. As with others who had come before, I was accepted, like a pilgrim at the gates of a mountaintop monastery, on the incontrovertible fact of having arrived. In a first-floor front room, I was assigned a mattress. Bathroom and lavatory were pointed out. In what would have been called the refectory on the mountaintop, food was heated in a casserole and scooped on to a plate. There was one American and some coming-and-going Europeans. Everyone was welcome, so long as the vibe was OK. It didn't have to be a good vibe: what mattered was that it wasn't a heavy one. "Heavy," like "uncool," could stand for a whole suit of negative characteristics, responses and consequences. But even that might be accepted on compassionate grounds. They were tolerant, the people of the Order of the Squatters: aspirant misfits and aspirant mystics, druggies and aspirant ex-druggies, drop-outs and, in one or two cases, aspirant drop-ins, secretly grateful for the unannounced arrival of a parental rescue squad.

During the week, I would begin looking for a job, with the end in view of advancing to Tunis in June.

II

My *Cain's Book*-style writings took on a new dimension in the upstairs front room at No. 9, becoming more naturalistic and introducing a named first-person narrator, Luke. I scribbled on a foolscap pad while reclining on the mattress on the floor, back propped against the wall. In the pages I have retained, I find the occasional marginal note to self: "May 10th 1973:

It is important that I begin to write systematically as soon as living circumstances permit, otherwise I will find myself lost in a tangle of ideas & sketches." Even in these little literary instructions, however—at once standing apart from the fiction, yet destined to be incorporated into it—I hear the voice of Trocchi.

Included in the story was a French freak I called Henri— "French freaks are rare, but French freaks are always the worst" is among the book's maxims—based on Dudley's friend Pierre, who was semi-resident at Poynings Road. I had often seen him with Dudley in Glasgow. They made journeys from south to north and back again in Pierre's illicit Austin van. Dudley told me that Pierre had taught him how to siphon petrol from other vehicles (before the days of secure petrol caps).

I disapproved. Dennis's lesson on the kibbutz—"You ever heard of karma?"—and the sour taste left by the petty theft itself were among my meditations at the squatters' monastery. The aura surrounding Pierre was alluring but not the one for Dudley, and by association didn't feel right for me. It was Pierre I had met in the street in Istanbul a year earlier, after being robbed by the German lorry driver. He was dark and spindly in appearance, electric in gesture and reaction, long-fingered and neon-lit, a kind of Jimi Hendrix without the genius, and he died similarly young.

Otherwise, I got on with everybody. I was on a more even keel than most, perhaps because I did not seek guidance in drugs, or not habitually, and drugs were a way of life at Poynings Road. Mandrax, hash, grass, acid, and various pharmaceutical concoctions that could be bought over the counter at the chemist's without a doctor's prescription. There were no junkies among the regular inhabitants of the street. But some came from neighboring squats to sit at the kitchen table in one or other of the houses—Nos. 9, 7, and 4 were the main ones—waiting on junk time, passing through junk space, speaking in junk speak, smiling mild junk smile, thieving junk goods. There was always someone willing to greet them with a pot of tea and a joint. People managed to sit around all morning, or, if they had managed to skip the morning by remaining asleep, all afternoon and evening, too. It was a form of junk meditation practised by some of the monks in this hospitable community.

Living in an adjacent room at No. 9 was a young Irishman called Gerry, basically decent, like so many, but the pawn shop on Junction Road housed not only every last personal object that Gerry suspected of having monetary value, but his soul as well. It was Gerry who said one day, apropos of I don't know what, "You're the most together person in this street." I mention it only to make clear that it isn't my intention to characterize myself as a near-miss, as someone forced into a choice between survival and perishing in this arena. I was there, but as a chiel taking notes. By now, the novel had a title: "Spread Eagle." I gave some of the characters the names of actual people from the street. This passage is based on a real event:

Gerry and I had dropped some medicinal high of which an amount comes one's way every now and then but with this the only buzz was a sore head and if we were laughing in the kitchen it was because of the brotherhood that develops between two beings in moments of adventure the more ill-advised the adventure the greater the bond. Gerry stood up to walk towards the sink but he only got as far as the oven and he fell against

Scribbling something or other, in a caravan.

it like he had been shot, with an excruciatingly painful countenance like he was being castrated and his fists clenched and teeth set together, his eyes rolling twitching all over and sliding down the front of the oven—Oh man he's OD'd Henri said—Gerry was on the floor now still twitching and having turned white green and now going blue and the four people who were in the room looking helpless and me and Henri worried because we had taken the same stuff without having any notion of the effects and me seeing my face in Gerry's face on the floor and going oh fuck I wish I hadn't and Gerry coughing and grunting . . .

In the story he died. The real Gerry rose again a few moments later and survived to make another visit to the pawn shop. In both fiction and life, the narrator suffered nothing worse than a sore head.

Several people in the street worked, and I was one of them. Work was not difficult to find and was untrammeled by bureaucracy. At eight in the morning, following the advice of a Poynings villager, I turned up at a builders' yard close to Tufnell Park Tube station, and asked the age-old question: "Need any men?" The foreman looked me over and posed his own inquiry in return: "Can you start right away?" That's why I'm here. "OK, go with him. He's another the same as you. *Jock!* Take this lad to the house in Prince of Wales and tell Bernie to get him mixing cement and on to the paving . . . At the *back* not the fucking front." And I was hired, no further questions asked, a blistering shovel affixed to my tender grip, cash to come on a Friday afternoon without the mediation of the taxman.

The job led me to Kentish Town, Primrose Hill, and other North London sites, and brought in more money in a week than I had earned at various places of toil in Glasgow in a month. I was thin and flexible and relatively fit, but after my first day of mixing cement, digging trenches and clambering up scaffolding, moving from left to right in Spiderman choreography, I returned to the house at Poynings Road and tumbled on to my mattress, a ball of pain. The sinews loosened quickly, though, and before long I was more flexible than ever.

The other Jock was an ex-convict, a red-haired, slight man with a mild nature and the marks of a broken life scrawled all over. He might as well have been covered in knots and crosses. An air of surrender clung to him. Of his conversation I remember mainly the hard labor of making time pass in a Pentonville cell. "Countin' thae bricks . . . Oh Goad, ah don' waant t' be doin that *ever again*, naw, naw. "

Simple, harmless Jock was one of my teachers, though he would never have guessed it. He, too, led by example, poor man: shovel in hand, forsaken eyes never tested by love.

III

When my purse had filled up with about £100—more money than I had ever had in my life—I made plans to be off. Go down to the road. Form the signature salute: right hand out (left, when in Britain), thumb raised. Head up, features open. Climb in with a grateful smile, careful to extend polite thanks when stepping down.

The direct route to Marrakesh would have led straight to the south of France, over the Pyrenees, with a stop at the peculiar Principality of Andorra, fathoming south through Franco-ite Spain to the port of Algeciras. There, the ferryman accepted tribute to spirit the traveler across water to Tangier, from this world to the other, the staging post at which one entered the much-desired zone of Difference.

In the hitch-hiker's personality test, however, France emerged with a low score and an unfriendly reputation; Spain, a fascist, fearful country, did even worse. People swapped stories of standing by the side of the road under the sun for six hours, waiting in vain for a lift. I knew that wait, and that sun. The delay was maddening, both for itself and for the fact that it permitted no deviation. You had to comply. Take a break—to read, to eat, to pee, to look around the nearby streets—and every car that whizzes by has the mark of being the one that could have plucked you out of this plight.

So I traveled via Germany, the most efficient hitching country. That way, I could cross from Northern to Southern Europe via the Alps, arriving in the unexpectedly snowy upper reaches of Italy. When I touched the outer tip of Europe, my magic thumb-travel would once again be interrupted by water: again the Mediterranean, though now the stretch separating Sicily from the Gulf of Tunis.

From Palermo, a ferry left for Tunis. From Tunis, a road ran along the Barbary Coast, through Constantine and Algiers, on into Morocco. I longed to be within the walls of Marrakesh, to see with my own eyes what had lit up my imagination when, in my chilly flat in Partick on a gray Glasgow Saturday after returning from the lunchtime session at the Scotia, Jimmy Dunn described scenes in the marketplace: storytellers with donkeys beside them on the ground, sly merchants unfolding soft cloths to reveal Goulimine beads and amber amulets, camels blocking the road. People had mentioned the town of Essaouira, to the west of Marrakesh. You could stay there cheaply, they said; few words were more likely to seduce me than that one.

On an autostrada slip road somewhere north of Rome, a lorry stopped and the driver asked, "Dove?" When I shouted up, "Palermo!" he said "Bene," and I got in. I stayed with him for two days. In a roadside restaurant filled with other long-haul drivers, he treated me to a meal of spaghetti with an unforgettable tomato sauce, followed by plump sardines bearing the stripes of the grill, and white bread with hard crust that softened under the cinder-flecked oil. We drank proper wine—not "the wine" in the Glasgow sense, nor the resinous yellow wine of Spetsai—something that had happened only a few times before in my life. There was a paper table cloth, which retained dark red rings left by the carafe, as I myself would have liked to retain them. I had seldom sheltered under such an agreeable web, spun by weather, food and drink, and companionship. I spoke just a scattering of Italian and he had little English. At night he slept in the cab, while I unrolled my sleeping bag next to the mammoth front wheel. He took me across the Strait of Messina in his cab and let me down monosyllabically on the other side, in Sicily.

The Tirrenia ferries left Palermo for Tunis only twice a week, something I didn't learn until arriving at the port and approaching the ticket office. I would have to bed down in Palermo for a few nights, which I did in the local campsite, sleeping on the ground in the open air, using a sweater on top of my sandshoes as a pillow.

Eventually, the ship cast off for a voyage scheduled to take ten hours.

On the quayside, as we waited to load, I had spotted a trio of Americans of about my own age, in a yellow VW campervan. Once aboard, I fell into conversation with one of them, Jeff, a dark-haired, squarely built footballer type, with a New World innocence not suggested by his rugged appearance. Jeff introduced me to his two traveling companions, the owner of the van, Russ, and his girl, Annette, and suddenly we were a convenient foursome on the open sea.

They planned to drive from Tunis, through Constantine and Algiers, all the way to Morocco. First, however, there were visas to be obtained for their American passports. The prospect made them nervous. "They'll speak English, won't they?"

"In North Africa the second language is French."

Russ and co. didn't know anything of that. They had barely a *oui* or a *non* among the three of them.

"And you?"

Yes, I did. By then, I had studied French for a Scottish

Higher certificate and had passed with a decent grade, moving beyond the low horizon of the final report card at King's Park Secondary (adjusted to make a modest 49 percent). From time to time, when we were wandering in Kelvingrove Park, Dudley would say, "Let's talk in French for a while," and we would play a game that involved approaching people in the street and asking for directions. If they didn't understand our elegantly phrased question ("Sauriez-vous me dire, madame . . ."), we would continue, seeking the way to "Sochi-aal Street" in broken English. "Ah, you mean Sauchiehall Street?" "Soo kee aal! Ben, oui!" I had enough to get the four of us served at café tables; enough, maybe, to talk to somebody in the Consulate about visas; enough to seek directions once we were on the road; possibly even enough to get us through an awkward situation at passport control.

That was one good reason for taking me on. Another, perhaps the main reason, was that Russ and Annette were fed up with Jeff, and he with them. It wasn't long before Jeff told me so himself. They slept in the campervan at night, while he lay outside, calm or storm. He and I quickly struck up a rapport, however, and I began to understand his irritation with the other two. Still, we were all going to be traveling companions, and it was best that we get along.

In order to obtain the visas, we had to spend a few days in Tunis. A place was found near the sea where we could park the van. On a visit to the neighboring coastal town of Sidi Bou Said, I inquired of a crepe-skinned, turbaned man squatting on his haunches outside a café where I could buy a stamp "pour l'Israël." I had a letter for Dennis, who was still on Kibbutz Mishmarot. The Arab snapped into an instant rage and struck my shins hard with his cane without rising to his feet.

At some stage I learned that Russ and Annette, once in Morocco, planned to travel into the Atlas Mountains in order to purchase a large quantity of hashish. They said they were going to smuggle it out of the country into Spain, then sell it in Europe. The scheme had been born in the US before they left. They had it all worked out. They knew where to go in the mountains to buy the hash, and even had the name of a seller, presumably passed on by some other dealer.

Cannabis was illegal in Morocco, as in Europe, but personal use was widely tolerated. People smoked openly in cafés and other public spaces. Sandal-clad travelers came from all over to indulge their habit freely. The markets in the city squares sold wooden pipes with ceramic bowls and earthenware chillums of the sort favored by cannabis connoisseurs. I had seen those connoisseurs in Glasgow and Poynings Road. Just to say "chillum" in a familiar way placed the user on a higher step.

It was equally well known that peddling drugs, or possession of a large amount, was not permitted in the country. The act of smuggling from Morocco into Spain was likely to be punishable by a long term of imprisonment. I felt about it the way my father felt about gambling and burglary: there must be easier ways of making a living.

Russ and Annette filled me in on the details of the scheme as we prepared for the journey across the Barbary Coast, projected to last several days. They planned to package the hashish in metal tins—labeled "poire" or "prune"—then to re-weld the tins. It was not a new trick. It was one that an old sniffer dog might have learned long ago. Why they told me about this reckless idea I don't know. Perhaps they hoped deep down that I would talk them out of it, or perhaps it was to seek temporary relief from the tension it generated inside them, and among the four of us, which was evident throughout our time together. Its effects were frequently directed towards Jeff.

Russ and Annette smoked dope every day. In a small public park in Sidi Bou Said—just a patch of parched yellow with a bob of scrub here and there—I accepted the joint, although my experience with Gerry, Pierre and the over-the-counter medicinal high at Poynings Road ought to have warned me off once and for all. I had told Russ I didn't smoke, but he insisted this was different: pure grass; there wasn't any tobacco in the joint, a gold-standard guarantee to certain potheads.

I inhaled and when it came round again I inhaled once more. I realized I was about to have one of my familiar sessions: of feeling that the natural world had been drained of all energy and capability, that the earth was gray and dead and that we were automatons moving through airless space.

All through the long Algerian days, Russ drew periodically from a joint as he sat at the wheel of the VW. He smoked in the morning and he smoked at night. The campervan had a mattress in the back, on which Russ and Annette stretched out when the day's driving was done. Jeff and I were usually content under the stars, but one night, at a stopping place on the coast between Algiers and Tipassa, it poured with rain so heavily that Jeff slid open the door of the van at 5 am and asked to be allowed to shelter inside. They said no. Our sleeping bags were dripping wet and we had no choice but to get up and stand under a tree, watching the rain batter the roof of the van, and the sea, hoping it would relent.

When it did, we went for a drying-out walk along the sand. The temperature rose quickly as it became light and we shook off our moisture. On the beach we came across an Arab fisherman who had just made a catch. A few words of French were exchanged—his was almost as pebble-mouthed as mine—and he invited us to share breakfast in his cabin. The freshly fried fish and hot black coffee, prepared over a fire built at the sandy threshold to the shack, eaten and drunk in sight and sound of the sea with the African sun coming up, cheered us so much that the downpour that had splashed us awake at dawn now seemed a blessing. On our return we enthused about it to the couple in the van, who responded by scolding Jeff again for having woken them up.

It wasn't our only experience of Arab hospitality in Algeria, but Russ and Annette were disinclined to be aroused by the esoteric world. What were they traveling for? Like other Americans I met on the road—the exceptions to the rule—they appeared surprised to discover that life wasn't arranged the way it was in Chicago and Washington DC, that *Time* magazine wasn't on sale in the kiosks under the arcades in Algiers, so reminiscent of Paris, that their Scottish traveling companion wasn't familiar with the nefarious maneuverings of their President and his outlaw band, that Coca-Cola was unavailable in the backwater café-cum-restaurant we would head to for an evening bite. To get to one of those rural places, Russ and I walked across a vast, empty patch of earth that was cracked like crazy paving, familiar from photographs I had seen in the pages of Jimmy Dunn's *National Geographic*, a sight I now found thrilling. Once inside, Russ asked in English for a hamburger and Coke, to the bafflement of the *patron*. Their only news was American news, their only history recent American history, their expectations domestic ones.

Somewhere along the 1,200-mile coastal route to Morocco, Russ and Annette smoked the last of the hashish they had brought with them over the border into Algeria. They discarded all traces of drug detritus, and the van was clean as it rolled into Zouj Bghal, the westernmost frontier post between the two countries. Darkness had fallen by the time we got there and ours was the only non-official vehicle in the compound. Somebody took a deep breath and said, "Here we go-oh." My companions showed the approaching officials their US passports with the newly issued visas.

They were freshly stamped and correct, but it wasn't enough for the impassive men in the military-style uniforms and peaked caps. Russ was asked to turn off the ignition and we were invited to step down and enter the office. The Americans were taken into a side room where they were strip-searched. For some reason, the British passport-holder was left alone. I picture myself—it might be one of those false screenshot memories but I'm sticking to it—leaning on the desk in the North African evening, chatting to the uniformed officers at the front counter ("Pas beaucoup du monde ce soir, hein?") while the others were subjected to a humiliating routine behind closed doors. Annette, too, by a pair of pretty female officers. The van was searched, as was the luggage, but in a haphazard way. No drugs were found, in their pockets, their bags or their innards. Even a small amount retained out of carelessness could have landed the lot of us in prison.

After an unexplained further hour's delay, we passed through. Not far from the border town of Oujda, we found a place to park and stretch out: Russ and Annette on the mattress inside the van, as usual, Jeff and me on the ground by the wheels.

In the morning—it was Morocco. As they let me down at the city wall, we shook hands and made promises and exchanged thanks: me for the longest lift I had ever had; they for the rudimentary but useful French. Jeff and I made a no-arrangement arrangement to meet in Marrakesh, which we kept.

A memory, in my relief at being free of the yellow VW campervan that I had first spotted on the quayside at Palermo a week before: that there were suddenly African men all around, distinct in gaze, gait and shape from the black people I had seen in London; and that the ankle-length djellabas and piled headscarves of the women on this side of the border were more colorful than they had been in Algeria.

I was *here*, like Jimmy Dunn before me, like Robin Williamson before him. Soon I would have my own tales to tell, of small sturdy glasses stuffed with mint leaves, of stepping out like a mad dog in the midday sun, of visits to an oasis, a word with biblical resonance. And indeed this oasis was surrounded by men and boys, goats and camels, out of *The Children's Illustrated Bible*. The bearded elders squatted on a mat in their thick-weave djellabas and turbans, sketching incomprehensible diagrams in the dust with a stick. That incomprehensibility made perfect sense to me. It was just what I had come for.

IV

Throughout my journeys in Morocco, south, west and finally north towards Tangier, I slept outdoors: on a sandy ridge by the side of the road, or in an unoccupied building—construction sites were particularly convenient, if I happened to be near one. From time to time, I granted myself the luxury of a night in a pension, with the intention of taking a shower, but at the level of accommodation I could afford I ran the risk of coming out the next day grubbier and more bug-infested than when I went in.

I got lifts without much trouble, and saw the Moroccan social spectrum from the passenger seat: one ride on a pot-holed road between two desolate small towns in the back of a pick-up at the wordless invitation of an illiterate goatherd; another in a Mercedes, across a good stretch of duel carriage-way with a French- and English-speaking charmer dressed in Polo shirt and sharp slacks. From him, I learned about Polisa-rio and a recent uprising springing from the Atlas mountains against King Hussain, and about the underground prisons in the desert housing prisoners with no name, no number. There were policemen at road junctions, stopping drivers, confiscat-ing documents and probably vehicles, too, smiling at bribes. But visitors from the north, half-clothed and unsheltered though we might be, went largely unmolested. We were a spe-cies of royalty, respected for our wealth. Drop-outs in our own lands, we were welcome drop-ins here.

Somewhere towards the south, as I was starting my voy-age back to Marrakesh from Essaouira, a man picked me up in the evening on a stretch of semi-desert road, with no other living thing in view but goats on the hillside. Here and there you would see them grazing the leaves in the branches of a tree. We drove a little way with few words exchanged. Then he stopped the car. With a questioning expression, he formed a circle with the thumb and index finger of his left hand, while making a poking movement with the middle finger of his right. My French, and my sign language, were up to a polite no thanks. I no longer had a lift.

It would soon be dark and there was nothing for it but to continue walking or to hope to be rescued by another driver.

The roads were practically empty, but eventually I came in sight of a cluster of flat roofs and angled walls, all at about the same height, all tinted dirty white or gray. Children stopped their kicking games and stared. Women stopped their sweeping and stared. Men passing by twisted their necks to stare.

After reaching into my purse for a beer and slab of indeterminate meat at a roadside lean-to café, to be consumed under the unrelenting gaze of the proprietor and his small son, I left and lay down on a dusty bank by the roadside on the outskirts of the village. I was in my sleeping bag, using my shoes for a pillow as usual, with pullover on top; comfortable enough. Let the cars roll through the night—I was in for a good sleep. Tomorrow, back to Marrakesh. Then Rabat. On to Tangier, Algeciras, Europe.

As it turned out, the cars were not the enemy. Before I could fall asleep, I heard a scratching next to my ear . . . then silence. Again a scratching . . . What is it? *Scratching* . . . silence . . . *scratching*. Could it be that scorpions live here? A noise at the other ear this time . . . at my feet . . . everywhere. I began to believe they were in my sleeping bag. When I stood up, the noise stopped. When I lay down, it started again. Could it be rats? Would I prefer a rat to a scorpion? I was briefly the hero of Maupassant's novella *Le Horla*, who goes mad from hallucinations of intruders. Eventually the scratching stopped and I fell asleep. If I dreamt, I dreamt of a soft bed raised safely off the floor in a secure bedroom.

It was because of my night with the rat or the scorpion that I responded to an invitation some days later in the course of my journey towards Tangier. After seven weeks in North Africa, more than half of it spent in Morocco, I was on my way. No map was needed for getting from Africa to Glasgow.

Just a rudimentary homing instinct: keep heading north to Rabat, the capital, skipping Casablanca on the way; follow a string of small towns up the west coast to reach Tangier. It was a distance of some 400 miles to the border post, three, at most four days' travel, allowing for poor roads, short lifts and a bit of sub-tourist loitering. Then I would be in Algeciras, back in the continent of pavements, streetlamps, sloping roofs and people who dressed lightly under the sun rather than piling on extra layers.

I had reached the outskirts of Rabat. The medina, where I had spent the afternoon looking round in desultory fashion, was conveniently to the north of the city, and as the sun sank swiftly I marched through a dusty suburb in hope of getting a lift to take me within reach of Kenitra, the next town of any size. The long-form hitch-hiker is always prey to temptation: that last lift of the day, the lure of a few more miles. If not that, then settling on a place to stay for the night, before resorting to some roadside café with scattered tables made from oil drums for a supper of chicken in soupy orange sauce and a glass of mint tea. Next day, under the sun, more cars, more curious or silent drivers; another hundred miles closer to Europe.

A small, swarthy man dressed in a beige bus driver's uniform fell into step alongside as I made my way through Rabat's final outpost. It was a stretch of road dotted on both sides with filling stations, open-front shops selling car tyres, wheels, slack jump leads and exhausted batteries to attach them to, entire engines, radio fronts without radio backs, dislocated television screens and cathode tubes, screws incompatible with neighboring screwdrivers, eternally tangled wires, goods of mangled metal waiting to be put to unimaginable use. These shops were all over Morocco.

"Take-i-reasi," he said. "Take-i-reasi. Où allez-vous?"

Take-i-reasi was practically the limit of his English. He must have seen the scorpions in my head. I told him in French that I was heading for Tangier.

"Pas ce soir!"

No, not tonight—there was still about 150 miles to go—"but I'll keep on for now, until I find a place to sleep."

"Américain?"

It was the eternal question. If not that, "Deutsch?"

"Scottish." It was the obligatory reply. "Ecosse." The name of the country meant nothing to him.

"Bretagne," I said. "England. Angleterre. Pas anglais, moi, mais . . . c'est d'à côté."

"Cous-cous." He made an eating gesture with fingers and thumb. "You like. Cous-cous. Vous. Faim." They were not questions.

Through smiles and gestures and bursts of repeated phrases, I let the image flirt with my hunger. I would be keen to eat from a plate of cous-cous in a Moroccan home, with a Moroccan family. A pleasant picture formed in my head. He invited me to follow him, and my stomach gave permission to do so.

The bus driver lived in a modest house fifty yards or so from the road, one of a row, painted blue on the bottom half, with whitewashed upper. I was always struck by the lack of even boundaries between the foot of a house and the sidewalk—you couldn't call it a pavement, for there were no defined pavements in poor areas; no concrete or slate, only hard earth, rock, or mud.

Inside, I found not a bus driver's wife but two girls of about thirteen or fourteen, surprised by the apparition from the Different world. They began to giggle, and continued giggling all through my stay, except when asleep. I could scarcely see what they looked like, because they were not allowed to be in the room with me or even to be seen with heads uncovered, but they embarked on a continuous procession of tiptoeing out of the kitchen or one of the side rooms in order to steal glimpses of the stranger.

While the driver and I collaborated on a duet of franglais and hand signals in the small living room, the girls set about preparing the cous-cous. If one had to pass from the kitchen, which was through an arch to the left of the living room where we were, to a room on the right, a colorful killim would be ostentatiously stretched and finger-pinned across the open space by the other, so that the first could dart, faux-furtively, from there to there. The accomplishment of these missions was concluded by intense bursts of hilarity.

When the food was ready, the driver and I ate together where we were, while the girls remained in the kitchen. There was no table. We sat on the floor. The cous-cous filled a white enamel basin of the type my mother once washed small clothes in. We used our fingers. There was meat and gravy and soft flat bread to scoop it up with. I patted my tummy in appreciation.

When it was all done, the driver produced some hashish and offered to make a pipe. After my dead-world experience in Sidi Bou Said, I had renounced even the social obligation of smoking. A few weeks before, at an oasis outside Marrakesh, in tribute to Davey Graham, I had accepted maajun—the sweet, sticky cake baked with hash, after which he had named one of his orientalist tunes—leading to the same old result. My excuse was that it was in honor of a hero. Davey's shimmering "Maajun" I could tolerate, but not the thing itself.

"Is it possible that I could have a drink of something or

other?" I asked my host. "Du vin, par exemple?" Ever since my magnificent dinner with the Italian lorry driver in the roadside restaurant north of Sicily two months earlier, I had grown fond of sun-and-south-suggesting red wine and its effects, so different from the weather-resistant heaviness of draught ale. In the cafés of Marrakesh, it had been easy and cheap to order a glass.

Not so easy now, though. He looked at me for a moment. Possible? Yes. First, though, he would have to telephone a friend. A man who knew how to acquire wine. We would go to meet him in the medina. "Dans le médina?" He assured me it was not that far from where we were sitting. "In Rabat?" I thought it was all a bit elaborate. All I wanted was a glass, two at the most. I wouldn't have mentioned wine had he not asked me first about the hashish. But another adventure, and why not? Things were going well. The cosy room. The giggling girls. The feeling of hot food in the neglected belly. The Moroccan night. The prospect of a bed, a bed, a bed.

A bed where, by the way? Which bed? Before I could take that train of thought further, he said, "Et bien?" I said, "OK." My host repeated "OK," with a conspiratorial smile as he got to his feet. He had changed out of his bus driver's uniform, and was dressed in a white, ankle-length garb.

"OK" and "et bien" were not all that were needed to get us started on the quest for a glass of wine. First, he told me, it was necessary that we take a shower.

The evening was turning out to be full of surprises. No wife. Happy girls. An offer of hash from a bus driver. A secret rendezvous in the medina of the Moroccan capital. I enjoyed making the imaginary link with the film *Casablanca*. Now a shower. And only then the wine! Who knew that the inkling for a glass could lead one into such a labyrinth? But why not? In any case, I hadn't had a shower since leaving the *riad* in Marrakesh.

The next surprise was that the shower was not to take place at home, since there was evidently no bathroom in the house. Instead, we walked through the neighborhood towards a public bathhouse. On payment of a small fee, we entered a steamy room full of cubicles with wooden three-quarter-length doors of a sort familiar from the Calder Street swimming baths in Glasgow, where I had gone during the school holidays with Jean and Phyllis. Each cubicle housed an individual shower. I made my way towards one with an open door. Inside, I pushed it closed—there was no latch—and undressed. In a flash my naked host was in with me. It was a small room, now rather full, and we were squeezed tightly together.

The bus driver prepared to soap his guest, but with only a little persuasion he found his own shower room, and all was well. When we reconvened in the waiting area, he seemed not at all put out by my insistence on taking a shower in private. We were clean, there was no denying it. And now . . . some wine?

We left the public baths and took a bus towards the medina, which was more or less deserted, though it was not yet nine o'clock. At a crossroads free of traffic, from which one could see shadowy colonnades and flat roofs in all directions—as if we had to be watchful for the police—we kept the rendezvous with our dealer.

As I was introduced to a dark-skinned Arab with a thin moustache, I had the uncomfortable sensation of being presented in an unaccustomed role, a guest of honor. In among the Arabic gutturals I heard the shuffling of words like "Deutsch" and "Américain," percolating down to "Anglais"—inaccurate, but this was no time for pedantry. There were nods and smiles. The messenger produced from within the depth of his djellaba a bottle of some sort, of which I was granted a glimpse before it was once again folded into safety.

How does that seem? "Ça va?" I could only shrug my shoulders. I knew nothing. Even if I knew something, I had seen next to nothing. "Oui, ça va." At least it was red.

From that moment on, it was an embarrassing assignation. The black-marketeer named a large sum, in Moroccan dinar—let's say the equivalent of ten pounds at the time, a hundred pounds or more in today's money. I was used to living on under a pound a day.

Excuse me, monsieur, but it's simply not possible.

Immediately, he reduced the price by half. But it was still far too much. I never enjoyed this kind of bargaining anyway, which was expected of the Westerner in Morocco and placed the native vendor in the role of con man. The wine seller came down again, but—I am afraid it's impossible. His good humor, such as it was, drained away, and he got angry with us for having wasted his time. What had he been led to expect by the driver? A meeting with "an Englishman," probably, with all that it implied. Poor chap—he had found only poor me instead. He turned and walked away without a farewell. The driver and I made our way out of the medina back to the house. I would have to live without a glass of wine that evening.

Inside, the little flat-roofed house was tidied up, dimly lit and quiet. The two girls were asleep already, or pretending to be asleep, and we were soon to follow. In the living room, the driver gestured towards the seat-cum-bed against which I had rested my back while we consumed the delicious cous-cous and meat.

So kind! Yet again. "Et vous?"

He pointed to the floor. There was a rug—we were standing on it—and beneath the rug, red tiles.

During the night, my host decided that the tiled floor was too severe to sleep on, and he tried to join me—clean as I was—in the bed. His own bed, after all. But no. For this night only, it was mine. As with the shower cabin, we would have found it cramped for two.

I would have liked to say, "You are like a scorpion, my host." But all I said was: "No, monsieur, but if you want we can change places."

He returned to his hardness on the floor.

Morning came and I swished my feet over the edge of the bed on to the cool, now vacant tiles. From the depth of their headscarves, the lovely girls served coffee and flat bread left over from last night's feast, with fig jam. Flavors: the crusty *batbout* in the palm; a sweet black syrup; a girl's shy smile saved up all through the night—impressions that endure through five decades. I felt—or imagined I felt—their aching to be free.

The bus driver appeared, dressed again in his beige uniform, ready for work. I thanked them all and went down to the road in search of a lift to Tangier.

12

THE MAGUS

I

On my return from Morocco, the Glasgow autumn already frowning, I took my seat at Jack's side in the Grosvenor Café in Byres Road once again and tried to come up with ideas for *GUM/Moving Review*. It was September 1973. The magazine had suspended publication over the long summer holiday. Jack continued working as a reporter in Clydebank, while Brian Hannan developed his interest in the new British cinema.

Jack and Brian appeared to me mainstream in their tastes, whereas to me the mainstream was a diversion. I cherished the identity of the dropout. At Langside College on the Southside, where I began to study for Highers and A levels in preparation for applying to university, I established my identity as the traveler who had just come home from Away. I had walked among the minarets of Marrakesh and seen the goats in the trees. I had tasted maajun. I had stood with a foot on either side of the Bosporus and plucked stringed instruments with turbaned minstrels. I had taken tea with modern British literature's most famous junkie. He had offered me a Danish pastry instead of a fix.

A book I read between classes was Jeff Nuttall's Bomb Culture. I was hungry for any news about Trocchi, and he and Nuttall had come together in the early 1960s, plotting to overthrow the oppressive system and change society. Co-conspirators included the alternative psychiatrists R. D. Laing and

David Cooper, the Fluxus artist John Latham, the sound poet Bob Cobbing, and our own Tom McGrath, who was then the editor of *Peace News*. The satanic majesty hovering above them all was Trocchi.

The name of the master plan was project sigma (subversively lower-case), otherwise known as the Invisible Insurrection of a Million Minds. Trocchi declared it a *coup du monde*, distinct from a *coup d'état*. The invisible insurrection would result in "spontaneous universities" shooting up like consciousness-raising mushrooms across the nation, and in power passing to the elect, which would in time include everyone. The semi-criminal drug addict Trocchi—a wanted man in the United States for providing narcotic drugs to a minor—would assume temporary leadership. After the fulfilment of project sigma, the leader's role would dissolve.

William Burroughs was among those who had made written offerings to the sigma portfolio. In fact, his "M.O.B.," which Trocchi had given me in typewritten Gestetner form, and which we were about to publish in *GUM/Moving Review*, was his contribution to the project: one junkie supporting another down the road to perfectibility.

"Let's get this clear," Nuttall reported Trocchi telling him one afternoon in a pub near Marble Arch. "What this is all about is the rejection of *everything* outside that door." Nuttall had misgivings about Trocchi and about the rest of the plan. Was he himself a dropout with the inclination to drop in? He wrote amusingly of his predicament, as he made his way to a weekend convention of project sigma at a country house rented for the purpose, in Oxfordshire, in 1964. "At Reading I missed the bus so started out on the Oxford Road. An old man gave me a lift; courteous, kindly, at peace with himself, he seemed the embodiment of all that was good about the way of life we were out to destroy."

Jack traveled to London to interview Edna O'Brien, "who guards the privacy of her London exile like gold dust," he wrote. His long article for the next issue of the *Moving Review*—Burroughs's "M.O.B." was on the inside-front page—was widely admired among the 1,000-strong readership of the magazine.

"I don't do many interviews these days," she said. "I find my time rather, um, precious. You must just have caught me in the right mood. The proper vibrations, eh? I don't like being interviewed by the professionals from Fleet Street. They know all the things they're going to ask before they come." She thought a moment. "Glasgow University, now is that the one where you have that man as your, what is it?"

She was referring to Jimmy Reid, who led the Upper Clyde Shipbuilders' work-in in 1972. The word she groped for was rector. Jack returned from the visit to her house in Chelsea with his pen full of fine phrases ready to be transposed to print, about her "loose-curled, gold-red hair," her neck "almost as long as one of those erotic Modigliani models." Her eyes, he wrote, "look to be green, but she winks and says ah, just put down gray like your own, love."

My own first contribution on returning from North Africa was a piece about press coverage of the October 1973 Arab-Israeli war, sometimes known as the Yom Kippur War. Jack suggested I was well-placed to write a commentary, and the bold-face intro reflected his newspaperly instincts: "Why has the British press been lying on an Israeli slant since the fourth break-out of the Middle East war? Jim Campbell, who has traveled extensively both in Israel and in Arab lands, argues for a more balanced sympathy in current newspaper coverage."

If I was an expert on anything, it was hitch-hiking, travel, Away—I could lead you from Piraeus to the bar of the Horse Shoe, through Yugoslavia and over the Alps, in five or six hard-earth nights, plimsoll-shod and lacking a compass. Still, I was keen to write, keen to learn to write. Jack and I discussed the matter while leaning on the bar at the Horse Shoe.

"How *do* you learn to write?"

Jack: "By writing."

"Any other way?"

"By reading."

I launched the piece with some remarks made by Bertrand Russell three years earlier—"What Israel is doing today cannot be condoned, and to invoke the horrors of the past to justify those of the present is gross hypocrisy"—and combined them with historical facts filleted from a pile of books in the Mitchell Library. In the *Guardian*, the *Express*, *Telegraph*, and other papers, I found little or no sympathy for the Palestinian cause. The word itself was seldom used at the time, giving way to "Arab." I bound my new-found knowledge together with impressions left by life on Kibbutz Mishmarot. It was untutored, no doubt a little glib, but not dishonest. It was, like the Trocchi piece, the result of hard work. I was finding out that that was a literary virtue in itself. Discrimination and restraint were guided by it; talent was futile without it.

It was dishonest, on the other hand, to have allowed Jack's flattering intro to my Arab-Israeli piece to go through, and I blushed when I saw it in print. But blushing teaches lessons, too.

At Langside, I would take classes that would lead towards exams that would lead in turn, I hoped, to university. There would be no report cards and no ink rubber, no disapproving father staring at the crudely improved marks, no Mr. Crawford to find me out and no desperate salvation in the shape of a rickety printing factory in the old Fruit Market. The Glasgow Corporation bursary was modest but sufficient for part of a year. The exams to come would not be hideous traps into which I was certain to fall, but stepping stones to higher learning. "I see and aim for better things," the old King's Park Secondary motto come home to roost.

An application to a range of universities had to be made halfway through the academic year—a term it was now a pleasure to hear myself say. My first choice was Glasgow, so that I could stay in close contact with Jack, Jimmy Dunn, Kate Reader, and others in a growing circle of literary and artistic friends in and around the university itself. After all, I still had some claims on an office there, with Jack, as co-editor of the *Moving Review*. All under vaguely false pretences. I'd had a happy time with vagueness. It had given me a decent run for my money. Now I wanted something more definite. After Glasgow, I put down Edinburgh University and after Edinburgh, Reading.

On the application form, I set out the courses I would be following at Langside: A levels in English and Sociology; Highers in Art, French, which I already had but wanted to re-sit to gain a better grade, and something called Modern Studies—politics, current affairs—which was advertised as an easy option. In response, each university applied to would say either No—the answer I quickly received from Glasgow and Reading—or Yes. That came from Edinburgh, on condition of specified minimum grades.

My parents were pleased at the idea, and I was developing a faculty that permitted me to be happy to see them pleased. The center of gravity was shifting. Instead of Gilmorehill, just a few minutes' walk from my flat, I was bound for the east coast. In the autumn of 1974, when I got there, I would have turned twenty-three. Another motto: "No reward without effort," in the name of which the father had forsaken the son and left him to wander among the Children of Israel. When I did come back, thanks to a Samaritan from Flushing, New York, he greeted me warmly: "The return of the Prodigal! We'll kill the fatted mince."

II

I had read John Fowles's novel *The French Lieutenant's Woman* before arriving on Spetsai. The story was set in the year 1867 in the seaside resort of Lyme Regis, a century before its composition in a farmhouse where Fowles lived, just outside. I knew nothing about the Dorset town in reality, only the dressed-up Victorian version at the center of the novel. The discovery, from magazine clippings I consulted—again in Glasgow's Mitchell Library—that Fowles himself now lived there, gave a shine to his fictional representation. As Trocchi was present in the New York City he described in the so-called novel *Cain's Book*—like his double Joe Necchi, he worked on a scow amid the commercial river traffic on the Hudson river—so Fowles the erudite puppeteer was an actor in his own nineteenth-century staging in Dorset.

I was bewitched by the illusion of the writer emerging from the writing—stepping out from the page to shake hands with the reader. It was the same thrill that I had felt with Cocteau and his mirror: choose to walk into the world of art; then choose to walk out again. Why separate the two? You could live an ordinary life in Byres Road and, at the same time, an extraordinary one in the pages of *Les Enfants terribles* or *Cain's Book* or *The French Lieutenant's Woman*.

The most famous feature of Lyme Regis is its long, curved harbor wall, the Cobb, which plays a role in Jane Austen's *Persuasion*: "... the principal street almost hurrying into the water, the walk to the Cobb, skirting round the pleasant little bay ..." In *Persuasion*, Louisa Musgrove loses her footing and falls down the stone steps at the side of the Cobb. *The French Lieutenant's Woman* takes the reader to the Cobb on its opening page, "a long claw of old gray wall that flexes itself against the sea." The enigmatic figure of Sarah Woodruff is standing "at the seawardmost end," staring out across the waves, "like a living memorial to the drowned."

Before I had left Glasgow in the June of 1972, with the intention of traveling to the Far East, a regular in the Three in One on Woodlands Road, the pub that Jack and I favored in the university area, had let fall a surprising verdict: Well, *The French Lieutenant's Woman*'s good, she said. But *The Magus* ... That's incredible. *The Magus* was the big one.

Apparently there was something I didn't know that I ought to have known. *The Magus* was his best book. "Remember?" our friend in the pub went on. "The house of the Magus, Maurice Conchis—*conscious*—and all that ..." I kept quiet. It was a poor show to be a Fowles propagandist and not to have read or even to have heard of *The Magus*.

During the time off from my labors over the pizza ovens on Dizengoff Street, I had looked for the big novel in the second-hand bookshops of Tel Aviv, which were well stocked with

English and American paperbacks. I found a copy, and when I returned to the kibbutz after my existential adventure involving the 300 Israeli pounds, I began to read it outside my cabin on Desolation Row.

About eighty pages into the story of Nicholas Urfe and his visits to the house of the Magus, I had an unusual experience, one that the creator of a fictionalized location perhaps does not intend to provoke in his readers, but which he surely ought to welcome.

> I came to the ridge again. The sea was a pearly turquoise, the far mountains ash-blue in the windless heat. I could see the shimmering green crown of pine trees around Bourani. It was about noon when I came through the trees out on to the shingle of the beach with the chapel. It was deserted . . . A long way south a plump caique thudded past towing a line of six little lamp-boats, like a mallard with ducklings. Its bow-wave made a dark miraging ripple on the creamy blue surface of the sea, and that was all that remained of civilization . . .

As I continued turning the pages, the island on which the Magus dwells began to assume the shape of the island where I had lived and which I had recently left, Spetsai. The Phraxos of the novel is small, with a single town, no cars and a pine forest through which one must pass in order to reach the beaches and caves of the south-west. I had walked through that pine corridor, decorated with smells of oregano, thyme, and other olfactory delights yet undiscovered in Glasgow, as well as the previously unknown sound of cicadas. As Fowles's narrator, Nicholas, puts it, "they racketed in a ragged chorus, never

The Anargyrios and Korgialenios School, Spetsai, lightly disguised as the Lord Byron School in John Fowles's novel *The Magus*.

quite finding a common beat." And "huge hornets, midges, bees, bots, and ten thousand other anonymous insects."

The Lord Byron School of the novel, where Nicholas is a teacher, was unmistakeably the imposing Anargyrios and Korgialenios School, which Jerry had pointed out from the saddle. It is the place where, the author tells us—as Jerry had told me—the future rulers of Greece receive their education. It didn't look like any school I had known in Scotland: a white-and-ochre cube, three or four stories high, with pilasters framing the grand entrance. If Jerry had said it was an army barracks, I would have believed him. Only later did I discover that Takis, owner of Romeo, Zorba, and the other horses—our patron, our exploiter, our victim—was one of its products. He would have been thirty-three or thirty-four when we worked for him on Spetsai. It is possible that he had been coaxed into his fluent, acquisitive English some twenty years earlier by the author of *The Magus*.

Six years after publication of the novel, the island in the story would have been recognizable to any attentive reader wandering over Spetsai itself. It was impossible not to see it. But unless they had been there and possessed some sense of curiosity about Spetsai's wilder parts, readers of *The Magus* would have been unaware that Phraxos was modeled on a specific place. Fowles had never made the information public. Spetsai was a popular destination in 1972, but not yet the over-stuffed tourist resort it would become. There was no airport; the boat journey from Athens took five hours (the rapid Flying Dolphin had yet to surface); beyond the port, there are no villages and no antiquities to speak of; the military junta of the Colonels was still in power.

The events that take place at Maurice Conchis's villa Bourani—the elaborate, staged masques of which the sole spectator is Nicholas, the Fowles character in all but name—are fantastical but, like Phraxos itself, the house is not a complete invention. To judge by the cartographical references provided by Nicholas in the novel, Bourani is the imaginary counter-part of a real house called Villa Yiasemí, situated in the area between the bay of Aghia Anargyri, past which I trotted every other day with a posse of happy riders, and another beach at Aghia Paraskevi, or Holy Friday bay. Sometimes we stopped for drinks beneath one of the tattered thatched umbrellas. If I close my eyes and rummage through my memory, spreading my legs over the saddle again, I can convince myself that I see the whitewashed chapel at Aghia Paraskevi, visible from the seaside track and frequently mentioned in the novel.

Villa Yiasemí (jasmine) was owned by a member of a well-established local family, Ioannis Botassis. In a journal entry dated November 30, 1952, Fowles described an accidental meeting with Botassis after a swim in the bay. He had encountered the house's owner on the sands, "bald but for a wisp, in shorts and a green shirt, brown-faced, freckled, with pleasant, amiable eyes." Fowles was invited to come for coffee after he had shaken himself free of the captivating sea. It was during the course of this visit to Villa Yiasemí that the seed of *The Magus* was planted.

In the fictional realm, the beauty of the site is heightened by a concoction of magic, menace, and eroticism. On first seeing Conchis at the villa with the mysterious sign nailed to a pine tree, "Salle d'attente," Nicholas regards him as "this man who had come to 'my' desert island."

I knew how he felt. In a back-to-front way, Fowles had come to mine.

III

"Why not John Fowles?" I said one evening when Jack was presiding over a Big Ideas meeting at the Grosvenor. "The most interesting English writer of our day." I felt confident in my approval of writers I liked, as I was assured in my disdain of those I had never read. Any mention of Sillitoe or Storey would draw a look of arrogant ennui, though I later came to admire both, and many of the writers associated with them. At the time, I was too provincial to appreciate their advanced approach to provincialism.

Jack liked my suggestion and I went out into the street with the lightness that comes of having a commission to fulfil. Fowles was rumored to be reclusive but, an old hand now,

I obtained his address from the publisher without any trouble and wrote a letter requesting an interview. His reply came quickly. "Fine, but I live a hell of a way from Glasgow, as you perhaps didn't realize when you wrote. Best wishes . . . John Fowles."

I realized it perfectly well. I had accompanied Nicholas Urfe, the hero of *The Magus*, to Conchis's house on the other side of the ridge on Phraxos in more than the usual imaginative sense. I wanted to share with someone the revelation that I had spent ten weeks in 1972 living in a fictional place, and who better to share it with than the author himself, the architect of "The Godgame," the novel's working title? That I wasn't a *Magus* crank who had traveled on purpose to Spetsai after falling under the book's spell, but had had an independent life there in the house up on the hill, with Jerry and the horses, made my discovery more piquant, more "weird."

A quick, nervous phone call from our student offices and it was arranged. Fowles suggested a date: December 8, 1973.

IV

After an overnight stop with my parents in High Wycombe, I stepped down from the train that Saturday morning at Axminster station, the nearest to his home, as instructed. But where was his home? I was without any information about transport—I realized only then—or even whether there was such a thing as a bus to shuttle me from Axminster to the domain of the Lyme Regis Magus. How big a town was Lyme Regis, and how would I find him? I had the name, Belmont House, but it could have been anywhere.

There was a public telephone on the platform and from

there I dialed the Belmont number, which fortunately I had brought with me. Fowles sounded intimidatingly grumpy. He didn't drive, he said . . . but . . . (a muffled off-receiver exchange) . . . his wife would come to pick me up.

Elizabeth Fowles was tall and warm and friendly. I can see now that she was accustomed to compensating with kindness. "Are you a Hardy fan?" she asked as she switched us down the rolling, wintry, rural roads. I wasn't. I hadn't read much Hardy. I hadn't even clicked that we were in "Hardy Country," as she called it. I could talk to her about William Burroughs, Alexander Trocchi, Jean Cocteau, Hermann Hesse, John Fowles. I had read *The Magus*, and I had accepted the invitation to inhabit its imaginary land. Half a million others had read it too but, unlike them, I had tramped the real-life terrain of which the story was a reflection: that shaded and scented and sea-washed place where the Mediterranean was "most itself." I was, like Nicholas Urfe, like Conchis, like Fowles himself—Elizabeth, too—a resident of Phraxos, the conceptual isle. I had come to Lyme Regis to claim my citizenship.

Having heard the crunch of gravel in the courtyard as Elizabeth parked the car, Fowles appeared at the door of Belmont House to welcome us. "Big, bearded and burly," I jotted down later. "He transferred his cigarette to his lips and his Scotch from right hand to left in order to greet me."

Throughout the day, Elizabeth treated me with benign patience, as she would have a peculiar nephew; only much later did I learn that it was an instinct in search of an object. "She has so many steady, earthy, commonsense qualities beneath the waywardness," Fowles wrote in his journal in 1953. "A gangling, elegant creature." I sensed her maternal warmth straight away, without having to explain it to myself. What might she

Belmont House, Lyme Regis. Fowles opened the door—"big, bearded and burly."

have seen? A slim boy with long blond hair in a military jacket and funny-colored trousers, half-starved, in need of a bath, probably, socially unformed but striving to be polite.

Belmont House, two stories high, washed in shaded pink, has the shape of a double cube. Built in 1777 as "maritime villa," it sits at the top of the hill on the main road leading into Lyme. At the back is a large, sloping garden, with a view of the Cobb. Fowles bought the place in 1968, moving from an isolated farmhouse, Underhill, not far away. He started *The French Lieutenant's Woman* at Underhill and finished it off here, in the room above the lobby in which I was now standing. He loved Belmont, but had loved even more the solitary existence of Underhill Farm. They had to leave, he explained, because landslips on the cliffside on which the house was perched had made staying impossible. Elizabeth, I discovered, hated the loneliness of her life in both places.

As we ate lunch in the spacious kitchen and I blethered on profusely, any residual nervousness now released, he made attempts to be chatty and cheerful, but it wasn't his proper mode. When he saw the tape recorder, he said, "Oh, you use one of those things, do you?" (For a long time afterwards, I made it a point of principle not to.) When my Scottish two-pin plug failed to fit his English three-pin socket, he scowled and impatience filled the air. Elizabeth stepped in and we drove together half a mile to an electrical goods shop on Lyme's Broad Street, sloping down to the sea ("the principal street almost hurrying into the water," as Jane Austen wrote), where she bought an adaptor. I would happily have spent the afternoon being shepherded round the town and on to the Cobb by her.

By the time we sat down before the fire in the living room in order to "get down to business," as Fowles put it, he had recovered his mood, and he spoke generously to his young interlocutor. "Some critics have said *The Magus* did not achieve what it set out to do." Did I really say that? What critics? Why did I pay attention to them instead of relying on my sense of gratitude and wonder? "No argument from me," Fowles replied disarmingly. At my prodding, he expanded: "You must remember it was a first novel and I tried to say too much."

Fowles had begun writing *The Magus* in the 1950s, several years before completing *The Collector* (1963), his publishing debut but not his first novel. After the success of that book, in Britain and the US (a film by William Wyler was released in 1965, starring Terence Stamp and Samantha Eggar), he resumed work on what was at different times called "The Godgame" and "The Magos."

"It was written by a young man," he said into my tape recorder, "who really didn't have very much experience of life,

John Fowles in Lyme Regis, circa 1973. *Courtesy of Sarah Fowles.*

but who had a tremendous love of narrative. It says so many things and nothing really is concluded. One thing that worries me about it now is that it's not terribly well written. One day I hope to rewrite it." Three years later, he did so.

He talked about his deep sense of Englishness. If anything, he felt part Greek and part French, but English all over—"not British."

"You are as much a stranger to me as any American."

Creative-writing courses were not yet a feature of university English faculties. Fowles would have hated them. He spoke disparagingly anyway of "the whole academic set-up" as a "grave block" to the writer. "If there's one gang of people I'd like to see thrown into the sea it's the professors of English Literature."

He had a belief that "capitalism must outgrow itself," but was not drawn to the idea of a "violent overthrow" of the system. "Because there's a massively powerful fascist element in Britain, and a potential disaster could occur." This is one of the ideas behind the action of *The Collector*. The central character

Clegg's feeling that he has the right to suppress the freedom of another, Miranda, grows out of his lack of understanding, and eventually hatred, of art and culture. It was one of Fowles's obsessions: the menace posed to society by philistinism, in which he discerned a nascent fascism. He went on to say that *The Aristos*, his carnet of personal philosophy, was "the sort of book a French writer would publish naturally." His editor had advised against it, "but you have to take the iron fist with publishers occasionally. I wouldn't want this American situation where your publishing editor dominates your life."

The information that I had just returned from Greece, where I was staying on Spetsai—"it's the same, isn't it? . . . it's Phraxos"—surprised him. He allowed a moment's pause in the middle of one of his diatribes against the ruination of Greece, as if his power of speech had unaccustomedly stumbled. Then he said, "Good Lord," and called for Elizabeth.

He had never returned to the island that the world knew as Spetsai, but which we—the elite assembly of Conchis, Elizabeth, Fowles himself, and now me—called Phraxos. He did not wish to visit Greece while the Colonels remained in power. Their influence was only slightly more oppressive than that other tyranny, tourism, which had overtaken Spetsai and many other Greek islands. Like others who loved Greece in the 1950s—Patrick Leigh Fermor, for one—he abominated the curse of progress. I knew little about the Colonels, who had not prevented me from discovering the pines and the tortoises, the "pearly turquoise" of the sea, the tavernas, the retsina and fasolakia, Romeo and Zorba. I was oppressed, rather, by the tyranny of rain and cold and wind, under which we spent our lives in the north.

The remainder of that long afternoon passed awkwardly.

The next train for London, the last of the day, did not depart from Axminster until a quarter to seven. I should have offered to take a walk by myself through the streets of Lyme Regis, but I might have wandered too far and then missed it. One or other of them could have volunteered to escort me down to the Cobb, if only to make the time pass more quickly for the relief of all, but no. Fowles gave me a tour of the house, which included his collection of nineteenth-century erotica. He mentioned a French tale of a black slave girl, dating from the early years of that century, which he would "one day like to translate into English." I asked him to repeat the title. "You won't have heard of it." He brought out *Ourika* by Claire de Duras (1826) in a limited edition four years after our meeting.

At some stage, unable to put up any longer with questions about which records he listened to and if he had a favorite pub—Miles Davis's *In a Silent Way* was one answer to the first question; to the second it was the Masons Arms in nearby Branscombe—Fowles disappeared upstairs to his study, leaving me alone with Elizabeth in the big kitchen. She cooked a cheese omelette, so delicious I've never forgotten it, fortifying me for the journey back to High Wycombe.

At just after six o'clock, we all three climbed into the car and headed for Axminster. Although he had chosen to live in out-of-the-way places, Fowles told me he would be "a menace behind the wheel." He had eyes only for wildflowers by the roadside, a butterfly or a bird darting overhead. He gave me a copy of his latest book, a collection of poems, published in the US. It has a cobalt blue cover, an echo of the sea surrounding Phraxos, with just *Poems* and the author's name.

As I stepped on to the train, Elizabeth asked me to be sure to send them a copy of the article when it appeared.

V

Not long after I returned from Dorset, it became clear that our magazine was headed for trouble. The Students' Representative Council had withdrawn its funding, not unreasonably, since the publication was no longer called *Glasgow University Magazine*, or *GUM*, but the *Moving Review*. Looking back at the issues we produced, I find a report by Brian Hannan on the film director Lindsay Anderson, "returning to work in his old stamping ground, the theatre" (*The Farm* by David Storey opened at the Royal Court in the spring of 1973); an interview with Stephane Grappelli ("*GUM* went along to meet the grand old man of swing"); a discussion of football violence in Glasgow. There was Jack's Edna O'Brien piece, and an interview with George Melly—again by Brian, a better writer than I had the decency to acknowledge at the time—my commentary on the Yom Kippur War, and a good deal besides. But there was hardly anything about local activities or student organizations. The very idea of acknowledging Freshers' Week or events of that sort would have embarrassed us. Of the principal figures involved in the magazine's production, only one, Brian, was studying at the university. The *Moving Review* had already moved itself in spirit out of Gilmorehill. Now it was going nowhere.

My Fowles piece, towards which I had been making notes since he and Elizabeth saw me off, clutching the signed copy of *Poems* to my breast, remained in limbo. It was to be another two years before I transcribed the tape in question-answer form and submitted it to an academic quarterly at the University of Wisconsin, which accepted it for publication.

I dutifully sent the typescript to Lyme Regis for approval, as required by the journal ("Mr. Fowles has seen and approved the text"). It came back with inky emendations on every page, and a letter. "I wish you could have given me more warning, as I feel it badly needs editing. I should hate to see it printed in its present verbatim form. I've done what I can to make it a little more coherent." For the first time, I felt offended by his characteristic bad temper, and huffily omitted to take on all the suggested changes—something I would never have done later without good reason.

Publication in the handsome Autumn 1976 number of *Contemporary Literature* went ahead. It was book-size, floppy and desirable, on good paper, with a scarlet cover. "An Interview with John Fowles" had top billing. I added a brief introduction:

> We conducted the interview before the fire on a winter's day after lunch. Mr. Fowles frowned when he saw the tape recorder. He speaks in an English public-school voice, which he punctuates with such gap-fillers as "you know," "I mean" and "sort of," quite often leaving his sentences incomplete and dangling in the air between the two speakers. He answered with impatience one minute and with friendly warmth the next, but in the end his confidence—"I don't need people, really"—is not difficult to believe.

*

A footnote: In 2006, the second volume of Fowles's *Journals* was published, covering the years 1966 to 1990, and I was asked to review it for the *New York Times Book Review*. I recalled his brief note to me, dated November 9, 1973: "Fine, but I live a hell of a way from Glasgow." Might he have made some record of our meeting? Unsurprisingly, I consulted the index in the book to see if there was any reference to it; equally unsurprisingly, I found none.

The entry for October 31, 1973, however—nine days before his reply to me was written—revealed that Fowles had just declined an offer to give the Clark Lectures at Cambridge University. In addition, he had received "a profile request from the *Sunday Times*. Also refused." The suggestion from a student magazine in Glasgow must have arrived a day or two later, and to this he acquiesced, giving up most of a Saturday to answer questions posed by a raw youth from a foreign country. It's hard to dislike that.

*

A second footnote: In 2015, forty-two years after Fowles had sat before the fire speaking into my mammoth cassette recorder, I received an invitation, in my capacity as a columnist on the *Times Literary Supplement*, to spend a night at Belmont. The house had been bought by the Landmark Trust from Fowles's widow, his second wife, Sarah, and after extensive renovation was to be launched as an up-market bed and breakfast. "We are about to open Belmont," the message read,

> which is John Fowles's former home in Lyme Regis. It is a beautiful place and he wrote much of his work there including *Daniel Martin* and *The Ebony Tower*. *The French Lieutenant's Woman* was completed and published while he lived there and the writing room has a view over the Cobb. I wondered if you could cover the launch of Belmont in a considered way, including its

history and Fowles's time there. We might even be able
to organize a night for you there, to absorb the setting.

I was tempted, and in response set out a little of my Fowles
history. "The house will be rather different to when you visited it before," came the reply. "However of course some of
John Fowles's books are there (the ones we could recover from
auction), some have his annotations. His writing room is still
there etc. Décor-wise it will be very different to last time."

I contacted Sarah Fowles (Elizabeth had died in 1990), who
told me she was not pleased by the changes the Landmark
Trust had made. "They have pulled down all he and Elizabeth lived in, ditto with me," she said. "They have cut down all
his trees, planted by him. The garden I have been told is des-
ecrated." She felt that Belmont had been turned into a "vulgar
villa," reminiscent of "a millionaires' row-style of house you
might find in certain avenues in North London. It's not John
Fowles's house, because they have pulled down all the part we
lived in."

In the end, I was unable to arrange a convenient time with
the Trust to stay overnight in Belmont, where I had heard the
gravel crunch under Elizabeth's braking wheels in December
1973, and where I beheld the bearded and burly Magus of the
south coast at the door a moment later. I didn't really want to
go anyway, as a pawn in a publicity stunt. Belmont was being
promoted as a house haunted by Fowles, in which things were
to be explained to would-be pilgrims in a mundane way. Better
to settle for the spirit in memory.

13

"HOW LONG . . . HAS THAT
TRAIN BEEN GONE"

I

Edinburgh University welcomed me for my first lecture on Monday, October 7, 1974. I was accepted in spite of paltry qualifications—age might have been taken into consideration—and gratitude has never faltered. On my arrival there I had the feeling of sheltering under a benign climate. My wish was to study for a four-year MA (Hons) in English Language and Literature, specializing in American Literature. The general Bachelor of Arts (BA) degree entailed three years of basic study in English, Philosophy, History of Art, and other subjects of the student's choosing. I was advised to enter as a BA candidate and to seek to switch to an MA, with the chosen specialization, after two years. That way I would avoid outright rejection on the grounds of insufficient qualifications, or because "the course you inquired about is full." It was predicted—correctly, it turned out—that some places booked in advance by MA candidates would be vacated after two years, either by a change of mind or through exam failure.

With Colin Nicholson and Faith Pullin in charge, I therefore began my study of American Literature in the autumn term, 1976. It was, really, a two-year course in reading books and talking about them with people who knew more than you did. We studied William Faulkner, John Dos Passos, Ernest Hemingway, and other writers of the 1920s, 30s, and 40s, not forgetting the nineteenth-century greats. Nicholson and Pullin also placed a stress on the literature of our own time. This was America, after all: a vastness still in the process of being discovered.

A feature of the course was the separation of literary work according to school or ethnic group. It was unusual in the mid-1970s in having a section on Native American novelists— N. Scott Momaday and Thomas Berger (author of the novel *Little Big Man*) were two—and in giving serious attention to African American writers. We read the one novel by Ralph Ellison, *Invisible Man*, as well as his essays, a novel and autobiography by Richard Wright, a play by Amiri Baraka (LeRoi Jones), two novels by the little-known William Melvin Kelley, which we all liked (*A Different Drummer* and *Dem*), and a book of short stories by black women: Paule Marshall, Gwendolyn Brooks, Alice Walker, and others. The contemporary emphasis gave our studies an up-to-the-minute feel, a sense of personal involvement with the author through the work. This turned out to be more than usually the case for me with one writer, in particular.

II

My father's job at British Rail in London had taken a turn into what he felt was a dead end, and my parents moved from High Wycombe back to Scotland in 1975, buying a house in the Perthshire village of Braco. They were also worried that Julie was not being tested sufficiently at her school in Buckinghamshire. The twelve-year-old Glasgow girl had merged with a Home Counties double. Now she would change back again.

For my father, it was convenient for the golf courses at

Gleneagles. For my mother, there was the subconscious attraction of its closeness to the village of Blackford, where she had lived as a child in the 1920s while her father worked as an all-purpose builder on the construction of the Gleneagles Hotel.

One Sunday evening, after Dad had seen me off on the train at Dunblane on the journey back to Edinburgh, I opened a book that was on the slate for discussion in the coming week. It was gratifyingly slim. The dedication itself was stylish:

> *for* James
>   James
>   Luc James

It consisted of a brief introductory text—"My Dungeon Shook: Letter to my nephew on the one-hundredth anniversary of the Emancipation"—followed by a longer piece; together, they amounted to under 100 pages. I had thought I was beginning a short novel but once settled in the carriage realized I was reading a personal testament. The opening declaration of the extended essay hit forcibly:

> I underwent, during the summer that I became four-teen, a prolonged religious crisis. I use the word "reli-gious" in the common, and arbitrary, sense, meaning that I then discovered God, His saints and angels, and His blazing Hell.

The cover of the Penguin edition of *The Fire Next Time* showed James Baldwin dressed in a sheepskin coat holding an infant black boy whom readers ever since have assumed to be his nephew. In fact, the child is an orphaned youngster whom

Baldwin had encountered on the day the photograph was taken (by Steve Schapiro) in 1963, while on a reporting trip in Durham, North Carolina. The boy's eyes wander away from the camera, as the photogenic author in profile gazes pensively downwards.

Not only did the essay at the heart of *The Fire Next Time* have a gripping opening, it came with an arresting title: "Down at the Cross: Letter from a region in my mind." These titles were all drawn from the words of Negro spirituals, in the scriptural shorthand of which the author had been immersed as a young man. Before reaching the end of the first paragraph, he has set his fourteenth birthday in an alarming context:

> What I saw around me that summer in Harlem was what I had always seen; nothing had changed. But now, without any warning, the whores and pimps and rack-eteers on the Avenue had become a personal menace. It had not occurred to me that I could become one of them, but now I realized that we had been produced by the same circumstances.

Unusual in many ways, Baldwin struck me as being unique in this: he held all his experience at the ready, both personal and ancestral, in a continuous and dramatic present. It was always at the front of his head, prepared for persuasive argument or for heated rhetoric, the one frequently following the other. The task of digesting this experience, making sense of it, or trying to, was a perpetual engagement. It meant understand-ing, or, as he might have said, "decoding," the actions of white people, since—as he strove to make readers see—his existence as a mid-century American Negro was at the mercy of their moves, whims, strengths and fallibilities. And his desire for change was directed at white people, too, often in a tone of sympathy. "Any real change involves the breakup of the world as one has known it, the loss of all that gave one an identity, the end of safety."

It was thrilling to be brought face to face with a contemporary writer at the front line of a modern existential conflict. Baldwin was an eloquent, patient, even tender guide. With the deftest of touches, he made social and historical "circumstances" mirror the circumstance of his own life. A line of Scripture, a snapshot of a school classroom, a parental lecture, a humiliating encounter with warm, budding girls so recently familiar from Bible lessons—these and other phenomena are brought into play in the first few paragraphs of *The Fire Next Time*. The words skimmed across the ocean that autumn Sunday evening to give the reader on the Dunblane–Linlithgow–Edinburgh train, four decades removed from the 1930s setting, a high-resolution picture of an unusually alert and sensitive Harlem boy.

From that slim volume I moved to others: novels, collections of essays and short stories. Quite soon I had read them all. Those that were hard to find, I sought in the library. Just the mention of a piece that did not reveal itself between the covers of a book—*Notes of a Native Son* (1955) and *Nobody Knows My Name* (1961) were the two main collections besides *The Fire Next Time*—was enough to set me on a quest. I studied every magazine article about him I could lay hands on.

There were book-length essays, too. One morning, I went to buy the newspaper at the newsagent across the street from my flat in Forrest Road and was amazed to see on the revolving bookstand a copy of *The Devil Finds Work*, Baldwin's disre-

garded book on blacks in the American cinema. I had ordered
it some weeks earlier in the National Library of Scotland,
where I had sat at a desk among scholars and browsers and
read it fleetingly. The discovery in McColl's lightened my day,
my week. I read *The Devil Finds Work* again, and then again.
The rhetoric rumbling through its pages was committed to
memory and recited to indulgent colleagues. "The grapes of
wrath are stored in the cotton fields and migrant shacks and
ghettoes of this nation . . . and in the eyes and hearts and per-
ceptions of the wretched everywhere, and in the ruined earth

of Vietnam, and in the old men, seeing visions, and in the young men, dreaming dreams . . ."

These light Corgi paperbacks fitted neatly into the pocket of a corduroy jacket and entered Edinburgh pubs, settling themselves at a table or on a barstool, desiring to be opened one more time. I would select something from the bookshelf, then set off alone on a Friday evening after the last lecture, intending to visit three or four different pubs, to read an essay in each, finding a fish supper in the interval. This way, I entertained myself. I was having a conversation with Baldwin himself. An essay by him was a storehouse of eloquence and charm, a lesson on style and dynamics—how to manage tact and presentation—a lecture on morality: "Notes of a Native Son," "Equal in Paris," "The Black Boy Looks at the White Boy" (about his bittersweet friendship with Norman Mailer), "Alas, Poor Richard" (a triple-decker on his mentor-turned-adversary, Richard Wright). There was pleasure in revisiting slighter essays—"Notes for a Hypothetical Novel," "East River, Downtown"—in the hope of imbibing again some neglected perception. "Hatred, which could destroy so much, never failed to destroy the man who hated, and this was an immutable law." What kind of personal ordeal bestowed the authority that allowed one to declare, at the age of about thirty, "this was an immutable law"? One day a friend from university entered my flat and, seeing a familiar book on the table, said, with an affectionate laugh in her voice, "Oh, Jim, you're not reading *The Fire Next Time again!*"

The Devil Finds Work had been practically ignored by the British press at the time of its original publication in 1976. Regarded in the mid-1960s as a whirlwind, Baldwin was now viewed—with relief by some, perhaps—as a storm played out.

Just an extreme weather event. The mood of the civil rights movement in the US had changed and its public face had hardened. The outstretched hand of James Baldwin was rebuffed by the clenched fist of Eldridge Cleaver; the Harlem boy's toothy grin was overshadowed by Stokely Carmichael's frown in dark glasses. It happened as early as 1966, when the Black Panthers began to occupy the limelight in the civil rights arena that had once belonged to him. Baldwin opened his arms to greet his younger brothers, but they didn't even share the same body language. Cleaver wrote menacingly about the "faggot" at the back of the room. Their militant posturing was miles removed from his natural stance, yet he strove to see things from their point of view. People began to ask: what *is* Baldwin's stance? As the years passed, the question became increasingly hard to answer. He was here (non-violence); he was there (militancy); suddenly he was nowhere to be seen.

Little by little, I uncovered facts about his present existence and the reasons behind the perception of him as a yesterday man. He had spent most of his adult life abroad, sometimes in Turkey but mainly in France. ("I was born in New York, but have lived only in pockets of it. In Paris, I lived in all parts of the city.") Settled since 1971 in the bijou Provençal village of Saint-Paul de Vence, surrounded by a camp of mainly non-literary friends and hangers-on, reading the newspapers at a day's remove, he could hardly fail to be out of touch with trends in America.

This happens to people tricked by time in all walks of life: the music changes, leaving them dancing the same old steps, looking mildly foolish. As a public intellectual, a worse fate had befallen Baldwin: he was boring his audience.

Leaving McColl's in Forrest Road with my neat black-and-red paperback of *The Devil Finds Work*, I had no cause to be occupied with these questions. "For I have seen the devil, by day and by night, and have seen him in you and in me . . ." At the end of a university seminar, a passing member of the faculty overheard me enthuse to Colin Nicholson about an earlier but equally neglected book, *No Name in the Street*. He regarded me with polite curiosity. "Is he still around?"

The question irritated me. I replied that he certainly was. Before long, I would be trying to have him around here.

III

The university had rewarded me handsomely, not only in respect of studies. In my early weeks as a student, in a Philosophy tutorial, I fell in love, a first experience of sublime passion. Her name was Diana, she was from another country—England—and the relationship fitted itself as a parallel to our education. Before the climax of final exams and degree, however, she decided she wanted to leave the university, to leave Edinburgh, to return to London to seek work in the theater, to leave me. We continued to be friends, but the great event was over.

I felt lonely, and particularly lonely at weekends. In order to outflank time, I invented ways to generate excitement. One Saturday morning, on the spur of the moment, I set off for Glasgow to watch Rangers vs Celtic in a League Cup Final at Hampden Park, expecting to buy a ticket at the ground— and did so, finding myself as a half-hearted Rangers supporter in a section of the Hampden stand reserved for wholehearted Celtic fans. I didn't hide my allegiance, and the surrounding spectators were open about theirs. When Rangers scored, I cheered. When Celtic did, I applauded. A whisky bottle was passed along the row of seats from hand to hand, with a small glass. I can't remember who won the match, but I have never forgotten the people who surrounded me. Ever since, when asked the question that inevitably comes a Glaswegian's way on the subject of football, I provoke bafflement by replying that I support Rangers *and* Celtic. It was only later that the facts of our family background came to light.

Sometimes I phoned my mother on a Saturday morning and said, "I was thinking of coming through . . ." Dad would pick me up at Dunblane. There would be drinks at six. A roasted pheasant on the table at eight. One of my sisters might arrive. The next morning, while Mum made her way to Ardoch Parish Church, where she would soon become the organist, Dad and I walked in the Highland foothills near Gleneagles. They were understanding about Diana, about whom Dad had said, "She's a looker, all right. The mystery is what she sees in you."

One morning I arose with a different idea of how to fill the yawning weekend hours: I would write a letter to James Baldwin.

This I did, at some length, trying to express in mature terms what his writing had meant to me. I rounded it off with an invitation: would he consider coming to Edinburgh, to talk to the students at the university? If so, we would be thrilled to have him. Sometime in May would be best.

I folded my letter into an envelope. Then I telephoned Diana in London. I had learned the previous year that a man she knew, a film-maker called Michael Raeburn, was a friend of Baldwin. They seemed to be part of a jet set that existed for me only in fiction and in the pages of magazines: meetings in London, in Paris, on the Côte d'Azur. Michael was trying to raise money to make a film of Baldwin's second novel,

Giovanni's Room, and they were writing a script together. I had met Michael at Diana's attic in Belsize Park, where I now went to visit, as she sometimes came to Edinburgh to stay with me.

I told her what I had done and asked if she thought Michael would be willing to pass on Baldwin's address. He obliged, and soon my fan letter (I would never have thought of it like that) was on its way to the south of France.

Did I expect to receive a reply? I think I probably did. It duly arrived one day in March, on a Saturday morning, suitably enough. There was stylish handwriting on the front, and the name and address in the top left corner: Baldwin, 06570 Saint-Paul, France. The brief message inside was not written by Baldwin himself.

Dear Sir,
  Mister Baldwin would prefer to speak to the students
  of the University of Edinburgh in April when he is on
  his way to California. The date would be between the
  15th and the 20th of April.

It was signed: "Yours truly, Bernard Hassell."

What was supposed to happen now? The reader may well ask, for I hadn't a clue. James Baldwin was coming, and I was to be his host. I would go to the pub as I had before: the Café Royal near Princes Street or the Bailie at Stockbridge, where I had dipped into his books and imagined myself in his company. But now *I would be in his company*. We would talk about *The Fire Next Time* and *Another Country*—not just in my Friday-night fantasy, but in reality. I had the letter from Saint-Paul de Vence. It said so.

I went to see Faith Pullin. With her assistance and that of

Colin Nicholson, we could easily find somewhere for him to speak. There were plenty of guest speakers at Edinburgh, but usually they were academics or local authors. Sometimes a prominent politician was invited. I have no idea if they were paid, but if they came from the south of France, on the way to California—never mind if they were world-famous or not—they expected to have somewhere comfortable to sleep, wash and dress, to be fed and otherwise refreshed, to be ferried from the airport when they arrived and back again when it came time to leave. To be put on an aeroplane and have the fare paid. No doubt to have all these things arranged in advance. *By me?* I had only been in the air once in my life, on the furtive flight from Athens to Tel Aviv.

Faith was enthusiastic, but she had few more ideas of how to go about hosting the great writer than I had. She suggested applying to the cultural wing of the American Consulate in Edinburgh. Perhaps they had a fund for events such as this? I did so, and received the written equivalent of a shrug. We talked to one or two people in the English department about it, but got scant interest in return, and no money. We did a brief accounting, and I jotted the results on the back of an envelope—the envelope in which the acceptance of the speaking engagement had arrived:

£20 students
£30 NAASP
£30 Eng
£25 Faculty

I wrote "understand not normal" and "course running B"— prompts suggested by Faith to persuade "other orgs" to help finance our project.

One hundred and five pounds: that is the sum we hoped to find in order to bring "B" to Edinburgh in 1978. The "£20 students" I assume was meant to be the proceeds of a whip round. The organization sheltering behind NAASP has escaped from memory. In the event, we raised none of it.

April was approaching ("The date would be between the 15th and the 20th of April"). If James Baldwin wanted to come to Edinburgh, I wasn't about to be the one to tell him not to. I consulted Michael Raeburn, who didn't seem unduly worried. "He might just appear out of nowhere and sleep on your floor. That's the kind of thing he does."

This was encouraging. It would have suited me fine. All the other stuff that didn't concern me—money, principally—I could assume, for a satisfying moment or two, did not concern him either. We would sort it all out once he got here.

April 15 came and went, without a ring of the telephone to say that he was on his way, or a knock on the door to announce that he was already with us, happy to bed down on my floor.

News arrived in the form of a Post Office telegram. I was at home when it dropped through the letterbox. It bore the date "18 Apr 78."

Nice/TF/STPAUL 25 18 1505
MONSIEUR JAMES CAMPBELL 22 FORREST
ROAD EDINBURGH /1
UNABLE TO MAKE THE DATES SET FORTH
IN YOUR LETTER PLEASE CONTACT ME FOR
LATER DATE
JAMES BALDWIN STPAULDEVENCE (93) 328 790

I was disappointed, though also relieved. I was touched by his considerateness, and by the suggestion of a "later date." It would give me more time to make the preparations, though I still had little idea of what they were. For now, there was the challenge of a telephone call to the South of France.

I made it one early evening, on the spur of the moment, as I passed a red telephone box near Tollcross. With a pile of coins at the ready, I dialed the number. A distant voice answered— a gruff, trochaic "Hey-lo" that would soon become familiar. This was followed by a voice that said, "May I speak to James Baldwin, please?" The words seemed to have been spoken by a person standing next to me.

He came on the line and I heard that low-slung, honey-and-brandy tone for the first time. I told him how much I had admired his most recent book, *The Devil Finds Work*. He acknowledged this with "You are very kind," a stock response which he imbued with a natural elegance. He was sorry not to have made it to Edinburgh. Something had turned up and he wasn't going to California, after all. As for the later date: "I thought I could come to Edinburgh in August, and speak to the students then."

That suited me fine, I said, but unfortunately it was a month when most of the students would be on holiday. Ah, then— here he used a phrase that was new to me—"It's a dead letter."

I understood what it meant. I was prepared to let it go. We wound up the call with polite formalities, and I left the telephone box.

IV

With the start of summer, something else turned up. At the conclusion of four years of study—in the library, in the lecture theaters of the David Hume Tower and in the eighteenth-century terrace of Buccleuch Place, I passed my degree exams and applied for a job. It wasn't much of a job, in respect of the money to be earned (hardly any), but in terms of the scope it offered for literary exploration, for a different reading of "trouble and travel"—experience, in a word—it was the best I could have wished for.

The editorship of the *New Edinburgh Review* (NER) had become vacant. The quarterly magazine was published by Edinburgh University Student Publications Board (EUSPB) but it was not a student magazine in any recognizable shape. Under the EUSPB constitution, the editorship had to be advertised every two years. The sitting editor was free to reapply, in hope of being re-elected. Those were the rules.

I had already been a member of the Publications Board— Gordon Brown was its dominant presence, with the air of prime minister-in-waiting even then—and I had been writing regularly for its weekly broadsheet, *Student*. I applied for the post of editor of the *NER*, for which I would be interviewed by people who were, in some cases, my friends. The same went for certain other candidates, including the current editor, Owen Dudley Edwards, a lecturer in the History department.

By then I had added to my portfolio by writing some pieces for the *New Statesman* and publishing a number of poems in magazines, including the *Scottish Review*, edited from Glasgow by Maurice Lindsay. In its pages, my lines appeared alongside those of George Mackay Brown, Norman MacCaig, Iain Crichton Smith and other Scottish poets to whose work Diana, the colonial girl from Kenya and Surrey, had introduced me. I wrote about Norman Mailer and Hermann Hesse for the *New Statesman*, about Andy Warhol for *Student*, and reviewed art exhibitions in the city. I tried to craft a prose style in which I would hear my own voice. The hardest thing of all in writing is to sound like yourself. Eventually, I reached an understanding that the kind of writing I liked kept its feet on the ground. It was a Scottish style: commonsensical, skeptical, impatient of cant, alert to the value of subterranean humor.

Somewhere amid these developing cadences I felt the air of a place where I might live. I wasn't reckless enough to refer to this possible future as a career, but I began to think I could mould my life to fit the contours of my sentences, if only my resolution were strong enough—to make a living by my pen, in short. A skimpy living, of course. But what else was I going to do?

I was not casual in my application for the editorship. On a Friday afternoon, I sat before the interviewing panel with sensible things to say about the direction I foresaw the *New Edinburgh Review* taking, about the people I intended to ask to write for it—all the poets mentioned above became regular contributors—and about what I saw as the weakness of its present state. It was not wide-ranging enough. There were too many single-theme issues. The articles—many by academics from the university—were monotonous and overlong.

Before the day was out, a member of the interviewing panel came to the door at 22 Forrest Road to tell me the job was mine.

V

My editorship was still in its early stages when a book arrived in the office: *The Making of Jazz: A Comprehensive History* by James Lincoln Collier. It didn't take long to decide what had to be done. I wrote another letter to Saint-Paul de Vence, tucked it into Collier's book, and put the parcel in the post. His writings contained many allusions to jazz, I pointed out to Baldwin (I felt entitled to write as if I knew what I was talking about), but he had never written a separate essay on the subject. "It occurred to me that you might welcome the chance to do so."

It took three months, by which time I had given up, but one day I went into the office to find my own letter on top of the in-tray. It had been returned to me with a message underneath, in large writing in black ink: "Would love to arrange to do a long piece: but cannot do it within the dead-line. Am not free before the end of May."

No "please contact me" this time. It was taken for granted that I would—weren't we old pals by now?—and, once I had worked up the courage, I did.

One rarely got straight through to Baldwin on the telephone. The call was usually answered by a secretary or a guest or a brother. They sometimes sounded gruff, but once I gave my name I was handed over. And the welcoming words were always warm and delivered in the same melodious tone: "Hey, baby, how are you?"

I said I was thrilled to learn that he would write about jazz for our magazine.

"I'd love to do that, baby. Can you send me the book?"

I pointed out that I already had. Baldwin said he must have lost it. Not to worry: I would have another delivered direct from the publishers. We agreed a date in July. I told him to write as long a piece as he wanted.

There was one other matter, which I thought best to settle now.

"This magazine . . . it doesn't have much money . . ."

There was a pause at his end. Then he came back with one

of those imperishable remarks that leave themselves engraved on memory, like Bruce Dryden's insistence to my father at the police station in St Andrew's Square that "Jim didn't steal anything."

Baldwin said: "Who mentioned money?"

I had consulted the higher-ups at EUSPB and it was agreed that we could stretch to £80.

"Eighty pounds? . . ." Another of his eloquent pauses. "That's OK."

I put down the receiver with a feeling of elation. James Baldwin. Writing for the first time about jazz. Commissioned by me. Who mentioned money?

VI

In the first few months of my editorship, I combined *New Edinburgh Review* duties with a summer job that I had held the year before and had enjoyed, as a driver for Edinburgh Council Department of Social Work. The garage, a vast hangar filled with cars, vans, single- and double-decker buses, was situated near the foot of Leith Walk, but daily duties took me all over the city and beyond. Sometimes I would park a van or small bus outside EUSPB's Buccleuch Street office, then dart inside to pick up the mail and send out suggestions for essays and reviews, or requests for stories and poems, to writers I admired. We published articles by Angus Calder (on African fiction), Douglas Dunn (on Hugh MacDiarmid), Allan Massie (on the resurrected James Kennaway), Tom Nairn (on the 1979 referendum on Scottish independence), the playwright E. A. Whitehead on Brecht, Rick Cluchey on producing *Waiting for Godot* in San Quentin prison, stories and poems by Ron Butlin, Edwin Morgan, Naomi Mitchison—a frequent contributor, and the only one born in the nineteenth century—and others.

My stated intention at the interview had been to blend a Scottish perspective with an outlook on the wider world. George Mackay Brown was generous with short stories, Iain Crichton Smith with poems typed in a mangle of red and black ribbon, on crumpled scraps of paper torn from other scraps, but always worth printing. Norman MacCaig sent poems with a covering note: "If they seem worthwhile, print them. If not, put them in the bin." I persuaded James Kelman to return to publishing after he had given up for some years in disgust and desperation. His story "Keep moving & no questions" was printed in the Winter 1979 issue, together with an article— at the opposite end of the Scottish intellectual spectrum—by David Daiches on Thomas Carlyle.

For the internationalist, there was an amusing account by Henry Miller of meeting his mother in heaven (Miller died on the day after the issue was published; I later found out, to my disappointment, that the piece had been published before) and a foreword to a new edition of *The Collector* by John Fowles. In London, I visited Trocchi at Observatory Gardens and heard from his own lips the admission—expressed with a great and weary "Ach!"—that his heroin addiction was "a drag." We went together to an afternoon drinking club, where Alex took delight in baffling the waiter by crying out, "A hauf an' a hauf, Jimmeh!" But I had no luck in extracting something publishable for the magazine.

Instead, I reprinted the short Burroughs article, "M.O.B.," that Trocchi had given me a few years previously, which had originally appeared in *GUM/Moving Review*. The *NER* contributors' budget being exhausted by then, I sent Burroughs my personal check for ten pounds. He forwarded it to his literary agent, who returned it to Buccleuch Place with an unamused note and demand for a larger sum. Pat Kavanagh was also Douglas Dunn's agent, and I asked Douglas what to do. "Drag your feet," he said.

On July 24—the arranged deadline for the jazz piece—I entered the office to find another telegram.

> I FEAR YOU HAVE AN ESSAY I CANNOT DO
> JUSTICE IN THE LENGTH PROPOSED HAVE
> BEEN TRYING TO CALL YOU PLEASE CALL ME
> JAMES BALDWIN IN STPAULDEVENCE (93) 328 790

Once again, I felt the elation, once again I picked up the telephone, and once again I heard a watchdog at the other end: "Who's calling?" Baldwin then came on with, "Hey, baby, how are you?"

I was fine. How was he? More to the point, how was the piece?

"You've given me something very important to think about. Something about my *life*." He was in earnest mode. He needed more space—was that OK? Of course it was. And more time.

"Call me Friday."

I did, taking a break from social-work driving duties to do so. He said, "I'm working on it, baby, I'm working on it. Call me Monday." And when I called him, he said, "I'm working on it, baby. Call me Thursday." I called him on every day of the week that he suggested. The introductory voices softened.

"Oh, Mr. *Campbell*! How are *you*? Jimmy's expecting your call. He's in the shower—oh, *here* he comes. He must have heard the ring tone."

July slipped into August. Our cover designer, Jim Hutcheson, came up with a nice scheme: a photograph of the star writer below the upper-case headline: "JAMES BALDWIN ON JAZZ." It looked great. All we needed was a piece to go with it. "I fear you have an essay." Was I about to be midwife to the new *Fire Next Time*?

"I'm working on it, baby, I'm working on it. But it's *very hot* down here." There was also his fifty-fifth birthday party in August to consider.

"Keep working on it," I said. "We've got the cover printed, with your photograph on the front. It looks terrific."

The electric jolt at the other end was transmitted all the way up through France, under the Channel to England and over Hadrian's Wall to Edinburgh.

"I'm on the cover, man?"

Well, of course he was.

"Oh baby."

One of those pauses.

"I'd better get to work."

He did, and the piece arrived, with, as so often, a wonderful title: "Of the Sorrow Songs: The cross of redemption." It wasn't the sequel to *The Fire Next Time*, nor was it as long as I had been led to expect. At the top was a date: 29 July, 1979. It began: "I will let the date stand: but it is a false date. My typewriter has been silent since the 6th of July, and the piece of paper I placed in the typewriter on that day has been blank until this hour." The false date was left because it was the birthday of his "baby sister" Paula (the youngest of eight siblings). The style was improvisational, occasionally shaky, but the tone was unmistakeably his:

The music called *jazz* came into existence as an exceedingly laconic description of black circumstances: and, as a way, by describing these circumstances, of overcoming them. It was necessary that the description be laconic: the iron necessity being that the description not be overheard . . . not be "de-coded." It has not been de-coded, by the way, any more than the talking drum has been de-coded . . .

I am attacking, of course, the basis of the language—or, perhaps, the *intention* of the language—in which history is written—am speaking as the son of the Preacher-Man. This is exactly how the music called *jazz* began, and out of the same necessity: not only to redeem a history unwritten and despised, but to checkmate the European notion of the world.

It appeared in the Autumn 1979 issue of the *New Edinburgh Review*. Baldwin was pleased. The author of *The Making of Jazz*, James Lincoln Collier, replied from New York at length, in mainstream terms, at the opposite reach from Baldwin's black-and-blue tone. "This music belongs on the auction block . . ." The check for £80 was sent to Saint-Paul de Vence. I doubt that it was ever cashed.

On the telephone afterwards, he said: "You know . . . I'd like to meet you one day."

I stammered a suitable reply.

"Because—*you*—are the most *persistent—person*—I have *ever*—KNOWN!" Followed by a great gale of laughter. He invited me to visit him in Saint-Paul, "if you happen to be down this way."

I was probably not the most persistent person he had ever

known. I simply thought that a writer, when he said he would deliver a piece, went ahead and did so. Nevertheless, I resolved to be "down this way" before long.

VII

It took over a year, but on a Thursday afternoon in July 1981, I entered a Post Office in the Champ-de-Mars area of Paris, where I was having a spring and summer sojourn, and asked to be put through to the number in Saint-Paul de Vence. I closed the collapsible door of the booth behind me and waited for a response to the piercing tone. I had been lucky, in previous communications, always to find Baldwin in France, for he was often on the road, in the US or elsewhere. It was his fate to be restless. His latest books had received lukewarm receptions. "Is he still around?"

And I was lucky again. The customary gruff answering voice passed the receiver to the honey-and-brandy one. "A little tight," Baldwin replied, in answer to my polite inquiry, "a little tight. But that's OK." I said I was in Paris and was wondering if I might come down to Saint-Paul, as he had suggested.

Baldwin barely hesitated. "I'd love that, baby."

I said I was thinking of the following Tuesday, which happened to be Bastille Day. There was space for a mental check.

"Toosday? . . . Tha'd be fine."

"Should I call you before I leave?"

"Only if you have *time* . . . only if you have time."

He made it sound like a gospel refrain. I left the Post Office knowing that I wouldn't have time. I had my invitation: why set myself up for a cancellation?

Early on the Tuesday morning, I boarded a train at Gare

de Lyon, ready for the nine-hour journey to Nice. I remember what I ate in the restaurant car—*petit salé aux lentilles*— the miniature carafe of wine I drank, whom I talked to, that I sat on the left-hand side of the carriage, facing forward, how north announced its change to south by way of the façades of provincial railway stations.

In Nice, I entered a café and requested a *jeton* from the barman.

For the first time in our by now extended telephone acquaintance, Baldwin himself picked up the receiver. He told me to take a taxi to Saint-Paul de Vence. "Do you have any money?" he asked with kindly urgency; I later learned that he was accustomed to people turning up with none. He said he would meet me at the Café de la Place in the central square.

It was a public holiday and the village was lively. Men played *pétanque* in the early evening sun on the sandy flat before a bank of café tables. I positioned myself at one of them and kept watch. Before long, a neat black man, not tall, wearing large sunglasses, appeared at the far corner of the square. As he paused to look around, I approached and extended my hand. Baldwin pushed the shades on to his forehead.

"Are you him?"

We crossed the square to his usual place, the Colombe d'Or, where he returned the greetings of staff and regulars with easy grace. We arranged ourselves at a snug table opposite the bar and had fifteen precious minutes to ourselves before the barman summoned him to the telephone. It was Bernard Hassell—pronounced Ber-*nard* Hass-*ell*—calling from the house. When he came back to the table, Baldwin explained that he had recently completed a piece for *Playboy* about the Atlanta child killings, then under investigation, and Bernard wanted to tell him that the editor had phoned from Chicago to say he liked it. The news put him in a happy mood. "They liked the piece!" he repeated, more than once, with a widening smile. The omens were good.

Half an hour later, Bernard joined us: a lithe, alert New Yorker in a white jump suit, zipped to just above the navel, with a skeptical but not unpleasant expression on his face when setting eyes on me. An amiable black American woman with tumbling locks came into the company, and when we walked downhill to the Baldwin residence, a quarter of a mile from the village, she accompanied us. Bernard insisted on carrying my bag, on top of which rested a Harris Tweed double-breasted jacket I had brought with me, in case I needed to appear smart.

"Where—are—*you*—going, with a tweed *coat!*" the woman asked. It was about 30 degrees. At the house, it seemed we were having an impromptu party. There were more drinks and Bernard began making preparations for dinner. Fireworks sounded from the village and spangled the sky. The woman departed, leaving laughter behind and talk of "Yves and Simone," who had a house in the village. Baldwin asked about Scotland, of which he displayed an almost complete ignorance. "It's joined to England, right? Not like Ireland." I offered some details of the centuries-long troubled relationship with the dominant neighbor, and Baldwin said something that took me aback: "So it's a bit like being a nigger?"

Nevertheless, he now had a literary connection to the country. Bernard told me that he had enjoyed writing for the *New Edinburgh Review*, and had agreed to do so because he was touched by my original letter, the one containing the invitation to address the students at the university.

I stayed at the house on Route de la Colle for six days—

James Baldwin and me, on the terrace outside "the torture chamber" at Baldwin's house in Saint-Paul de Vence, July 1984. On this occasion I was there to interview him for *The Times* on his sixtieth birthday. *Courtesy of Fanny Dubes.*

"Where we goin' to put this chile?" Bernard had asked, before going ahead and making up a bed in the spare room—during which there were dinners and all-afternoon lunches (Baldwin usually rose around noon) and late-night talks over the daily bottle of Johnnie Walker Black Label. Baldwin told me that he owned the portion of the L-shaped house in which he lived. The other part still belonged to his former landlady, Mlle Faure, an elderly local woman from an old Saint-Paul family— she was the author of a small book about the village—with whom he was on affectionate terms. He planned to purchase the remainder in due course.

The land attached to the house covered about three acres. It ran wild in places but the garden areas were pleasantly cultivated. Bernard was responsible for the arrangement of trellises and paths and rockeries, and there was also a young Algerian who went around singing Arabic songs softly in a low voice as he worked.

The village was popular with café society and celebrities. Dirk Bogarde had a place nearby. Simone Signoret and Yves Montand were regular guests at the house. Baldwin mentioned casually that Georges Braque had once had his studio where we were sitting now, but this proved hard to verify. The local Fondation Maeght contained works and architectural designs by Braque, Miró, Chagall and Giacometti. Baldwin seemed vague about it; his attention was consumed by his predicament. "The very time I thought I was lost, My dungeon shook and my chains fell off" . . . day after day.

"Are you James or Jim or Jimmy?"

I said I was usually Jim, but didn't object to any.

Baldwin gripped my wrist and said with a sudden intensity that I came to recognize as characteristic: "I will call you *Jamie*."

I had brought the current *TLS* from Paris (easy to find there) and I fished it out. The lead article mentioned *Uncle Tom's Cabin* and Baldwin's 1949 essay "Everybody's Protest Novel." It included a phrase I was happy to pass on: "Flaubert would have understood Baldwin better" (that's to say, better than the author of the book under review). He pushed the paper back in my direction and, leaning with his elbows on the outdoor table, said, with typical good humor, "Oh well . . . I'm up for grabs again!"

He loved to talk, but not to answer the telephone, and in a bit of role-reversal I found myself lifting the receiver in the living room when Bernard was absent—Baldwin's bedroom and study, "the torture chamber," was at a level below—and asking, "Who's calling?" in as gruff a voice as I could manage.

There was a certain tension between the two. Baldwin thought—or at least was encouraged by his brother David to believe—that he was being taken advantage of by Bernard, who was supposed to perform secretarial work. If he didn't do as much as expected, it was partly Baldwin's fault, for he was in the habit of hiring friends to do what would have been better left to professionals. Once when I mentioned something about the arrangement with Bernard—in a favorable light—he looked away and mumbled, "That's something else I've got to get sorted out." On another occasion there was a female friend of Jimmy's (we were on first-name terms now) from 1940s Paris days staying at Saint-Paul, who did not get on well with Bernard. To me, he referred to her with a chuckle as "Jimmy's girlfriend," which I, thinking it was amusing, thoughtlessly passed on. Jimmy was not pleased. "He said that, did he?"

Bernard stuck to his post. When, some years later, I asked about him during a meeting with Baldwin in London, he replied, "He's indestructible," with mirth in the voice but not in the sentiment. (Bernard was not indestructible; he died of complications from AIDS in France in 1992.)

But Bernard was fun. "The Côte d'Azur is back in business!" he would exclaim at the sound of a telephone call or the appearance of an unexpected guest. He used to stand on the balcony of the gatehouse, where he had his quarters, and sing operatic airs. It was he who told me to stay on when I offered to make myself scarce. Perhaps, unwittingly, I relieved the pressure. The evening before my departure, there was a party at the house of an American expatriate near Nice, to which we drove in the chauffeured Mercedes Bernard called on in these situations. On entering, Bernard had his hand grasped by a well-known English thriller writer. "James Baldwin! I'm so

Bernard Hassell, Baldwin's secretary, stands lithe and alert, "a skeptical but not unpleasant expression on his face," with Baldwin at Saint-Paul de Vence. *Courtesy of Carlos Freire.*

pleased to meet you." The grip was disengaged. "I'm Bernard Hassell. That's James Baldwin. This is Jamie Campbell."

Stylish as always, Jimmy took the now awkward hand and offered, with almost imperceptible irony, "Enchanté."

There were conversations lasting most of the day and half the night but I took few notes. When once or twice I sat on a wall near the Colombe d'Or to jot a few things down, I felt as if I were betraying the occasion. When I said so many years later to a friend, Darryl Pinckney, he replied: "You did the right thing. You didn't take notes: you hung out."

The following remarks are derived from what I scribbled into a notebook in 1981.

Norman Mailer: "Norman has absolutely no sense of humor." Later: "The problem with Mailer and Hemingway is the problem of homoeroticism."

Gore Vidal: "A ridiculous man."

Naked Lunch: "It's not a book; it's a convulsion." Later: "Bill would take people and get them strung out and then leave them there . . . And you can't do that."

Trocchi (in anger): "I hate him. And if you see him, tell him that from me."

Allen Ginsberg (shaking his head affectionately): "He's a beautiful man."

In Cold Blood: "I sent Truman a telegram: It's a dead end. Congratulations, baby."

"England is on fire!" (There were riots at the time in several cities.) With a perceptible sense of having been neglected: "If you'll forgive me for reminding you: I told you so."

Mrs. Thatcher: "I would like to coat her in chocolate and turn her into an éclair" (bit mysterious, this one).

Ralph Ellison: "He doesn't like me." Does he like him? "I'm glad he's there." *Invisible Man* was the winner of the National Book Award in 1953, which he believed to be the reason *Go Tell It on the Mountain* did not win in the following year.

Marlon Brando: "We were never lovers. We no doubt should have been lovers . . ." He said the same thing about Bernard.

Scott Fitzgerald: "The most overrated writer of all time—apart from *The Great Gatsby* and a few of the short stories."

Between the two bards of east coast suburban life, Cheever and Updike, he chose Cheever. "There was something there I could relate to. We now know what it was." Laughter. (Cheever's homosexuality had recently come to light.)

On "The Death of the Beat Generation," the name given to a party in New York arranged by his friend Robert Cordier: "I wasn't sure that it had ever been born, but if it had been I was sure it should be dispatched with a minimum of fuss."

"You cannot *learn* how to touch a woman unless you *know* how to touch a man." (This came on the first evening, after I had rebuffed his advances.)

"In Italy, people are not afraid to touch—one—another."

"People fear love more than they fear death. *Think about it!*"

"Be true to the clown in yourself."

I said that in November I was planning to visit America for the first time. After New York and Philadelphia, I wanted to go south to New Orleans.

"Be careful."

Was I likely to be in danger?

Jimmy's eyes widened. "I'm just a nigger." His sense of drama, and his timing, were exquisite. "You're a traitor."

The now taboo word was not used sparingly at Route de la Colle. Bernard would come out with "This nigger don't know which way his ass is up," or "The trouble with these niggers is . . ." At the Saturday night party in Nice, there was an African American woman with heavily pancaked face and dyed and straightened hair. She seemed mild and pleasant to me, but the next morning Bernard referred to "that lady with the brown face," which brought a knowing chuckle from Jimmy. I was, in their eyes, an innocent, someone who had never been to America, not really a "white" person at all, in the sense in which they used the term. At one point while we were sitting on the terrace outside his work room, Jimmy went off on a riff about white people this and white people that. Seeing the unease on my face, he placed a hand on my knee, and modulated his tone. "I'm not talking about you, baby. I'm talking about the people who think they are white." As with many things Baldwin said, the meaning of this seemingly cryptic remark became clear later.

In the event, I was mugged on that trip, held up at one in the morning on East 12th Street, New York, by a boy and girl who were not far advanced in their teens. The girl poked the barrel of a small gun in my face, withdrew it and poked again. They took a wad of dollars from my pocket and ran off. I told Baldwin about it at our next rendezvous, and he regarded me sadly. "Were they black?"

During that first week and on future visits, as well as during meetings in London and elsewhere, Baldwin assigned me a role in his company: "one of my editors." It was said with a twinkle in the eye when he introduced me to people. It pardoned me for having barged in, in the first place, and cleared me of any suspicion—on my own part as well as that of others—that I belonged among the hangers-on.

I see now, though I was too young to see then, that I could have taken this role more seriously, that I could have accepted it as a responsibility. He needed editing, and he wanted it. He had relied on his brother David to assure him that *No Name in the Street* was ready for publication in 1972, when really it is a sequence of notes in search of an arrangement. In the central place of Saint-Paul and in the Colombe d'Or, he was regarded as a celebrity catch, a segment of local lore—Yves and Simone, phlegmatic Bogarde, Matisse settling his bills at the Colombe with a drawing, Jeemy *le noir Américain*—but he lacked everyday contact with literary people, ordinary conversation, agreement and disagreement. There were old friends aplenty, with new ones arriving on the doorstep, among whom might stand a fugitive lover—"Are you him?"—but there was no one with the critical resolve to say: This is too shrill, Jimmy; this is off the point; you are being repetitious.

That editor would have found much to do. Baldwin talked to me about a trio of works in the pipeline. One was a novel, "No Papers for Muhammad"—the melodious gardener, an illegal immigrant, was behind it. He was also working on a play, "The Welcome Table"—the one and only work to which he gave a Saint-Paul setting—and a "triple biography" which took the working title "Remember This House." Its subjects were the three great stalwarts of the civil rights era, Medgar Evers, Malcolm X, and Martin Luther King, all assassinated between 1963 and 1968: a first, second, then a third and almost fatal blow to the heart of the man sitting opposite me at the table on the terrace—what some chroniclers have seen as "the welcome table" itself—in the garden at sunny Saint-Paul de Vence.

He gave me poems to read in typescript and hinted strongly that they were available for publication, "in magazines like yours." Two I remember were "Staggerlee Wonders" and "Christmas Carol." The second pursued a longstanding theme: the conversion of Saul to Paul: "how bright is the light / of the unchained night." There was nothing more basic in Baldwin's personal theology: confession, followed by conversion, leading to delivery from what he had elsewhere called "the sin that cannot be forgiven," slavery, which held Americans in bondage, black and white, as he had written in his *NER* essay, "until this hour."

That boyish eagerness when he asked the next day: "Did you get a chance to read the poems?" At the outdoor table we discussed them, and I said something about poetry allowing his voice to be "released from discourse." Jimmy repeated this pensively more than once, as it was his habit to do, staring at his interlocutor in the meantime. "Released from discourse . . . Released . . . from . . . discourse."

I've told myself since that I should have taken "Staggerlee Wonders"—now quite a well-known late Baldwin piece—for the *New Edinburgh Review*, even though I didn't feel enthusiastic about its addresses to "Duke Wayne" and "towering Ronald Reagan" and "the Great Man's Lady," as well as its scattered references to China, Russia, and Patty Hearst. My test was to ask if I would have accepted it if it had arrived in the mail with an unfamiliar name attached. I was turning down decent work by local writers all the time, for lack of space to print it. Could I justify accepting something I didn't care for, just because the author was famous? (Relating this story to a young Baldwin scholar much later, I heard myself say, "It was by James Baldwin, for chrissake!")

One afternoon, after the usual long lunch, he indicated to me and to the housekeeper Valérie that he was about to go down below to the "the torture chamber" and "la machine à écrire"—making typing motions with his fingers before the adoring Valérie's eyes—in order to work on the "Medgar, Malcolm, and Martin book."

I excused myself by saying I would go up to the village to read and have a beer, to fill the hot, vacant hours while he worked. Jimmy immediately changed his mind and said he would come with me. It was after five, a beautiful July evening in Provence, just before the hour when the landscape changes to offer the idler a deeper understanding of Impressionist light. On the quarter-mile walk uphill to the Café de la Place, he began softly to sing a blues.

"How long . . . how long . . . has that evening . . . train been gone.
How long . . . how long . . . baby, how long."

It is one of my most precious memories, but I knew even then it was not the way to go about writing the new novel and the triple biography. In the eight years that elapsed between drafting a letter to his agent in which he set out his initial thoughts for what he called "the Martin–Malcolm–Medgar book" and his death in 1987, he produced a sheaf of about thirty pages. "Since Martin's death . . . something has altered in me," he wrote in his account of the tumultuous period, *No Name in the Street*. "Something has gone away."

And yet, something positive and volatile remained. Something that one sensed could be "grasped in handfuls, tapped for electricity, bottled, used for blasting, set fire to," as Patrick Leigh Fermor wrote, not about a solitary, small man in a temporary setting, but an eternal geographical region, the Mani, in the southern Peloponnese.

I departed on the Sunday at midday, with careful directions from Bernard as to which train to take to Marseille, where I wished to spend a few nights, and how to find a hotel once I got there. I had been in the presence of a force that could be used for blasting, tapped for electricity, for all its altering and cutting-down. It happened each time I was in Baldwin's company, and I began to look forward to it as much as to anything else: the moment of stealing away with the electric beat still pulsing inside.

14

LEWES PRISON

I

It was one of those seemingly inconsequential events, almost a non-event, that by the end of the afternoon on which it happened has changed your life, in that the rest of your life can be seen in retrospect as depending on it.

I can date it precisely, even pinpoint the time, as I can with certain other events: April 8, 1980. I was on one of my regular, brief visits to London. Under my direction, the *New Edinburgh Review* had produced several issues, with a new one in preparation. I had persuaded James Baldwin to contribute to the magazine but had yet to make the expedition to Saint-Paul de Vence. Here I was at five minutes to 1 on the Tuesday after Easter, walking eastwards from Holborn Tube station in the direction of the curious little turning into Lincoln's Inn Fields called Great Turnstile. It had an appealing Old London ring when I saw it given as the address on the editorial page of the *New Statesman*.

By this time, I liked to think of myself as an almost familiar face on the third floor at Great Turnstile, where the arts and book reviews were discussed, commissioned, edited, proofed, and made ready for the printers. I had first gone there a year before, to see Julian Barnes—deputy literary editor under Martin Amis, but by that stage in more or less sole charge—and to deliver my review of a biography of Hermann Hesse by hand. When Julian left to take up an equivalent post at the *Sunday*

Times, I had applied for his job and had been interviewed as one of a shortlist of three. The other candidates were Paul Binding and Craig Raine. "You were second," Julian told me later. "Craig"—the front runner—"was just too mad." It went to Paul, who began work at Great Turnstile under David Caute, the new literary editor. How grand they seemed, those job titles, when spoken aloud in Edinburgh.

I continued to write for the books pages. And now I was swerving through the lunchtime crowd on Holborn, on my way to keep an appointment with Paul Binding. It was press day. He would be busy but not too busy to see a contributor. I had telephoned to say I was in London and we had made arrangements to have lunch. I would enter by the small door in the alley, always open, make my way upstairs without impediment, to be greeted by one of the secretaries, Gillian or Angela, or by Paul or even David Caute. I met Christopher Hitchens there for the first time, and overheard him ask Caute, "Who's running the paper next week?" before suggesting that he "telex" his article from Cyprus. To have such questions in one's mouth as part of one's daily bread. To be integrated into such important matters. "Who's running the paper?"

On a different afternoon, I entered the room to find Salman Rushdie leaning against the table that was always covered in newly arrived books, spines upwards. "Perhaps you know?" he said, without introduction. "We've been trying to remember the first name of Raskolnikov in *Crime and Punishment*." To my regret, I did not know.

Now I was back again. As I came within fifty yards of the narrow entry, a figure emerged from it and stood at the traffic lights in an almost frozen state of agitation, waiting to cross Holborn. It was Paul. As I was arriving at the office, three minutes before the appointed time, he was leaving it. Had I boarded the train at Tottenham Court Road after the one I did board, I would have missed him. Had Paul left the office a minute earlier or had the green man lit up thirty seconds before he did, I would have missed him that way, too.

I approached and said, "Paul?" leaving a baffled question mark inside the syllable.

His agitation all at once became visible. He was on his way to the *Times Literary Supplement*'s offices on Gray's Inn Road, just a few minutes' walk away (more like fifteen), to read and correct the proof of his article on Isaac Bashevis Singer for the issue due out at the end of the week. Angela had instructions to relay his apology and ask me to wait. "I'm so glad to have caught you," he said. Would I perhaps walk with him?

The green man gave his permission and we made our way into Red Lion Street. This was a new adventure. I could just about put aside my queasy recognition that I had been on the point of being stranded for an hour upstairs at Great Turnstile between two politely embarrassed secretaries. When we walked into the open-plan office of the *TLS* in the building it shared with *The Times*, the *Sunday Times* and the other supplements, we were greeted by Blake Morrison, the fiction and poetry editor, who was overseeing Paul's review. Blake, a Yorkshireman, was slight in build and reserved in manner but immediately friendly. He knew of the *NER* and had read the symposium "On Reviewing" that we had run the year before. He said: "Maybe you could do something for us?" and invited me to pore over the books shelved irregularly by his desk while he returned his attention to Paul.

I picked out three that appealed to me straight away: a collection of essays by Robert Creeley, with the likable title *Was*

That a Real Poem (the hidden subtitle being "or did you make it up yourself?"), an assortment of interviews with Creeley's Black Mountain associate Edward Dorn, and a non-fiction book by the Beat poet Gary Snyder, which reflected his interest in Native American traditions.

"Maybe you could link them all together," Blake said.

I could. And without much delay, once back in Edinburgh, I did.

As we were leaving the office, Blake introduced me to the paper's editor, John Gross. He, too, was reserved in that already recognizable way of English intellectuals but, like Blake, in a not disagreeable way. It was a body language I was becoming accustomed to—tight smile, folded arms, questions asked in order to avoid giving answers—as I was growing used to other curious English habits.

"I see Blake's given you some books," John Gross said, in his gentle fashion. Under the headline "Musing from the Mountain," my Creeley-Dorn-Snyder piece appeared in the *TLS* of May 30, 1980, the first of many reviews and articles to appear in the paper.

Just under two years later, John left the *TLS* to take up a position as a commissioning editor at Weidenfeld & Nicolson. One day in Edinburgh in early 1982, I opened an envelope to find a letter typed on Weidenfeld headed notepaper, with his neat signature at the foot. In a few brief sentences, he set out his reason for getting in touch. Was I thinking of writing a book? If so, could we discuss it?

I had never received an invitation like this before, but I knew when to keep my head. As luck would have it, I did have a book in mind. It had already been rejected, as a proposal, by Collins. I wanted to make a tour of Scotland, by bus, by train, by thumb, and to write about the places I saw, the people I talked to, folding my evolving literary experience into the narrative as I went. Edwin Muir had done something like it fifty years earlier and had written *Scottish Journey*, a book I admired.

I wrote back. Perhaps encouraged by the recognition that I was ready, John said he liked the idea. We met and talked about it some more, and Weidenfeld offered a contract: *Invisible Country: A Journey through Scotland*, with an advance of £2,000, payable in three instalments.

The book was published in April 1984, by which time John Gross had left Weidenfeld and taken up a different literary job. Another John, a genial man called John Curtis, an old hand, took over his authors—they were few, but I was one—and he invited me to suggest a follow-up.

"Something keeps saying to me, 'Ireland,'" this John said, thinking, as publishers do, that a form of continuity is desirable in an author's work. It didn't take me long to understand that I wasn't up to that. I considered a return journey across the Barbary Coast, in backwards motion, from Morocco to Tunisia, starting at Tangier, pausing for recollection at the border post near Oujda, dawdling under the Francophone arcades of Algiers, investigating Constantine while drawing old Istanbul breath in readiness for an expedition to the country's vast desert interior. Rolling forward in the VW camper, Jeff, Russ, Annette, and I had skipped it all, preoccupied with drugs (them), with getting *there* (me), mistaking a real land for the Land of Away, contenting ourselves with a flat exterior. Now I had changed, the times had changed, writing about remote regions was in vogue. But I soon admitted to myself that I wasn't up to that either.

There was a third notion, and this one stayed with me. In

terms of physical movement, it was the opposite of a travel book. It was a journey of a different kind, to a different sort of interior.

II

On a drab morning in November 1984, I stepped down from the train at the station in a pretty Sussex town, crossed the railway bridge, turned left, and took the steep road uphill. I was on my way to work at Her Majesty's Prison Lewes. It was my first day and they were expecting me.

After much maneuvering, repeated requests and meetings with prison governors and Home Office officials, I had received permission to enter a prison in order to write a book. Thanks to the governor-in-chief at HMP Lewes, it was this prison. Denis Brown's acceptance of my proposal had had to be ratified by the same Home Office official in London who had done his best to put me off the project altogether. In the end, though, he went along with Mr. Brown's welcome, and now, at 9:30 am, under a gray sky, I was hammering on the door of a high security English prison, asking to be let in. A peculiar kind of freedom.

The idea was to write a book with "the atmosphere of a novel," as I had put it to John Curtis. Non-fiction making use of the strategies of fiction was in fashion in the early 1980s: Ryszard Kapuściński did it; Bruce Chatwin did it. My hope was to do it, too. The intention was to mix freely with prisoners, to fathom the "inner life" of the prison. I would have preferred to write about a Scottish prison, but my request to the relevant department north of the border was rejected out of hand. When we met in a pub near Victoria Station in London, the press officer at the Prison Department of the Home Office—a Scotsman, as it happens—tried to rule it out, too. On practical grounds, he said. It would be necessary to have a member of staff assigned to me at all times, to ensure my personal safety. There simply weren't the numbers. The workforce was already stretched. Open-and-shut case. It was nice meeting you.

I was disappointed but I wouldn't have wanted a prison officer on my tail anyway. An official shadow would restrict my movements and thoughts, and make candid conversation with inmates impossible.

I kept at it, and someone with experience of the Prison Department gave me useful advice: you are going about it back to front. The thing to do first, he said, was to find a prison governor willing to take you in. Then return to the Home Office with a ready-made plan in want of a rubber stamp. The Governor of HMP Lewes was recommended as a relatively liberal sort. I wrote to him and he replied with the invitation to come down—in a homely phrase that still makes me smile— "to spend the afternoon and evening with us."

I did, and found Mr. Brown as likeable and open-minded as his phrasing suggested. Eventually, the necessary permissions were obtained. Even that afternoon-and-evening reconnaissance visit had required Home Office approval, but in retrospect my acceptance into HMP Lewes, a Category B prison—high-security, though not the highest—seems astonishingly free of bureaucratic impediment. I was going to be in a place where people are confined for large parts of the day, with four gates to be unlocked and passed through before the incomer reaches the core. Once there, however, no one tried to prevent me wandering from place to place on C Wing. It housed 150 long-term prisoners, roughly a third of them lifers.

Within the confines of the Benthamite panopticon—in theory, ever-observed—I went from kitchen to classroom, gym to chapel, library to laundry. In the evening, during the recreation period, between 6 and 9 pm, I often returned to the main gate after a light supper in a pub or at the house I had rented in town, sauntering on to the wing, where prisoners watched television and played games. If invited—I often was—I made up a foursome at table tennis or billiards with three cons; or I went into a cell to sit on the edge of a stark bed, waiting for a cup of tea.

Mr. Brown issued a pass which enabled me to turn up whenever I wanted, to enter through the twin flat-topped towers that flank the main gate—exchanging a friendly greeting with the officers on duty—and step into the yard.

All this took place before there was such a thing as the writer-in-residence at British prisons. The poet Ken Smith came under that rubric later, and wrote a book about HMP Wormwood Scrubs, published in 1989. I was in residence, and had hopes of calling myself a writer—but "writer-in-residence" had no currency as a phrase in this context. To those who asked, I liked to call myself a reporter in a forbidden zone. I thought of it as a second travel book, in which the traveler was confined to a walled city.

Just over a year earlier, I had started a part-time job as an assistant editor at the *TLS*. My duties took me there on Mondays and Tuesdays, leaving the rest of the week free. So I began to divide my time: two days of sub-editing and proof-reading at the *TLS*; three or four at Lewes prison, sometimes spilling over to Sunday as well. I attended services in the prison chapel. On Christmas Day, I was invited to call out the numbers for the pre-turkey bingo. A prisoner took me on an impromptu tour of the laundry, as the purser on a steam ship might offer

HMP Lewes, main entrance. Day after day, for six months, four gates were unlocked to allow me to reach my cell.

to show a passenger the engine room. Before long, I began to look forward to my march uphill in the direction of the well-made building, solidly installed in the 1850s, to a day of exchanges with people whose company was in some cases stimulating, in others indifferent, seldom uninteresting and only rarely hostile.

I was assigned an office: a cell, in fact, which until my arrival had served as a barber's shop. A chair was provided, and a small table—the only furniture in this stark little oblong with bars on the high-up window—on which I placed my tape recorder and notepad. Nothing was taped without the speaker's consent. After a week or so, I was used to friendly cracks of the "Back again? You must like it here" variety. On Christmas Day, I came through the main gate to find a Scottish prisoner clearing snow from the yard with a shovel.

"What are you doin' here? It's different for us. We get paid for it."

When I left the prison on that first day in November, I bought a newspaper, went into a pub and drank a pint of the local Harvey's Best Bitter at the bar. Half an hour later, I was on my way to the train. Seated in the carriage, I was able to choose between writing up my notes or reading the paper or a novel by John Cheever: *Falconer*, based on his period as writer-in-residence in Sing Sing, New York. Looking from the window at the scatterings of the town illuminated in the darkness, I thought of my new acquaintances and the multifarious forms of confinement they were about to introduce me to.

Gate Fever was published in the spring of 1986. It had a mostly warm reception, including two reviews—one in print, the other on the radio—from Britain's most famous ex-prisoner, Jimmy Boyle. Memory tells me that the least favorable notice was in the *TLS*. I remember complaining that Laurie Taylor had treated the book as sociology, something I had been desperate to avoid. I had suggested to the editor of the *TLS* that he ask the crime novelist Patricia Highsmith to review it, a favorite writer of mine and a regular reviewer for the paper. It was not done for authors to choose their own critics, however, and the idea was ignored. Looking back, I see that Laurie Taylor remarked that the author "fearlessly records the actual nature of inmate life in the cells," which is what I wanted to do. Memory, as I've been finding out lately, can act like a trickster.

During the six months of passing in and out of Lewes prison—sitting in my barber-shop office, perched on the edge of a bunk on C Wing, praying in the chapel, visiting some wretched solitary soul in "the block," where prisoners were sent for punishment—my mind would occasionally wander to the six hours spent with Bruce in the police cell in St Andrew's Square in Glasgow, twenty years earlier. Now I was on the other side of the lock. The key had turned in the opposite direction for me. In the basement at Boots, I had tried to fool the police officers with one of the most inept presentations of an alternative identity they had surely ever experienced: the hapless James Gunning. But in the end, thanks in part to the integrity of Bruce Dryden—and thanks to all the other people involved in that miserable drama, in particular my parents and sisters, not forgetting the exasperated schoolteachers at King's Park and even the St Andrew's Square policemen—I had forged another identity, an alternative to the delinquent

James Baldwin at the Edinburgh Book Festival, in conversation with me before a live audience, August 1985. We had quit the bar of the Roxburghe Hotel at five o'clock that same morning. Baldwin charmed and thrilled the audience nonetheless. *Courtesy of Fanny Dubes.*

schoolboy I had seemed to be then: some sort of existential entity I could claim was "me."

A few months before *Gate Fever* was due to be published, James Baldwin and I had sat at tables in the large tent in Charlotte Square at the 1985 Edinburgh Book Festival. Our mid-morning interview before a large audience had ended. Now he was half-hidden behind pillars of books, pen in hand. A queue formed and people came forward with copies of *Go Tell It on the Mountain*, *Another Country*, and other books. Jimmy greeted each in turn with some kind words, a twinkle in the eye, and his miraculous, healing grin.

Suddenly, the reader in front of him was my father. He and Mum had traveled through from Braco to be present. Dad thrust forward a paperback copy of *The Fire Next Time*.

"I'm pleased to meet you, Mr. Baldwin. I enjoyed your talk very much."

Jimmy gave him his full-attention stare.

Dad nodded in the direction of the other figure sheltering behind the table. "That's my son."

Jimmy looked at me, looked back at him. Then he took the book, which I have before me now, and wrote: "For Harry Campbell: God bless."

ACKNOWLEDGMENTS

Morris Dickstein, Lindsay Duguid, Jennie Feldman, Douglas Field, Diana Maxwell, Maren Meinhardt, Robert Messenger, Quentin Miller, Marjorie Perloff, and Faith Pullin read parts of this work while it was in progress. My sisters Jean, Phyllis, and Julie did so, too. Craig Raine of *Areté* in Oxford and Alan Taylor of the *Scottish Review of Books* in Edinburgh published portions of it, in different form. Chapters 3 and 5 appeared in the Autumn 2021 issue of the *Hudson Review*. My cousin Norma Young helpfully supplied family documents. Jerry Robock and Dudley Cole recognized themselves in the portraits found here. Jerry went in search of old pictures from our Spetsai days. Martin Smith and Jo Evans were on hand to scan them and others. My thanks go to Robin Williamson for gracious permission to quote lines from "October Song." For current information about Robin and Bina W. Williamson, see their website www.pigswhiskermusic.co.uk. I am grateful to all.

The telling of this story goes back to the one-to-one French lessons I began with Viviane Blanchard in 2011, continuing to the present day. In tackling the mechanics of the French language, we talked, listened to one another, and read aloud. And from time to time I presented Viviane with a short memoir. I would read a little episode from my past, paragraph by paragraph, and she would patiently correct it. At one stage, these tales emerged weekly or fortnightly. Short memoirs became longer. There was something unexpected in reading about oneself in a foreign language. I found that my use of the first person singular was different from my use of it in English. The tone of the writing was new and I was free to write things—and say things, since they were read aloud—that I wouldn't have written or said in my native tongue.

Later, I translated some of the pieces into English, partly for the amusement of my sister Phyllis, partly for my own. I tried at first not to take advantage of the greater fluency of my own language, and to keep something of that new tone. The narrative of *Just Go Down to the Road* has undergone many developments since then, but there are still traces of its origins beneath the surface.

It was my friend and former editor at the *TLS* Peter Stothard who, several years ago, first urged me to write a memoir. Warm thanks are due to Judy Moir for her sensitive copyediting and structural suggestions, and to Neville Moir, Alison Rae and others at Polygon, as well as all at Paul Dry Books.

I am indebted most of all, and in every way, to Vera Chalidze.